D0083746

Citizen Participation in Resource Allocation

Urban Policy Challenges

Terry Nichols Clark, Series Editor

Cities are critical. From the Los Angeles riots of 1992 to the Hong Kong reversion of 1997, cities represent in microcosm the problems and potentials we face at all governmental levels.

Focusing on cities can help clarify our most challenging issues. Most key decisions affecting our lives are made locally. Although national governments collect the majority of funds, most welfare state programs around the world are provided by local governments. Urban leaders play key roles in encouraging economic development, maintaining quality public services, and mandating reasonable taxes.

And they are pressed to do more: provide attractive physical environments, improve amenities such as bike paths, help encourage recycling, assist disadvantaged groups to achieve broader acceptance and access to public facilities, keep streets safe, and fill the gaps in health and social services.

Books in the *Urban Policy Challenges* series will explore the range of urban policy problems and will detail solutions that have been sought and implemented in cities from around the world. They will build on studies of leadership, public management, organizational culture, community power, intergovernmental relations, public finance, citizen responsiveness, and related elements of urban public decision making.

These approaches to urban challenges will range from case studies to quantitative modeling. The series will include monographs and texts, as well as edited volumes. Although some works will target professional and student audiences, many books will elicit attention from thoughtful public leaders and informed citizens as well.

BOOKS IN THE SERIES

Citizen Participation in Resource Allocation

William Simonsen

Mark D. Robbins

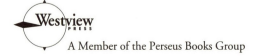
Westview
P R E S S

A Member of the Perseus Books Group

Urban Policy Challenges

Copyright © 2000 by Westview Press, A Member of the Perseus Books Group

Published in 2000 in the United States of America by Westview Press, 5500 Central Avenue, Boulder, Colorado 80301-2877, and in the United Kingdom by Westview Press, 12 Hid's Copse Road, Cumnor Hill, Oxford OX2 9JJ

Find us on the World Wide Web at www.westviewpress.com

Library of Congress Cataloging-in-Publication Data
Simonsen, William, 1957–
    Citizen participation in resource allocation / William Simonsen, Mark D. Robbins.
        p. cm.—(Urban policy challenges)
    Includes bibliographical references and index.
    ISBN 0-8133-6840-5 (hc.)—ISBN 0-8133-6824-3 (pbk.)
    1. Budget—United States—Citizen participation.   2. Government spending policy—United States—Citizen participation.   3. Political participation—United States.   I. Robbins, Mark D.   II. Title.   III. Series.

HJ2051.S494 1999   99-044626
336.3'9'0973—dc21

10   9   8   7   6   5   4   3   2   1

Contents

**4   How Fiscal Information and Service Use
     Influence Citizen Preferences   71**

5   Conclusions: Lessons for Governments   115

Appendices   125

Figures and Tables

Figures

Tables

Acknowledgments

As with any project that goes through many reincarnations and revisions, this book represents the contributions of many persons in addition to ourselves. We wish to thank Bas Denters, Lawrence Rose, and Pat Ingraham for their helpful comments on early portions of this book. We would also like to thank Edward C. Weeks, who codesigned the surveys that we analyze in Chapters 3 and 4. We deeply appreciate the help and support of Terry Clark, editor of this series. Last but far from least, we greatly appreciate the support of our wives, Robin Rhoades and Doreen Simonsen. Rick, Becky, and Nicole Simonsen also provided great inspiration.

William Simonsen and *Mark D. Robbins*

Introduction

This book is about public participation, citizen surveys, and government decision making. The book spotlights two very important areas where there is a lack of current research. First, it provides an overview and synthesis of state-of-the-art techniques for involving citizens in decision making. Second, this book provides a set of analyses of three innovative surveys of Eugene, Oregon, residents. We hope to contribute some interesting social science research while at the same time providing a guide for government officials.

Much attention has been given to creating processes by which citizens can be reengaged in government priority setting. This has come in large part as a response to the disaffection of the public, as demonstrated by low voter turnout and citizen distrust, and the continuing pursuit of tax limitation efforts. According to the National Association of State Budget Officers, in 1996 (the last year for which complete data is available) voters passed new tax limitation measures in eight states—Arizona, Arkansas, California, Florida, Georgia, Louisiana, Oregon, and South Dakota (Mazer, 1996). Although complete estimates of the economic effects have not been prepared, these limitations result in substantial revenue reductions for the affected state and local governments.

Some innovative processes have been used by governments to engage the public in a debate that moves beyond reliance on public hearings and toward the active deliberation of the citizenry. These efforts are predicated on the belief that the public, presented with realistic and detailed information, can make informed judgments to guide decision makers.

These techniques try to reach beyond gridlock and find new ways to engage the public in decision making—but these ideas and approaches do not come out of a vacuum. There is a long legacy of citizen involvement with government in the United States. The lessons learned from this earlier work shed light on contemporary participatory efforts. This book places the contemporary attempts to involve citizens in government in the context of theoretical themes and historical reforms.

Our interest is in the relationship between citizens and local government budgeting as it is broadly construed. We are more concerned in this book with the ways in which citizen preferences may affect resource decisions than we are in reviewing specific approaches to budgeting. Thus, this book moves beyond the exclusive consideration of citizen participation in budget processes themselves. It is a review of citizen participation in government administration and an empirical analysis of one of the most sophisticated contemporary participation approaches to date.

Mutual Distrust

Governments and the citizenry have developed a mutual distrust, as the public's perception that elected officials have distanced themselves from those whom they represent is too often a reality. In some cases, officials have traded the interests of the public for financial or other rewards.

In *Who Will Tell the People? The Betrayal of American Democracy*, William Greider (1992) presents several examples of how the decision-making structure of the United States has become increasingly beholden to corporate and moneyed interests. He further laments that the people and institutions traditionally expected to alert citizens to this kind of behavior have either been consumed by this power structure themselves or been made ineffective by its size and influence. Meanwhile, he contends, the citizen's role has been forced into the most narrow definitions of participation:

> If citizens sometimes behave irresponsibly in politics, it is the role assigned to them. They have lost any other way to act, any means for influencing the governing process in positive and broad-minded terms. . . . Citizens have been pushed into two cramped roles in politics, neither of which can satisfy their own aspirations or the requirements for a functioning democracy. . . . In the one role, citizens are the mindless mass audience that looks so dumb—the faceless crowd that speaks in politics mainly through opinion polls. . . . The other narrow role open to citizens is as special pleaders, defending their own stuff against other aspirants. (p. 18)

These "mindless masses" and "special pleaders" are citizens with whom elected officials are familiar. These are the people who cannot identify the Bill of Rights.[1] These are the people apparently swayed by negative campaign ads and political coverage that characterizes policy as a series of narrowly defined choices with simple distinctions. These people, to whom elected officials are ultimately accountable, are the respondents to opinion polls and the members of interest groups. These are the people who go to the voting booths to elect their representatives.

These same citizens, scorned by public officials as ill informed, feel reciprocally that their leaders are doing a poor job looking after their interests. If citizens are consumers of government, they are bargain hunters fed up with department stores that can no longer deliver the services that they want at prices they can afford. Citizen belief in government's ability to do the job has reached the point where only 21% of citizens surveyed

FIGURE I.1   Trust in Federal Government

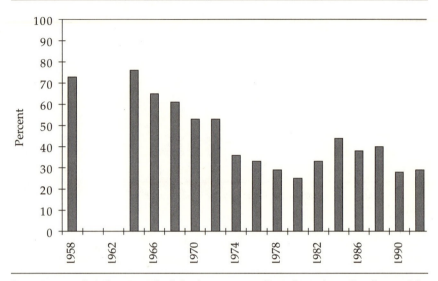

Percent responding they trust the federal government "just about always" or "most of the time" to the following question:

> "How much of the time do you think you can trust the government in Washington to do what is right—just about always, most of the time, or only some of the time?

NOTE: 1962 data was not available.

SOURCE: The National Election Studies (1997; http://www.umich.edu/~nes/nesguide/toptables/tab5a_1.htm)

trust the federal government "most of the time" or "just about always" to do what is right (see Figure I.1).

Thin Democracy

These same citizens are making dramatic statements not only through their comments to pollsters but in their turnout at the polls. Across the past twenty-five years, only 50% to 61% of eligible voters have turned out for presidential elections (see Table I.1).

Frances Fox Piven and Richard A. Cloward (1988) explain this phenomenon in terms of fundamental barriers to participation, and disaffection. Anthony Downs (1957) argues that the rational person finds no self-interested reason to cast a ballot. Raymond Wolfinger and Steven Rosenstone (1980) look for some explanations for this phenomenon in their work *Who Votes?* noting that education is stronger than either income or occupation

TABLE I.1   Voter Participation, 1968–1996

Election Year	Percentage of Eligible Voters Reporting Registered	Percentage of Registrants Reporting Voting	Percentage of Voting Age Population Voting for President
1968	74.3	91	60.9
1972	72.3	87	55.2
1976	66.7	89	53.5
1980	66.9	89	52.8
1984	68.3	88	53.3
1988	66.6	86	50.3
1992	68.2	90	55.1
1996	65.9	82	49.0

SOURCE: *Statistical Abstract of the United States*, 1992 and 1996, Tables 456 and 458; 1998, Tables 483 and 485.

as a predictor of whether or not a citizen will vote. Their explanation is an interesting one:

> Education increases cognitive skills, which facilitates learning about politics. . . . Better educated people are likely to get more gratification from political participation. . . . Finally, schooling *imparts experience with a variety of bureaucratic relationships:* [emphasis added] learning requirements, filling out forms, waiting in lines, and meeting deadlines.

What has developed is citizens who are not connected with government in productive ways, who feel that their governments are not doing a good job, and who increasingly abstain from voting. Our elected decision makers find that the financial demands of campaigning make it more and more necessary to engender the support of large corporate and other moneyed interests. Meanwhile, governments of all sizes are facing times of austerity that often require painful resource reduction decisions to be made (Lemov, 1991). It is reasonable to assert that this is not a satisfying state of affairs for either party.

Although it may be argued that electoral participation or a lack thereof may not be one of the greatest importance for the health and legitimacy of governments, the absence of a connection with the public can affect governments in profound ways. This is particularly true with regard to the vast financial commitments that governments make to deliver public services to the citizenry. Such obligations require the tacit and often explicit support of the public. If declining voting were simply a function of increased work behavior, for instance, and those who voted were well prepared to make careful and considered judgments about the trade-offs associated with different government initiatives, one could argue that there is no cause for alarm. Richard Topf (1989) looks at the democracies of Western Europe and argues, for instance, that not only is there no crisis of electoral participation associated with low voter turnout but the decline itself is simply a function of institutional and demographic changes that by themselves do not indicate a decline in the capacity to engage citizens in government. Alternative interpretations of voting patterns, however, offer little to reassure governments that they can secure the support they need from the citizenry to honor their commitments and responsibilities. The truth remains that many citizens express dissatisfaction and disengagement with government, and this disengagement has consequences.

In *Strong Democracy: Participatory Politics for a New Age*, Benjamin Barber (1984) describes this broad set of circumstances as "thin democracy." He describes it as not only ineffectual but fundamentally unsatisfying for participants and threatening to our civic culture. In *Coming to Public Judgment: Making Democracy Work in a Complex World*, Daniel Yankelovich (1992) describes the political system as "not functioning in good faith with its own ideals and principles" (p. 406) and brands this "mock democracy." Others note similar symptoms (Cronin, 1989; Piven and Cloward, 1988), diagnosing a problem not only of a lack of political depth but also of an absence of complex and considered opinions. Governments care about the quality of citizen judgments because what governments do is often complex and interrelated and much of it requires ongoing public support.

Citizen apathy and distrust of government—"thin democracy," if you will—have led local governments and concerned groups around the world to develop innovative ways to engage the public. Some actually seek to develop the capacity of the citizenry to embrace the inherent complexity of the public mission. Others pursue participation processes to improve the image of government. In either case, some level of public participation in decision making is employed in the hope that the suspicion and lethargy of the citizenry can be overcome.

A logical place for such involvement has been in the realm of budgetary decision making. Nowhere is the sting of a disconnect between government and the citizens more acutely felt than when the leaders of local goverment fail to make the case for voter approval of revenue or debt measures. In such cases, decision makers care less about the thoughts and more about the actions of the citizenry, a concern well characterized by Topf (1989): "In the last resort, it is not what people believe *per se* which will shape the future of our democracies, but what they do, and do not do, as the result of their beliefs and perceptions" (p. 53). Decision makers may feel that they are better informed about the relative merits of certain projects or the trade-offs inherent in certain budgetary decisions than those who are voting. Absent some mechanism to mitigate this asymmetry, however, those decision makers are simply out of luck when they present projects or tax measures to the public for which the benefits are not readily apparent.

One of the problems that becomes immediately apparent to the student of public opinion in the United States is that there is often a fundamental schism between the public perception and the factual reality of the costs and responsibilities of government. A healthy debate in the literature explores whether this disconnect really exists as a manifestation of a citizen desire for a "free ride," whether it reflects a lack of information and understanding about government, or whether it is an artifact of survey mechanisms.

Something for Nothing?

How realistic are public perceptions of the choices governments face? Jack Citrin (1979) finds that residents were apparently satisfied with the level of public services at the time of Proposition 13 in California,[2] yet astoundingly "fully 38 percent of the Californian electorate believed that state and local governments could provide the same level of services as previously with a 40 percent reduction in their budget" (p. 115).

Floyd Fowler (1974) explores the common belief that citizens seek tax reductions concurrent with their increasing demands for additional services. He surveyed residents of ten U.S. cities to measure the level of this effect. Among his research conclusions (made before the first series of tax limitation measures swept the United States) is the observation that citizens did not uniformly share the belief that local taxes were too high. In fact, only four of the ten cities he surveyed had a majority of residents expressing concern about tax levels. At the same time, there were few services that residents were willing to cut.

When citizens are asked whether they prefer continuing or enhancing services, lowering taxes, or increasing government efficiencies, they typically emphasize lowered taxes and more efficient government rather than a smaller public sector per se (Beck et al., 1987; Citrin, 1979; Courant, Gramlich, and Rubinfeld, 1980; Ladd and Wilson, 1982; Welch 1985). Government efficiency is a popular choice, particularly where interpreted by the respondent to mean a free lunch—lower taxes while maintaining or enhancing services.

The free lunch notion that citizens prefer both increased services and decreased taxes is explored further by Susan Welch (1985) in her work on public attitudes toward taxes. In research seeking to determine the extent of the coexistence of public desire for increased spending and decreased taxes, she found that (at the local level) only a small percentage (7%) of those desiring increased services were not willing to tax, assess fees, or reallocate local aid. Her work suggests that such a paradox exists but makes up a small relative portion of the attitude base toward taxes and spending. L. A. Wilson (1983) finds that those requesting service enhancements are sincere: Citizens are willing to pay more to receive more government services.

Gauging citizen preferences presents some profound difficulties that we address in more detail later in this book. Among the difficulties is that absent some connection to real outcomes, the solicitation of citizen preferences seems too abstract to provide much guidance for decision makers. On the other hand, most government decisions are not made through the direct action of citizens. Divining ways to produce informed public consideration of difficult government problems is one of the challenges that we discuss in the pages to follow. All of these matters are complicated by the fact that the citizens whose opinions are being solicited may be differentially affected by the resulting guidance provided. This situation is further confounded by the revelation, for which we offer some evidence in this book, that citizens provided with information about the costs of government programs make *different* decisions about those programs from those who are not provided with such information.

Citizen preferences appear to have more texture than suggested by the characterization "something for nothing." The public will is complex; citizens have opinions and are able to make judgments about their relative taxing and spending priorities. Citizens have their own understandings about government and what the administration of the programs that they care about should look like. At the same time, citizens are distrustful of their governments and the ways that governments conduct their business. Incorporating this input in the process of governance and the administration of programs has been the nut that innovators in citizen participation have attempted to crack.

This book has two key foci. First, in Chapters 1 and 2 we provide a look at the history and theoretical underpinnings of citizen participation and describe various citizen participation and survey efforts around the country. The remaining emphasis centers on the detailed analysis of three unique citizen surveys conducted in Eugene, Oregon. The analysis focuses on two research questions and several subquestions:

- How do citizens balance the budget when provided with an approximation of the necessary trade-offs? Do citizen characteristics, such as income, age, gender, and so on, relate to preferences for services and revenues? Primary data for this analysis will be provided by the Build Your Own Budget (BOB) survey (an instrument designed to allow respondents to "build their own budget"; see Appendix A). The policy implications point to the possible natural constituencies for budget cutting, service enhancing, and so on. We examine these questions in Chapter 3.

- What is the support for specific city services? Does fiscal information provided to respondents influence preferences for services? If so, does the information effect interact with citizen characteristics? For instance, does fiscal information have a different effect on choices made by older compared to younger people or people with higher versus lower income? Knowledge of how fiscal information affects support for services could influence how much and what type of information is provided to citizens. That is, less principled individuals could "rig the game" by withholding or providing fiscal information to affect citizen responses. We also explore how service use may influence citizen preferences for services. If the frequency with which citizens use city services affects support for collective services (such as administration or police and fire protection), then service elimination, privatization, contracting out, and other strategies that reduce the self-identification of the citizen as a government service user might lead to decreases in the support necessary to undertake some of the basic functions of government. We examine these issues in Chapter 4.

In Chapter 5, we summarize and discuss the implications of our results and consider directions for future research. We begin by turning to the theoretical and historical underpinnings of public participation in governmental decisions.

Notes

1. Sniderman, Brody, and Tetlock (1991) note studies showing that two of every three Americans would not recognize the Bill of Rights and that sizable numbers of the public are poorly informed about major issues.

2. California voters passed Proposition 13 in June 1978 by nearly a two-thirds majority (about 65% of voters). The measure set a property tax rate cap of 1% and rolled back assessed values for tax purposes to their pre-1976 levels. Further tax growth was limited to 2% per annum over the previous year's tax bill, and reassessment was permitted only when properties were sold. It also introduced a supermajoritarian (two-thirds) requirement for the legislative approval of statewide tax increases. Proposition 13 reduced local property tax revenues by approximately $6.1 billion (53%) in the first year alone. Elements of Proposition 13 were subsequently introduced in similar measures in Massachusetts, Michigan, Oregon, and throughout the country.

1

Theoretical and Historical Context of Public Participation

Before considering the host of contemporary techniques that governments are using to bring citizen participation into their decision-making processes, we pause to consider how we have arrived at our present understanding of citizen involvement processes. In the earliest days of the republic, the notion of a randomly selected sample of citizen judgments on budgetary dilemmas was nonsensical. Local decisions were citizen decisions by definition when town meetings were the dominant form of local government. The definition of a citizen, and of representation, was relatively narrow. A series of developments in U.S. history, including the swift and dramatic increase in the size of the states (in population and land area) and the government (number of governments, employees, and responsibilities) interacted to produce a unique relationship between the citizen and the decision maker. In this chapter, we consider the ways in which citizen participation has developed in the United States, how the citizen has been regarded in the developing scholarship of public administration (much of which reveals a gap between administration and citizen considerations), and some of the most common responses that governments have developed to fill this "citizen gap."

Mary Kweit and Robert Kweit (1981) describe three crises of participation in the United States corresponding roughly with the period of western expansion, the attack on the political machines at the end of the nineteenth century, and the social crises of the 1960s. Participation in its contemporary manifestation is traced to this last period.

Kweit and Kweit (1981) describe this understanding of participation as individualist—as opposed to collectivist—in its understanding of the public interest.[1] Individualists argue that legitimate decision making

1

must represent an aggregation of the demands of individuals. Collectivists, such as James Madison, argued that such a summation of and ac-
cession to citizen concerns would represent a preemption of the public
will. Theodore Lowi (1969) argues that (individualist-motivated) interest
group liberalism "deranged" expectations of democratic institutions by
applying notions of popular decision making to administration.

Although collectivists trust administrators to be stewards of a public
will quite separate from public opinion, individualists believe that it is
the combined involvement of the citizenry that must prevail in preserving the public trust. Emmette Redford (1969) argues that a government
acting without the universal participation of its citizenry lacks democratic
morality. He writes in response to the revelation that a unitary and centralized elite no longer prevails in government decision making. In such a
decentralized climate, a coalition of like interests is a legitimate expression of democratic will. But factors other than the fragmentation of power
contributed to the predominance of the individualistic ideal of citizen
participation.

The civil rights movement in the United States revealed to many citizens the degree to which basic rights were being disregarded. It also
brought two issues forward in our collective consciousness. One lesson
was that groups of citizens joining together could openly resist, and ultimately prevail against, a government that was refusing to act justly. The
other was the corollary revelation that citizens could no longer assume
that governments would act morally, or even legally. Although this is a
now a standard assumption, it marked a dramatic shift in trust from even
a few years earlier. By the 1970s, citizens had witnessed the protracted
suffering and loss of American and Vietnamese lives in a war that their
government perpetuated without popular consensus. With Watergate
and the near impeachment of President Nixon, citizens were exposed to
an equally grim side of their government, one where its leaders conspired
to commit and cover up felonies.

Frederick Mosher (1974), writing on behalf of a panel of the National
Academy of Public Administration, notes that most of the participants in
the Watergate scandal had no prior history of illegal acts, and he suggests
that the political and administrative systems may themselves have contributed to those events. He argues the possibility that such events were
less an aberration than a culmination of abuses based on a centralization
of power, the roots of which he traces back as far as the Bronlow Committee of 1937. Vincent Ostrom (1989) characterizes the Watergate crisis as
the manifestation of a concomitant increase in the centralized power of
the executive and a decline in constitutional government. Regardless of
the source of the corruption, the Watergate period appears to have pre-
cipitated an erosion in the already-dwindling public confidence in the

federal government. This is most dramatically evident in the decrease in those responding that they trust their federal government to do what is right always or most of the time from 65% in 1966 to 33% in 1976.[2] Those no longer trusting government to do what is right must either suffer its decisions or cause it to act otherwise.

We believe that the circumstances under which citizens have participated in government have played out in the context of certain recurring tensions inherent in the (U.S.) democratic system. The history and intellectual tradition from which this debate has proceeded are best described through three sets of these tensions: representation versus participation, politics versus administration, and bureaucratic expertise versus citizen access. These tensions frame the theater in which government is administered (see Figure 1.1). They are of critical importance as they trade off against one another and frame the ways in which notions of participation have evolved. Questions of governance and the legitimacy of government administration have not always been framed in terms of participation. In this chapter, we use these tensions to examine participation from the perspective of government administration in the United States across time. Understanding the tensions and the developments and character of the periods from which the tensions evolved informs us as we consider the nature of the contemporary call for citizen participation. We believe that these tensions also illuminate a citizen gap whereby distinct citizen interests fail to be incorporated in government. After reviewing these tensions and their historical antecedents, we turn our attention to some of the familiar forms of participation that have evolved.

From the perspective of state and local government administration, citizen participation connotes extraordinary involvement processes that occur outside of the business of everyday governance. Citizen participation was

FIGURE 1.1   Tensions

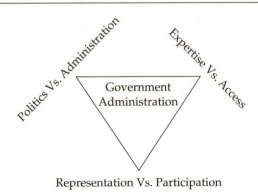

not always a supplemental or compensatory notion. In fact, Kweit and Kweit (1981) argue that the efforts of citizens defined government itself up until the ratification of the Constitution.

In Europe, the governments existed and citizens were born into an established political order. In the United States, however, with few exceptions, communities existed before their governments, and the people were required by necessity to participate in constructing their own government structures and the laws that would be enforced.

Absent a centralized authority for decision making, and largely preferring none, citizens, through their collective efforts and resources, agreed on the rules by which society would operate and the goods that would be publicly provided. These factors helped to set the stage for some of the ongoing struggles of participation. A series of constitutional and legislative efforts, coupled with growth in the size and scope of government administration, have removed citizens from what had been (until the time of the Constitution) a very direct control of government. Efforts in these domains (local, legislative, constitutional) have attempted to return some of this control.

Representation Versus Participation

The founders of the United States dealt with the immediate concern shared by many: how to create a government that would ensure the sovereignty of a nation while at the same time guaranteeing that this government would not oppress its citizens. The method selected was a process that involved citizens indirectly, through the election of representatives.

James Madison believed that representative government created a dependent, and therefore sympathetic, reliance on the public (Madison, in *The Federalist*, 52, Hamilton, Madison, and Jay, 1982). Even Thomas Jefferson (1984), although believing in the regular evolution, even revolution, of government by the people, was uncomfortable with the notion of the direct election of representatives. Legislating for the entire union required talents and skills that might not be found in those popularly elected. The outcome was that citizens would elect national and state representatives, state legislatures would select senators, and electors were to pick presidents.

By establishing an executive branch, the Constitution created a new governmental relationship: that between the citizen and the administrator. Early views about the executive office, whether in favor of absolute term limitation (Jefferson) or perpetually renewable tenure (Hamilton), turned on the impact on the citizenry and the ability to preserve citizens' influence in government affairs. Once the government was established, Hamilton believed its administration should be highly professional and insulated from the citizenry.

Leonard White (1948) describes the ensuing debate over the structure of government as one between Hamilton's federalists and Jefferson's republicans. The federalists saw strong executively controlled administrative functions as essential to the development of a strong economy. The republicans argued that the power of government action to enter into the daily affairs of citizens should be exercised locally, where those affected would have the most control.

Hamilton and his contemporaries could not have imagined the size and scope that administration would assume even a few generations later. Citizens may have been content with representation alone in a government of local scope and discrete federal duties. Along with the creation of large bureaucracies came the realization that governmental actors who are not elected have the ability to make decisions that could change people's lives.

By the time of the Jacksonians, the federal government had become relatively large and centralized. Citizens were moving west to take advantage of available land and resources, and they found themselves in need of the collective services that a distant government could not easily provide. To understand these circumstances, do not visualize the "Wild West" of American film but rather a junior high school class with a substitute teacher. The idea of a distant sovereign (be it a central government or a school principal) was inadequate to provide the structure to accomplish the work that needed to be done.

The Westerners found themselves in need of political structure and created governments where they were needed. The struggle for the removal of obstacles to voting and office holding that ensued has been described as the first participation crisis in U.S. history (Kweit and Kweit, 1981, p. 17). Broadened suffrage rights and the development of the party system created opportunities for greater control and input for the citizenry. President Jackson, himself a Westerner, eliminated the privilege component of appointment to the bureaucracy and established party loyalty as the sole criterion for such jobs. The citizens at large were then represented by the participation of their peers in the bureaucracy.

Participatory or democratic crises, whether resulting from economic catastrophe or political scandal, have boiled this soup from the same set of bones: Is citizen participation through representation and administration alone adequate to ensure the pursuit of the public good? In *Public Administration and the Public Interest*, Pendleton Herring (1936) argues that neither the administrators nor the citizens and others with competing demands for government can declare themselves sole proprietors of the public interest. They will either substitute their own judgment for that of the people or assert their personal interests. Herring relies on the open scrutiny of administration and the wisdom of administrators to identify and secure the public good. There is no notion of direct participation here, simply the idea that administration becomes representative through vigilance and stewardship in the absence of direct electoral accountability.

Questions about the ability of elected officials to secure the public good led to the reforms of the early twentieth century. Particularly dramatic in terms of the ability of citizens to have increased input in public decisions were the establishment of the ballot initiative, referendum, and recall.[3]

States allowing initiatives require a certain number or proportion of citizens to sign a petition that places statutory or constitutional changes on the ballot. States with referenda have a provision whereby existing statutes or constitutional provisions are placed on the ballot for voter approval. This may occur through citizen petition or by referral from the legislature. States with recall provisions set a threshold for petition signatures that triggers a vote on the removal of an elected official. It should be noted that none of these provisions are substitutes for a choice by popular vote (election), but rather increase the frequency of such opportunities.

Clearly, such methods of "direct" democracy ensure increased citizen participation in government decision making. The claim that citizens get what they expect from the resulting elections is more troublesome. Thomas Cronin (1989) contends that the evidence from California's (1978) Proposition 13 and Massachusetts's (1980) Proposition 2½ reveal that "voters knew what they wanted to do, and subsequent studies suggest that these tax cuts did not hamper economic development or severely impair city services" (p. 87). These same arguments are harder to make in more contemporary ballot measures such as Oregon's (1990) Measure 5 and (1997) Measure 50, the impacts of which were complex and very difficult to judge in advance. Furthermore, the use of professional signature gatherers and other commercial petition-generating methodologies have blurred the line between citizen and commercial interests to such a degree that it is unclear whether the benefits of such measures accrue in any manner that correlates with the proportion of votes cast.

Cronin (1989) argues that these provisions, although generally used responsibly by citizens, have failed to go far enough to secure citizen input in federal decision making. He reviews the arguments for and against the establishment of a national referendum to create binding federal law.[4,5]

Such provisions at the state level already reach ridiculous proportions and are easily subverted by the rapidly burgeoning signature solicitation industry that was partially responsible for the inclusion of a record twenty-three ballot measures in the Oregon elections of November 1996. Opponents of these reforms argue with the founders of the Constitution that there is a difference between public opinion and the public interest. Voting for representatives, these opponents believe, is adequate input, particularly where citizens may have neither time, talent, nor inclination to come to informed judgments.

Thus, since before the Constitution, the degree to which citizens are to be spoken for, or looked after, by government leaders, has been an unresolved tension. Attempts to "reinfuse" the democratic process with greater degrees of citizen input or control are by no means the result of a consensual understanding of the theoretical traditions of the nation. Instead, such innovations represent one understanding on a continuum between two points.

Politics Versus Administration

Citizen participation occurs in the middle of the tension between politics and administration. If politics is completely separate from administration, and administration implies neutral expertise, then the legitimate role of citizens might normatively be confined to the political process. If some blurring of this distinction is conceded, this role can be more broadly construed.

When Woodrow Wilson (1887) wrote about the administration of a constitutional government, he discarded the prevailing orthodoxy that administration was a political function (and one unworthy of scholarly pursuit) for a belief that administration was a distinct function (and one justifying the attentions of political scientists).

Frank J. Goodnow (1900) held a contrary view. He argued that the separation of politics and administration does not work. He saw the contest between the powers (judicial, executive, administrative) to express the will of the state as counterproductive. Thus, administration was simply another player in the political arena, competing for influence. He advocated an independent but limited administration. He argued that administrative powers should be ample to complete the tasks determined necessary to execute the will of the state but not so broad as to usurp popular government. From this perspective, citizen participation is confined to political activity. Where this activity occurs through political parties, citizens might find themselves having direct influence in both the expression and execution (through patronage) of the state will.

The separateness of the administrative function became a new orthodoxy, and scientific management became the hegemonized ideal. Although not directly questioning scientific administration, Mary Parker Follett (1924) questioned the ability of administrative officials to actually represent the will of the people. To Follett, the citizen was the irreducible base element of democratic governance. She argued that citizen input must be elicited at many points throughout the administrative process and that the interrelatedness between government activities and the persons acting and receiving those services ought to be recognized.

Pendelton Herring (1936) describes the equity agenda of government as its primary and most sacred purpose. He argues that administration should be set apart from the people, who should make their entreaties to the politicians whom they elect. He views the bureaucracy as reliant upon experts and their skills. In light of burgeoning interest groups, he argues that public sanction must compensate for the accumulated grievances of special interests that rise in opposition to administrative acts unfavorable to them. In this view, the role of the citizen is clearly defined as the power of the vote and the ability to form coalitions that influence politicians. Herring makes cautionary allusions to bureaucracies run wild: those that become remote and unyielding out of a necessity to shield themselves from the whims of advocates. Later reforms have tried to break down this shield.

David Lilienthal (1944), while lauding the efforts of the Tennessee Valley Authority (TVA) at citizen inclusion in an apolitical administration, chronicles the fact that citizens were not decision makers but were installed on numerous boards and committees with oversight for aspects of TVA projects. It is of course ironic that Lilienthal writes about the value of a strong citizen participation element to administration while overlooking the fact that democracy marched right over thousands of small farmers and landowners in efforts to dam and flood basins to provide cheap power and water to larger concerns elsewhere. The importance of his work to the development of notions of citizen participation is in the amount of participation he advocated, not necessarily its quality components. Among his normative arguments is the endorsement of the TVA policy of prohibiting authority employees from political speech or action (other than voting).

Philip Selznick (1949), also writing about the TVA and grassroots organizations, has a more pessimistic view of such citizen involvement. Selznick writes of co-optation, his term for the phenomenon whereby special interests interject their agendas in place of that of the agency. He describes a series of trade-offs between the agency and citizens or other interests that affected the ways in which values, goals, and administrative procedures became institutionalized. In essence, the TVA's administration, designed to be free from the burden of political governance, became political.

One measure of the variations of political involvement required for government action, according to P. H. Appleby (1949), is the degree to which government function is exposed to the citizenry. Administrative activities that are exposed to large numbers of the general public will become more political than those affecting only a few. Appleby views administration as complete and distinct from politics. The role and influence of the citizen, according to Appleby, is to focus popular concerns through participation in political activity and to vote responsibly.

Norton Long (1949 and 1952), like Herring, sees the decision-making process as heavily influenced by executive and legislative politics, ultimately leaving gaps for administration to fill, particularly in pursuit of special program interests. This notion is echoed by the constitutionalists in a more contemporary public administration debate (Rohr, 1986, p. 40; Wamsley et al., 1990, p. 46). Administrators are faced with the responsibility of running what amounts to a fourth branch of government. They rely on their skills and talents to do so in a fair and expert fashion. Long argues that bureaucracy is itself representative and must rely on itself to check the other powers of government. Thus, whereas Long's faith is in the professionalism and separation of the administration, Appleby's is in the wisdom of citizens in their political choices and the ability of the public servants to act in citizens' best interests.

Emmette Redford (1969), in *Democracy in the Administrative State*, argues that it is administration that touches citizen's lives and administration is where their influence should be felt. Redford describes the formation of interest group coalitions, in addition to voting and party membership, as legitimate ways in which citizens may participate in their government. But only certain kinds of interests are likely to be represented by such coalitions, specifically those of sufficient intensity and quantity to allow for easy aggregation and organization. In this understanding of government, the citizen without large economic stakes or majoritarian concerns is largely left out of the process. Redford sees administration as checked by citizen involvement, but he warns of the limitations of such processes.

Theodore Lowi (1969) argues forcefully that the dominance of interest group politics has served to erode work toward the public good. This erosion has primarily occurred in the functions of administration, where well organized and financed groups have been able to usurp justice and fairness in the policy and planning processes by substituting their own agendas.

All of these theorists are responding to the same essential truth: Bureaucracies persist and they are large and (descriptively if not normatively) political. The political process designed to balance powers and protect citizens from tyranny does not always work as intended. The citizen is faced with different roles in relationship to these bureaucracies, depending on the views of the theorist. Herring's citizens are at once apart from and protected by administration. They are only to be heard from by politicians. Appleby's citizens have more responsibility—responding to administrative acts by coalescing like-minded citizens in groups for political action. Goodnow's citizens may participate directly in the administration of the public will as a reward for political activity. Redford's citizens are members of interest groups applying their influence directly on administration, but both Redford and Lowi note that only those most affected by the work of an administration will be motivated to participate in such groups.

And thereby public administration leaves another gap, the citizen gap. In none of these scenarios are citizen interests (as distinct from special, political, or stakeholder interests) incorporated in the administration of government in any manner larger than a colonial or protectivist notion of the public will. Even here the public will is defined by either administrators or politicians. When contemporary decision makers, public managers, and citizen activists speak of inserting citizen input and deliberation in administrative decision making through various methods, they are speaking about this gap.

Bureaucracies and Expertise Versus Citizen Access

Those centralized and professional bureaucracies that are highly independent from political functions may also be distant from the public. In some cases, this seems a reasonable fit with their mission. Few would argue that the Departments of Defense or Energy should look directly to the public for guidance about what choices to make and how to pursue their goals. In other cases, bureaucracies make many decisions affecting the daily lives of citizens but are perceived as equally centralized and impervious to the entreaties of the public. A paradox—between the growth in the need for expertise in a complex society and the concurrent growth in the cries of citizens for access to the decision processes—has contributed much to the structure of the contemporary citizen participation process.

When President Jackson gave his first State of the Union address, he argued that there was nothing special about the public service and that it could, and indeed should, be conducted by typical members of the citizenry at large (Jackson, 1837). Why then, do some theorists trace the dawn of the bureaucratic age in American government to this administration (Nelson, 1982)?

Greater representation in the context of the growth of the bureaucracy was appealing to many citizens. The direct beneficiaries of this perspective, however, were those granted patronage appointments in the civil service. Thus, just as revolution had served to exchange one administration for another, Jackson's purge of expert, elite, and isolated bureaucrats traded them for a bureaucracy characterized by political spoils and executive allegiance.

Michael Nelson (1982) argues that later reforms were just as pernicious as earlier bureaucratic excesses in their delivery of unintended consequences to citizens. The Pendelton Act of 1883 led to the professionalization of the civil service. At the same time, it removed from political accountability the fastest-growing sectors of government. Bureaucracy was now more stable, and therefore more influential in the affairs of administration, than politics. Despite Jackson's efforts to the contrary, the shape of these bureaucracies remained true to the Hamiltonian vision: vertical, hierarchical, and removed from the public.

Appleby (1949) describes this hierarchy as increasingly pitched against expertise and in favor of politics, particularly at the top of administrative organizations. In his view, citizens frustrated with government and its administrative responsiveness were unrealistic in their expectations. What is reasonable for citizens to achieve, according to this argument, is what you can persuade politicians to accomplish on your behalf. Any more direct access, as by means of national referendum, would impede the process of governance (Appleby, 1949; Cronin, 1989).

If our contemporary society faces growing demands for the technical competence of its workers, as some argue that it does (Reich, 1992), then we may expect the government also to find it demands these kinds of skills. Such needs for expertise may serve to further exacerbate the existing tensions between governments and citizens. As more government processes open up to citizen input, the need for citizen education and the need to provide citizens with the highest quality of information become more pronounced. Even with such efforts, governments will continue to require expertise beyond that which citizens generally find accessible. Citizen participation efforts, where they occur, will continue to operate in this environment.

Tensions

Recall the tensions characterized in Figure 1.1. These tensions—representation versus participation, politics versus administration, and bureaucracy and expertise versus citizen access—represent the field on which participation is played. Each tension encroaches on the relationship of citizens to their government and each feeds it. All have remained relevant, and descriptive, when applied to the contemporary challenges of citizen participation in government.

Each set of tensions competes with the others for the ability to frame government administration. If the idea that government is representative of the citizen takes hold, citizens and government alike may be less concerned about participation. As the representative notion wanes, as evidenced by growing distrust of government, so also does the acceptance of the ideal that the citizens may rely solely on representatives to make their case for government change.

The reliance on bureaucratic expertise balances against the ability of citizens to directly access the administration of government. This balance is arguably a perceptual one with deep cultural and traditional roots. Western European democracies are far more comfortable with professional administrators in higher levels of government than are citizens of the United States. Consequently, the fulcrum of balance for those countries would be further from citizen access than in the United States. The balance of these elements influences the climate for, and structure of, citizen participation. The politics/administration dichotomy presents a third set of tensions that influence participation. If administration is a fundamentally political action, as the U.S. federal government shifts more responsibilities to local levels of government, the politics/administration debate may be reinvigorated yet again. Here citizen trust may interact with the shift in responsibility to affect the shape of governance. Citizen distrust of local administrators to deliver services may lead to further calls for direct citizen involvement. Changes in the balance of these tensions, whether as the result of historical accident or public persuasion, will affect the desire for additional citizen participation and the room for it.

Given the way these tensions have changed over the past thirty years, it is not surprising to see the development of a plethora of citizen involvement efforts beyond what is required by law. The politics versus administration tension affords no obvious role for citizens, leaving them largely out of the decision-making arena. Trust in representatives has declined, and with it the acceptance of the ideal that the citizen may rely solely on representatives to make important decisions, providing further impetus for increased meaningful citizen involvement. In addition, the ability of citizens to directly access government balances against the increasing reliance on bureaucratic expertise in an increasingly complex world. This increasing need for specific expertise and knowledge provides an incentive for inventing sophisticated means of involving citizens such that the problems are presented and deliberated in the context of their complexity. Many governments, seeking citizen assent, have undertaken the design and implementation of citizen participation projects. These projects operate within these tensions in influencing government administration.

Tensions cry for release, and problems for solutions. Scholars and practitioners have therefore turned their attention over the years to techniques for involving citizens with government. It is to the development of the earliest of these techniques and the events and ideas driving them that we now turn.

Public Hearings

John Clayton Thomas (1995) notes that the concept of public involvement as integral to administration is a novelty of these modern times and efforts. Tracing the growth of involvement programs through the expansion of the Great Society, he concludes that even though the antipoverty programs proved disappointing, the public input attached to such efforts continued to grow and broaden, particularly due to federal program requirements. Thomas relates an increasing demand for citizen participation to the increased educational level of the public. Although education levels have increased over the past fifty years, trust and electoral participation have declined, suggesting a complex and interrelated causal structure to the blossoming of forms of participation.

It was during a period of deterioration in the public trust that the shift to government-sponsored citizen participation in decentralized bureaucracies first appeared. Distrust and an increase in government responsibilities bonded to make way for an explosion of interest groups. Interest groups, particularly where well organized and mobilized, have been very visible in public hearings. Public hearings have been a predominant source of citizen input in state and local government—particularly in administrative areas. Hearings, as idealized, allow administrators and politicians to get a "sense of the community"[6] on particular issues and activities of government (Cole and Caputo, 1984). They are an effective method of raising concerns that may otherwise not be heard, particularly when the decision-making process is exclusively reliant on experts. At the same time, hearings often frustrate both bureaucrats and citizens. Bureaucrats, faced with increasingly complex decisions, are unlikely to find citizens with relevant expertise in areas necessary to provide substantive guidance and consequently may discount citizen opinions. Citizens find that their testimony often has little if any observable impact on the policy direction of the agencies compelled to solicit it. They often find their involvement sought too late in the process to have much impact and may choose not to participate based on such experiences.

The world of environmental activism provides many examples of this frustration. Unable to influence the administrative process through hearings, many citizens have taken to participating in direct actions such as protests and blockades in an effort to reinsert their voices in the process. This has become particularly characteristic in timber use decisions and in the siting and construction decisions involving waste dumps, nuclear power plants, and high-energy power lines (Van Valey and Petersen, 1987).

Advisory Committees

The advisory committee is another classic method of public participation. The advisory committee is established in response to a statute or to create a group that can help to inform decision makers of the views of a select group of citizens. Often, these citizens are selected on the basis of their expertise or interests and appointed by the decision-making body. Hearings typically add public comment to an administrative process that is issue specific and of limited scope. Advisory committees meet to deliberate and make recommendations on multiple issues. Kweit and Kweit (1981) find that of these two forms, it is the committee that has the stronger claim of impact on government decisions (as ranked by government officials). Advisory committees, as vehicles of citizen involvement, are typically found in low- to mid-level governments and may be associated with political or administrative functions. Such committees include budget and public safety committees that meet regularly over the course of the year and those with a specific charge, such as task forces and ad hoc committees. (Advisory committees at higher levels of government are typically constituted of experts and political appointments and are not considered further in this discussion of citizen participation.)

Grassroots Versus Government-Sponsored Participation

In the section below, we consider the role of citizen agencies, which although created by statutory dictate, don many attributes of grassroots organizations. Before that discussion, however, it may be helpful to make a distinction between the government-sponsored participation approaches we consider in this book and grassroots participation movements.

There are substantial differences between grassroots and government-sponsored participation. Typically associated with grassroots or "bottom up" participation are the activities associated with neighborhood and activist groups. Much of the attention on citizen participation in the contemporary literature focuses on the efficacy and influence of these types of grassroots or neighborhood projects. One fine source exploring the issues and accomplishments of such efforts is *The Rebirth of Urban Democracy* by Jeffrey Berry, Kent Portney, and Ken Thomson (1993; see chap. 2, "Gauging Results of Citizen Participation Efforts"). This work compares cities with and without substantial neighborhood organizations. Recent work by Janice Tulloss (1995) in this area draws some distinctions between types of participation, noting that by achieving legitimacy, such groups often sacrifice autonomy (p. 533).

Table 1.1 compares important characteristics of government-sponsored and grassroots efforts. Government-sponsored and grassroots citizen participation efforts represent different constituencies. Participation forms sponsored by governments aim to elicit the input of the broadest possible public, whereas those of grassroots origin bring together persons sharing a specific concern or the same geography. The narrowness of the grassroots interest is axiomatic. Such efforts develop strength and clarity where their focus is specific and their membership is limited to those who care about the issue selected. Such efforts become diluted and fail to succeed when

TABLE 1.1   Grassroots Versus Government-Sponsored Citizen Participation

Government Sponsored	*Grassroots Sponsored*
Characteristics of Participation	
Broad/representative constituencies	Narrow/interest-based constituencies
Sponsorship/commitment from decision makers	Advisory to/challenging decision makers
Jurisdiction based	Neighborhood based
Employs experts	Employs experts and advocates
Organized to inform	Organized to persuade
Most Effective Use of Participation Form	
Issues affecting entire jurisdiction	Issues affecting local, contiguous, and homogeneous groups
Jurisdiction-wide acceptance important	Neighborhood acceptance important
High levels of community-wide disagreement, low levels of local interest, e.g., citywide budget prioritization	Low levels of community-wide disagreement, high levels of local interest, e.g., neighborhood land use decisions

membership is broader and issues are less clearly defined (similar statements can be made about stakeholder groups).

The structure and intent of the two kinds of processes are likewise poised to satisfy different functions. Government-sponsored participation efforts are organized to inform both the public and decision makers. Members of the public optimally gain a deeper understanding about the dynamics of the problems facing government and decision makers ought to exit the process having gained a real understanding of what solutions the public supports. In many cases, experts from inside or outside of government are used to help both groups reach this level of understanding. Grassroots efforts, by comparison, are poised to persuade governments that their specific concerns are powerful and their numbers great enough to justify action on behalf of the public. Experts may be employed here as well, but in an effort to inform and persuade.

Finally, grassroots actions to engage citizens to participate in the lobbying of government are most effective when the concerns of the very local group are more pointed, acute, and uniform than those of the public at large. This might be the case in a neighborhood land use decision where those in one precinct are gravely concerned about the abutters to a park whereas those in the rest of the town are somewhat ambivalent. One or another solution to the local problem may prevail without much disagreement from the larger community. Government-sponsored participation projects are suited to a different type of problem, namely, one generating great levels of controversy jurisdiction-wide but not divided into obvious neighborhood or single-issue interests. The budget dilemmas facing local government today are typical of problems of this type. There is likely to be community-wide disagreement about what combinations of tax increases and service cuts to pursue when balancing a budget, but little locally distinct interest.

Both forms of participation, grassroots and government sponsored, may have important positive effects on the provision of government services. We focus here on government-sponsored efforts because they normatively capture the ideas and deliberation of the public at large. We now return to our discussion of participation mechanisms with a consideration of the citizen agency.

Citizen Agencies

Community action agencies or community action programs (CAAs) are citizen agencies that evolved as a result of the mandate for the "maximum feasible participation" of residents and affected groups in the Economic Opportunity Act of 1964 (Cole, 1973, p. 13; Kweit and Kweit, 1981, p. 5). This mandate quickly spread across many government services and spawned the citizen agency as a method of citizen participation. Prior to this time, government-sponsored participation had been limited to the public hearings and advisory committees described above. The focus of this new approach was to give participation as well as power to the poor in implementing the war on poverty at the municipal level. To accomplish this, local agencies were established in ways that encouraged the recipients of agency services to participate in decisions regarding the distribution of antipoverty resources in their areas. The local boards were given direct control over the federal money allocated for these programs.

A common public response to the CAAs was that they were given too much power and autonomy (Cole, 1973, p. 118). Conflicts arose between local governments and these largely independent CAAs. The direct allocation of funds to citizen boards was discontinued in favor of a process whereby money would be allocated through the auspices of a local elected official, typically a mayor. Succeeding programs, such as Model Cities, softened the structural requirements for participation to ensure that the programs operated under the jurisdiction of local governments. Ultimately, the direct allocation of federal funds to such agencies was terminated in favor of state and local revenue sharing.

David Greenstone and Paul Peterson (1973) examined the character and effects of CAAs in various cities. They found, among many other things, that the establishment of a citizen participation mechanism did not ensure participatory policies in the governments that housed them. This was true even when members of citizen agencies were able to use the power of their agency to help them to elect ideological allies (p. 264). Greenstone and Peterson also found that in the machine cities of the 1960s (Chicago, Philadelphia, New York) the influence of citizen participation groups corresponded with the balance of power between machine politicians and reformers, the reformers being more open to citizen influence. In reform cities (Los Angeles, Detroit), the influence of CAAs increased with the strength of the minority community. This, the authors argue, led to different political outcomes with CAAs in the different locations (p. 231).

The CAAs marked two key changes in citizen participation. The first was the shift to actions occurring at the administrative level and away from the focus on the political policy-making process. The other was that citizens attained, through the administration of these antipoverty programs, some connection to power. Although critics of these programs have complained that the existence of such power caused additional and complicating conflicts among citizen participants, and between them and their governments (Cole, 1973), the fact remains that their decisions were directly implemented. Such a connection to power has never again been achieved.

The view of government administration is framed differently across different forms of participation. Participation confined to hearings relies primarily on an expert and representative administration for the execution of the public will. Citizen agencies such as the CAAs, on the other hand, reflect a different order in which direct access and the direct political influence of citizens frames the way that government programs are administered. It is within the context of these tensions and within a historical context that citizen participation emerges as a distinct form.

Discussion

> The omnipotence of the majority, and the rapid as well as absolute manner in which its decisions are executed in the United States, has not only the effect of rendering the law unstable, but it exercises the same influence upon the execution of the law and the conduct of the public administration. (de Tocqueville, 1838/1899, p. 275)

In governance and administration, de Tocqueville viewed the extent of citizen influence to be a fundamental flaw of democracy in the United States. How, one might ask, did the nation proceed in its evolution to develop since that time even more opportunities for citizen input and oversight in government? Our answer to this question has come in postulating and posing the answer to another: How have the forces creating certain classic tensions in public administration exerted themselves on the structure and extent of citizen participation in the United States?

The contemporary context of citizen participation involves few of the same material concerns, but the same tensions frame the struggles in the 1800s, 1970s, and 1990s. We have discussed in this chapter how the founders of the United States struggled to create a government strong enough to act as a sovereign but with enough citizen input to prevent tyranny and oppression. The rapid expansion of the nation and the need for government institutions far from a central authority combined with a disaffection with spoils politics to create a more directly represented citizenry. Calls for populist reform many decades later sought to create methods that allowed citizens to bypass elected officials and vote directly on certain ballot measures. The contemporary concern that the exercise of public judgment is overtaken by celebrity and celerity in such measures echoes the debate of the framers of the Constitution regarding the degree to which citizens represent or are represented by their government.

Grappling with the implications of an administration separated, if not wholly apart, from politics has evolved with the size and industry of the nation. Challenges to the strictest tenets of scientific management brought with them some recognition that the citizen worker and service recipient were inseparable elements of a well-functioning production system. Nearly half a century after the zenith of scientific management and its arguments for technical efficiency, writers such as Redford return to citizen input as both an element of successful administration and also a remedy for inequities of interest. In the working out of this tension between administration and politics, a citizen gap appears in the sense that the public will remains defined by representatives or administrators regardless of the form of remedy each generation of theorists embraces.

Certainly, the need for experts has increased with the complexity of the tasks facing government administrators over time. The development of more bureaucratic forms of governance may have ultimately created more room for expert residents, but these forms blossomed from the seeds of discontent with an isolated and erudite government.

Subsequent reforms to shift government employment from the well connected to the well trained did not by themselves ensure citizens a voice in how those services would be delivered. Competence in production does not by itself create comity in consumption. In the production of public goods and services, the citizen is inseparable from that which is being produced. The struggle to bring talent to governing and keep government responsive to public concerns is as much a concern today as it was when Jackson first assigned friendly faces to tasks they were not prepared to undertake.

When we turn our eyes toward federal administration alone, it would appear that the federalists prevailed, creating a government largely insulated from direct citizen entreaty. Local governments have made, or have been caused to make, greater strides toward the incorporation of a citizen view in their endeavors. The methods of so-called direct democracy are but one example. Certainly, the advent of the community action agencies in cities throughout the country in the 1960s changed the nature of the relationship between local citizen groups and their governments. Although the immediate effect may have been substantive and resource focused, the enduring contribution of these regimes may lie in the legacy of tolerance for direct citizen influence in certain areas of government.

The earliest extrarepresentational techniques for citizen participation briefly discussed in this chapter (public hearings, advisory committees, and citizen agencies) are typically responses to statutes or other authorities that cause them to be put into use. None of them are routes to forming a valid representation of the will of citizens at large. Citizen agencies, in the form of the community action programs became, in many ways, authorities of their own. Nonetheless, all represent efforts to fill a citizen gap widened by the growing population, the size of the government, and innovations in techniques to infuse the decision-making process with moneyed interests.

De Tocqueville worried that the fancy of the public was too easily captured by popular issues, thus creating circumstances in which important government obligations could be neglected. As it turns out, it is difficult to determine how one might gauge what neglect is benign and what reflects an abdication of government responsibility. Parties with different interests are unlikely to agree on the criteria. Citizens may simultaneously subscribe to associations with different positions on the same issue.

The modern results of the search for citizen participation may not have satisfied the critics of burgeoning democracy. They reflect the struggles of this democracy to find, in administering the public will, methods to ensure a connection to the preferences of the citizen. Such methods may make democratic government more vulnerable to fashion than are other forms. The hope is that they also help to reinforce the trust in and legitimacy of a government that must provide services to a profoundly eclectic electorate. In the chapters that follow, we explore some contemporary and innovative techniques of citizen involvement in government administration and evaluate their potential merits.

Notes

1. There exist different uses of the terms *individualist* and *collectivist*. We use them here to be consistent with Kweit and Kweit (1981) in referring to a public interest defined by aggregated individual desires versus a public interest defined by a concern for the broader public good. We are not attempting to evoke allusions to

communitarianism, collectivism, or utopian ideals as expressed, for example, by Rousseau or More (see Rousseau, 1987; More, c. 1555/1988).

2. University of Michigan National Election Study. 1990 (http://www.umich.edu/2nesguide/toptables/tab5a1.htm). A similar survey conducted by the Gallup organization in August 1995 shows that this trust has dropped to 23%.

3. A thorough review of these techniques and their implications is provided by Thomas E. Cronin (1989).

4. Cronin (1989) ultimately rejects the national referendum and initiative petition on the basis that they would be too difficult to monitor for deception and access.

5. There may be a financial cost to governments subject to the provisions of direct democracy. Zax (1989) finds that the existence of the initiative petition pressures decision makers to increase popular spending, although Farnham (1990) notes little if any such effect.

6. The idea of taking a "sense of the community" or "sense of the meeting" as a method of participation and consensus formation may be attributed to the tradition of the Society of Friends (Quakers), whose meeting form of governance relies on the use of such a technique. Although no leader is elected, a clerk is designated to find and record the collectively acquired insight of the members at "meetings for worship with a concern for business" (see Society of Friends, 1999).

2

Contemporary Techniques for Citizen Involvement

The current governmental climate is one in which interest group politics largely prevail in decision making and citizen trust is low. Some citizens perceive a peremptory arrogance in the demeanor of officials. Many government officials, whether elected politicians or professional staff, describe public hearings as dominated by angry and uninformed residents and activist groups. This climate exists concurrent with budget deficits and eroding public tolerance of taxation. Lost in these participatory opportunities are the insights of the vast majority of citizens, who are unable or unwilling to attend hearings. These are people with low-intensity or low-quantity interests (Redford, 1969) or little rational reason for participation (Downs, 1957). Contemporary efforts in citizen participation operate under the theoretical assumption that governments should reach out to include the public in their decision making. The further assumption made by many such as Daniel Yankelovich (1992) and Alan Kay and his colleagues (1992) is that citizens' opinions and insights may be captured in ways that reflect a considered judgment, as opposed to a cursory or reflexive response.

Polls are one way to reach such citizens. Polls have had their own impact on contemporary citizen participation. Public opinion research has allowed decision makers to know at any point in time what a majority of the population thinks about a variety of issues. As a result, decisions can be made that reflect the changes of attitudes over time. This can be considered one method of participation, but for many it is a rather unsatisfactory method. The veteran pollster Daniel Yankelovich (1992) argues that public opinion gathered in this manner is unstable and uninformed and that techniques of deliberation need to be employed to move citizens to a more developed stage of discourse. Voter participation rates are low. Trust in government continues to decrease. If the goal of polling is to bolster trust in government or increase participation, it has not worked.

Precisely how to incorporate citizen preferences in decision making, or even to identify them in a meaningful way, is the challenge of contemporary citizen involvement programs. We have reviewed various attempts at involving citizens meaningfully in decision making across the nation, and indeed internationally.[1] The vast majority of the projects we have found are citizen satisfaction surveys, geared to provide "customer" feedback to local governments, and are not included here. A few of these projects brought citizens together in groups to discuss their attitudes about various government issues. Only a very few of them involved deliberation, or active dialogue between participants. In many cases, participants were not selected randomly but were encouraged to attend or respond based on a newspaper article or a flyer. A smaller number of governments have used citizen preferences to help guide their budget processes, but only a handful of them have made attempts to constrain the choices presented on the basis of the existing budgetary limitations.

The projects described here are a small subset of the citizen input activities that have occurred across the past several years. Most of these have been collected with a particular eye toward their implications for budget processes or resource allocation. We have not included activities such as standing committees, advisory committees, and neighborhood groups (such processes could fill a book of their own), focusing instead on the discrete, time-limited activities that governments employ to gather input and gain public understanding for specific problems. These fall into two basic types: citizen surveys or forums and citizen juries or panels.

Citizen Surveys and Forums

Citizen surveys apply the contemporary methods of survey research to the problem of noninvolvement. Through the use of random sampling, governments may identify representative groups of citizens and gauge their support for various services, as well as their willingness to pay for them. Sampling may be stratified such that respondents reflect the diversity of the citizens in a given region. At their best, these methods provide a real gauge of citizen opinion and support, based on a consideration of the actual constraints facing decision makers. At their worst, such efforts are not representatively drawn and simply reflect a (typically overstated) expression of citizen satisfaction with government services.

Citizen forums typically involve the invitation (random or public) of citizens to one or more sessions where problems facing local governments are explored or community attitudes are assessed. During the sessions, various techniques are employed to determine citizen attitudes about a variety of issues. Large gatherings are often broken down into smaller groups that pursue list-making, prioritizing, or budget-balancing techniques.

During 1991 and 1992, **Eugene, Oregon,** employed an innovative combination of public forums, budget-balancing exercises, and representative surveys to determine public support for a variety of spending and budget-balancing alternatives. The fundamental mission was to provide guidance about how to balance the city's budget in a way that was sustainable over time. The citizen involvement process was known as Eugene Decisions.[2] Eugene Decisions was iterative in that there were multiple rounds of citizen input. It was deliberative in that it was designed to give citizens opportunities to make judgments about their preferred strategies after considering the set of fiscal circumstances facing the city and in some cases after having structured conversations with other citizen forum participants.

Similar to Eugene Decisions was a process replicated in 1996 and 1997 in **Sacramento, California**. A representative sample of citizens were telephoned about their budget preferences, and all residents of the city received a budget worksheet to complete and submit to the city. The city also conducted open forums in which citizens were able to come together and deliberate on the effects of different budget reduction strategies. Seventy-five percent of the (representatively sampled) respondents included revenues in their budget-balancing strategy, but support for any one strategy failed to exceed 45%. In the midst of this process, statewide voters passed Proposition 218, requiring a public vote to increase any tax or fee. In subsequent rounds of the Sacramento process, revenue strategies were dropped from the areas of inquiry.

In 1993, **Lexington, Kentucky,** conducted eighty-nine town meetings that solicited input from citizens about their family and household concerns, neighborhood issues, larger community issues, levels of activity in the community, and the legacy that they wished the region to build (Vanhoose, 1993). This process, called Speak Out Lexington 1993, was a follow-up to a successful citizen input process from the previous year. Both efforts focused on gathering general public views about a diverse set of issues and developing a sense of what people felt were the appropriate roles of government. The participants, who were not randomly selected, were overwhelmingly positive about their region and its potential. Many expressed ways in which they felt government could be more responsive. A survey included in the meetings asked participants questions such as "What three things do you like most about your neighborhood?" and "What would make the community better?" The process produced a long list of one- or two-word responses based on these questions and the open sessions.

Direction 88 was a project conducted by the city of **Springfield, Oregon,** to garner public input in its ongoing budget process (Leblanc, 1988). In addition to a representative community opinion survey of 1,500 residents, citizens were brought together during a week of public meetings to review the results and identify areas of concern for the city council. This information was used by the city council in the annual goal-setting process, and these goals guided the formation of the city budget (Collier, 1987; Portal, 1987). Among the results of the process were the establishment of service priorities for fire protection, emergency medical response, police enforcement, and the repair of sanitary sewer lines.

Chattanooga, Tennessee, conducted Vision 2000, a series of public forums and information sessions that garnered 1,700 participants across twenty weeks. The purpose was to determine the will of the people regarding the health of the community. In 1992, the process was further developed with ReVision 2000. Meetings were held in neighborhoods throughout the city to gather more citizen ideas in a collective effort to revitalize the community (National Civic League, 1994a). The results have been concrete and implementable designs for many aspects of the Chattanooga community structure. Participants were not randomly selected.

Fort Collins, Colorado, combined the input of citizens and stakeholders in Challenge Fort Collins, a planning process designed to identify high-priority projects for improving the community, which ultimately identified nine projects for the city to pursue. One proposed project, Riverwalk, would build urban pathways along the Cache la Poudre River, which runs through Fort Collins. Challenge Fort Collins revealed that a majority of residents support such a project, despite the vocal objections of some community activists (National Civic League, 1994b). Again, the citizen participants were not randomly selected.

In 1986, the city of **Sparks, Nevada,** mailed 18,000 households a "budget ballot" on which citizens could indicate their preferences for the spending allocations of their municipality (City of Sparks, 1986). Residents were presented with a tentative budget in the form of a (budget) pie chart with spending separated into eight categories (in decreasing size order): public safety, health and sanitation, general government, public works, leisure services, debt service, municipal court, and contingencies. Respondents were asked if they agreed with the tentative budget as presented. Thirty-one percent agreed, 51% did not agree, and 18% were undecided (1,061 responses were received). But when citizens were queried about possible increases or decreases, no majorities existed for any but the status quo responses for public works, health and sanitation, and leisure services. Public safety and general government had, respectively, 47% and 48% of respondents indicating that they sought no change to these categories, with the remainder of respondents divided between increases and decreases. Responses for debt service, courts, and contingencies were not solicited (City of Sparks, 1986).

On the revenue side of the Sparks budget ballot, residents were asked whether they would support additional taxes for specific service enhancements. In reply to response options of "not needed," "might lend support," and "necessary and I would support," 43% supported additional taxes for a fire station and 58% supported increases for additional police officers. In both cases, 18% felt such additions were not needed (Melton, 1986). The approach taken by the city of Sparks is also conceptually similar to the budget pie (see "Preferences Under a Budget Constraint" later in this chapter).

Michael Meshenberg (1989) notes that cities such as **New York, Boston, Las Vegas, Cincinnati,** and **Dayton,** together with **Johnston County, Kansas,** have provided budget information to residents and actively solicited their input through methods such as random sample surveying and neighborhood meetings. More recently, significant public input has been noted in the budget processes of **Dayton, Ohio; Saint Paul, Minnesota;** and **Portland, Oregon** (Hallman, 1992). The public processes in these cities centered around democratically elected neighborhood governing boards and district councils. One of the twelve "general lessons" learned by Hallman in reviewing the budget processes of these cities is the need for "balancing parochial and city-wide perspectives" (p. 5). He notes that by involving those active in neighborhood associations in the citywide budget process, "macro" and "micro" viewpoints are combined such that citizen support is built for not only the services that the city provides but the revenues necessary to support them.

Fort Worth, Texas, took an unusual step in attempting to fill the citizen knowledge gap when it came to the budget process. The city issued a computer diskette containing a program that citizens could run to see the impact of their budget choices on taxes and deficits. This created an individualized forum, of sorts, that residents could participate in at their own pace and leisure. The budget simulator was well received by the public, and there was unusually little citizen opposition to the resulting budget—which included tax and spending increases (McKinney, 1996).

The city of **Tempe, Arizona,** conducted an extensive random sample survey of local residents, measuring such things as service satisfaction, usage, and spending priorities. When presented with twenty-two services, at least 90% of respondents indicated that they would like to see at least the same or more spending on all but three of the services. Only public art had more than a third of respondents seeking less funding (34%). Fully one-quarter (25%) of respondents replied that they felt that the city wasted money, although overall most (85%) agreed with the current spending priorities (Merrill, 1995; Yantis, 1995).

In addition to the municipalities listed above, many others presently employ or have employed survey methodologies in gathering citizen input in recent years. Some of these include **Scottsdale, Arizona; Pasadena, Santa Clarita, Ukiah,** and **Upland, California; Thornton, Colorado; Longwood** and **Orlando, Florida; Decatur, Illinois; Gaithersburg, Maryland; Blue**

Springs, Missouri; and **Henrico County** and **Virginia Beach, Virginia.**
Typical of these efforts is that of **Knoxville, Kentucky,** which conducts an
annual budget survey, querying residents about their quality of life and
satisfaction with and concerns about various city services (Lyons, 1994).
This information is available to elected officials when deciding on the priorities and financing strategies of the city government.

The city of **Auburn, Alabama,** provides another example of the use of
citizen surveys in setting budget priorities (Watson, Juster, and Johnson,
1991). In 1985, Auburn institutionalized citizen surveys as a way of providing feedback to city departments and the city council. After five years,
the process evolved to produce the following results: Council budget decisions are based in part on survey results and the survey techniques
themselves became increasingly sophisticated.

Although well-designed surveys may reveal preferences at a given
point in time, we expect the results may be volatile and preferences overstated in the absence of forced trade-offs or a budget constraint (see "Preferences Under a Budget Constraint," later in this chapter). Small group
deliberations and forums may mitigate these effects, where present.

Peter deLeon (1992) advocates the concept of democratized policy
analysis, which he calls "policy sharing." Policy sharing requires decision
makers to devise and practice ways to include citizens' values and preferences in formulating policies. It implies that citizens have access to planning and policy decisions. Furthermore, it suggests that citizens' opinions
will be heard and considered. Unlike Benjamin Barber (1984), deLeon
does not advocate opening the decision-making process to the many.
Rather, policy sharing includes the opinions of a representative group of
affected (although not necessarily knowledgeable) citizens in formulating
a proposed decision. We now turn to two related forms of potential policy decision sharing: citizen juries and citizen panels.

Citizen Juries and Panels

Citizen juries and panels are conducted through the random selection of a
representative group of citizens who come together to deliberate for a
discrete period of time about a particular issue. The concept driving this
form of citizen participation is that most citizens do not possess the information and cannot afford the time to come to well-reasoned judgments
about the complex issues facing government decision makers. These
processes provide a small, representative group of citizens high-quality
unbiased information and the (often compensated) time to deliberate and
consider this information thoroughly. The resulting decisions are expected to represent what the broader group of citizens would conclude if
they were subject to the same ideal conditions. The hope is that citizen

panels and juries will gain moral authority that will then influence policy makers. Voters will be able to trust the results of such processes, as those deliberating are representative of the general public and independent of the special interests that typically dominate public debate. Participants have expressed great satisfaction with these processes and with their freedom from bias (Crosby, 1993).

The faith of citizens in these juries and panels, together with the inherent independence of these bodies, should influence decision makers to act in accordance with the views they express. These qualities are also the Achilles' heel of such an approach. For all of the effort and expense involved, where they are not sponsored by decision makers, such citizen efforts may not be given any attention. In response to this difficulty, Crosby and others (Simonsen, Johnston, and Barnett, 1996; Watson et al., 1991) have noted the need to involve the media in such approaches as completely as possible.

Boulder, Colorado, convened a citizen panel for a transportation-planning process, using statistical sampling techniques to gather a representative group to overcome some of the problems of traditional citizen participation processes (Kathlene and Martin, 1991). This group of participants completed an extended series of exercises designed to provide them with the information required to make informed recommendations. This process involved many iterations of interviews and surveys in addition to the panel work of the selected participants. The results, in addition to providing cost-effective input, provided a master (transportation) plan with very little citizen opposition despite some of its more "radical" provisions (Kathlene and Martin, 1991). The vast majority (86%) of panel participants stated they would join the panel again because "they thought their participation 'made a difference in the decision process,' it 'felt good' to be a part of the community and 'to be linked to government,' and it was an 'interesting experience'" (Kathlene and Martin, 1991, p. 57). When the decision makers' opinions differed from those generated by the citizen panels, they were forced to explicitly justify their policies.

Ned Crosby (1991), president of the **Jefferson Center for New Democratic Processes** has developed a process called Citizens Jury[SM]. This process relies on stratified random sampling to select citizens who are subsequently paid to come together and deliberate about specific issues or elections. The jurors are issued a "charge," or statement of the problem that they are to explore. Information is presented to the jurors from several different points of view. A neutral moderator facilitates these sessions to ensure fairness and clarity in the presentations. Finally, jurors deliberate based on the information they have received and in relation to their charge. Based on the information presented and decisions required, this process may take between ten hours and ten days (Crosby, 1991).

Citizens Juries have been conducted on such diverse topics as global warming and political candidate contests. One of particular interest for budget applications was the Citizens Jury conducted by the Jefferson Center on the topic of the federal budget (see "Two National Projects on the Federal Budget Deficit," later in this chapter).

An effort sponsored by the Illinois League of Women Voters and the University of Illinois at Chicago established that those who were reached by their voting project were "more interested in the election, more likely to consider themselves well informed about the election, and more likely to vote" (Rundquist, Fox, and Strom, 1995, p.9). This process, conducted by the **Illinois Voter Project** (IVP), included a telephone poll asking open-ended questions about important policy problems and solutions, fourteen focus groups (organized by urban or suburban residence, race, and age cohort, with other groups for homeless men and women making the transition from welfare to work), and citizen panels.

Ortwin Renn and his colleagues (1993) developed a **three-step citizen involvement process** and applied it to a public facility siting process. The theoretical understanding underlying this process is that the quality of decisions will be improved by the combined efforts of stakeholders, experts, and citizens. A process that combines such points of view balances three forms of knowledge: that derived from personal experience, from technical expertise, and from social interests. The first step used in this model is the solicitation of criteria and objectives for evaluating options from stakeholders. These are structured by project staff into a hierarchical "value-tree" that each stakeholder group must approve. The second step of the process calls for expert judgment about the performance of each option based on the indicators agreed on in the first step. Groups of experts work together on this process, and time is allowed for the groups to deliberate independently and as a whole until consensus is achieved. Discrete differences can be maintained and moved forward. Arguments and evidence in defense of the resulting scale of values are videotaped. This step of the process is designed to be accomplished in one or two days.

The final step creates citizen panels from a random selection of directly and indirectly involved citizens. Stakeholders and public officials appear as witnesses in a process similar to Citizens Juries. Citizens receive information through videos, field trips, written presentations, and lectures (Renn et al., 1993). They process the information in small group discussion, through hearings and the receipt of testimony, and through consensus-building exercises. The participants are asked to use the values identified by the experts in their deliberations but are free to add more of their own. They may also add outcome options. Each value criterion is weighted against every other criterion, producing a matrix of relative weights and utility measures for each option. These calculations are completed by the participants individually and in small groups. The numerical results are used to aid the participants in coming to their final judgments about a desired option.

Renn et al. (1993) report very successful use of this method in West Germany, particularly as applied to energy policies. The project attempted in the United States appears to have been somewhat less satisfying. The authors worked with the New Jersey Department of Environmental Protection to apply this process to the siting of a proposed project for the land-based application of sludge. They note that "the envisioned program for the citizens panel was radically altered after the participants, in particular the land owners abutting the site, made it clear that they rejected the project of land application and that they felt more comfortable conducting their own meetings without assistance of a third party" (p. 204). These authors attribute this outcome to differences in culture, noting "clear evidence that the U.S. audience is more sensitive to process and methods of participation" (p.205). A lesson we draw is that processes should be matched with decision needs. Answers to questions such as "How safe is it?", "How much opposition is there to it?", and "What is the larger public interest in this project?" could likely be answered without such an elaborate process. This approach may work better for less parochial concerns, such as soliciting values for a national energy policy.[3]

Two National Projects on the Federal Budget Deficit

Many national polls have attempted to gauge citizen support for various government officials and policy options. Few have looked at developing an informed public opinion on issues facing the country. Before moving on, we note two such efforts relating to public budgets. One was a Citizens Jury, and the other a telephone survey.

The Citizens Jury brought together a representative group of Americans for a weeklong series of sessions in which the participants were provided with information about the federal budget as well as testimony from Democrats and Republicans. After receiving this information and asking questions, the jurors deliberated. The participants found themselves in support of greater tax increases than the Democrats sought and greater spending reductions than those proposed by the Republicans (Jefferson Center, 1993).

Similar results were obtained by a survey of Americans conducted by the Americans Talk Issues Foundation (ATIF) in 1991. For considering the federal budget deficit, ATIF designed a survey to model the Congressional budget process. This budget exercise reflected an option available to Congress but not to municipal decision makers: Expenditures could exceed revenues. Participants could make broad cuts across all areas or target specific programs. Current and historical levels of spending were presented. The goal of deficit reduction was stated at the outset. The interviews were long (thirty-six minutes) and complex, involving a series of interrelated and nested questions, the responses to which determined what questions came next or were deleted. The results of this survey of 1,000 randomly selected respondents from forty-eight U.S. states revealed

- An average net cut in the deficit of 21%
- Support for a balanced budget amendment to the U.S. Constitution
- A reduction of the deficit from $360 billion to $137 billion
- Cuts in spending of $140 billion (11.5%)
- Increases in revenues of $82 billion (7.8%)

When confronted with the real added costs of additional interest, 30% of respondents went back and made additional revenue increases and spending cuts (Kay et al., 1992). The results of the poll were reported to Congress.

Organizations with Ongoing Efforts in Citizen Participation

Some organizations have dedicated all or some of their efforts to improving the public dialogue, increasing citizen participation, and promoting citizen deliberation. **Public Agenda** is a nonprofit organization dedicated since 1975 to "bridg[ing] the gap between leadership and the public" (Bradley, 1995, p. 1). The work of this group has two missions: to reveal the public view on current policy choices and to provide for the kind of citizen education that leads citizens to make better informed, more thoughtful decisions (Public Agenda, 1995). Public Agenda conducts issues and opinion research and uses this information to present citizens with balanced and understandable materials about the issues selected. Working in partnership with many project partners, this organization has made high-quality nonpartisan materials available on issues across the complete policy spectrum, including education, health care, and the public debt (Walters, 1993).

Public Agenda has worked with the **Kettering Foundation** in developing the materials for National Issues Forums. The product of this collaboration has been a litany of policy books that seek to explain in a clear and fair voice the pressing public policy issues of the day. The forums are run like town meetings across the country and are designed to inform the widest audiences possible about the issues and dilemmas facing society and decision makers.

As previously mentioned, the **Jefferson Center for New Democratic Processes** is also concerned with the quality of the public debate and committed to methods of improving and influencing decision making. The interests of this organization and its founder, Ned Crosby, have been focused on methods of deliberation, as principally developed in the Citizens Jury.

Many organizations are interested in and pursuing electronic participation, typically through projects that use the Internet for linking citizens with each other and their governments. One of these is the **Center for Civic Networking** (CCN, 1995). This group provides information and technical assistance to those pursuing a wide variety of citizen participation endeavors, with a particular emphasis on electronic methods.

The University of Oregon's **Deliberative Democracy Project,** headed by Edward C. Weeks, has conducted or consulted on citizen participation projects in Eugene, Oregon; Fort Collins, Colorado; and Sacramento, California. The project "aims to give citizens the chance to participate meaningfully in public policy making" through the development and implementation of new models of deliberative democracy (Weeks, 1995).

The **Americans Talk Issues Foundation** pursues ongoing efforts in citizen participation through the extensive use of computer assisted telephone interviewing (CATI). This method allows interviewers to present respondents with much more realistic and detailed information about which to make choices and express preferences. The foundation has conducted numerous surveys of the public using this methodology. In most cases, the choices of respondents are constrained to reflect the limits with which decision makers are also confronted. Researchers note some remarkable similarities as a result of conducting research in this fashion. The data are

> remarkably self-consistent; [they exhibit] common sense and collective wisdom; [they are] sometimes complex and sophisticated; [they change] in response to major events that supply new information but otherwise [they are] extremely resistant to changing; [they often reveal] strong majority support for policy positions NOT the same as the positions or opinions expressed by any of the leaders of either political party or by any widely recognized news reporters, editors, or commentators. (Kay et al., 1992; p.40)

Preferences Under a Budget Constraint

Aaron Wildavsky (1988) notes that expenditure opinions, to the extent they exist, will not be foremost in people's minds as they enter the polling booth. Consequently, representatives are elected whose preferences may vary greatly from the electorate's. In many ways, surveying has stepped in to fill this gap. According to Wildavsky, "Public opinion polling . . . has made it possible to ask whether citizen preferences do or do not generally accord with those expressed in consecutive budgets" (p. 26). Preference surveys have become an important way of connecting decision makers with the public will.

Many surveys of local government service preferences are fundamentally flawed because they do not contain a budget constraint or, at least, information on the cost of the service. This leads to an overstatement of preference that is volatile once other conditions are imposed (Clark, 1974, p. 13). Indeed, Thomas Miller and Michelle Miller's (1991) meta-analysis of 261 citizen surveys of service delivery in forty states found uniformly "good" ratings. We wonder what would happen to these ratings if a budget constraint or the cost of service were known by respondents? This question is addressed in Chapters 3 and 4 using Eugene Decisions survey data.

The imposition of a budget constraint can be helpful in two ways. Constrained respondents must trade off support or allocation increases against corollary decreases. This will ideally check the overstatement, particularly if the other items are ones respondents care about. Budget constraints also provide the opportunity to present respondents with a "reality-based" experience, one that reflects some of the essential dynamics of the actual policy choice facing decision makers. In this way, the choices of respondents to a survey on budget allocation may be presented in much the same fashion—and with the same trade-offs—as those confronting the decision makers themselves. Budget pies present one method of imposing a constraint, visually requiring that respondents allocate funds for various services with totals equaling 100% (a circle is presented to facilitate this choice).

Based on the concept of budget pies as presented by Terry Nichols Clark (1974), John McIver and Elinor Ostrom (1976) explore the application of the process to a field experience based on police spending. Respondents divided a circle into pieces representing their preferred allocations for aspects of this service. To correct for overstatement (respondents may rank things highly because they like a service or because they are dissatisfied and want more emphasis in that area), control variables based on negative and positive experiences with the police were introduced into the model. Once the data were differentiated, some positive relationships were observed between the budget allocations of those served and local police expenditures.

The great strength of these methods is their high degree of representativeness. The two major weaknesses are the great resource and financial cost of conducting such processes and the difficulty in getting "lower socioeconomic status groups" to participate, a concern expressed by McIver and Ostrom (1976). These surveys are difficult to design in a manner that avoids cultural and question bias. Among the strengths of citizen surveys are the ability to obtain residents' service, policy, and revenue preferences unencumbered by the loud protests of an activist few. Additional information about the citizen population may be learned as well. Such efforts are not always possible or appropriate. The cost of such procedures is high and the technical requirements are often daunting. It is against these considerations that a decision to proceed with such a survey must be made.

But what about the relevance and reliability of these data? Are they useful for informing decisions or simply another way to legitimize a foregone administrative action? Harry Hatry and Louis Blair (1976) explore these questions and other pros and cons in their examination of citizen preference surveys. They argue that problems of cop-outs and manipulation are larger than even the financial and technical difficulties of such efforts. Cop-outs occur when decision makers use surveys as a pseudo-referendum to justify government actions. Citizens too often lack the information relevant to the decisions that they are asked to make. Even when citizens are presented with a budget constraint, the possibility exists that they will not understand the trade-offs that they are being asked to consider. In these circumstances, "responses to such questions should not be considered to provide rational, specific allocation decisions" but represent gut reactions conceived of the moment (Hatry and Blair, 1976, p. 136).

Gauging the Results of Citizen Participation Efforts

Each of the projects described above is a product of its own time and place and the presenting problems of the jurisdiction in which it was employed. We suggest that nonrepresentative survey efforts offer little beyond the process satisfaction derived by the participants or perhaps help in developing political constituencies for project implementation. Among the more sophisticated techniques, the circumstances of the situation drive the choice of a method. Evaluating such efforts is therefore a difficult business. Several lessons can be learned from examining and reviewing the conclusions of those who have undertaken these evaluation and classification efforts.

S. R. Arnstein (1969) proposes an eight-rung ladder of citizen participation hierarchically spanning levels from nonparticipation, such as "manipulation," to real citizen power, such as partnership, delegated power, and citizen control. Burns, Hambleton, and Hoggett (cited in Atkinson and Cope, 1995) expand this to twelve rungs in an effort to recognize different levels of participation within different spheres of influence and areas of decision making. Either approach suggests the same truth: A continuum exists within which citizens participate in their governments, and these levels of participation reflect some combination of the needs of the citizens and the needs and openness of the government. These efforts, whether citizen surveys, forums, juries, or panels, share one essential goal: to enter the knowledge, opinions, and judgments of citizens in the government decision-making process. All share the theoretical assumption that the voice of citizens belongs in this process.

John Clayton Thomas (1995) argues that surveys are good tools when a representative sample is required without a need for shared decision making. Such methods exceed public meetings in expressing the public will. The disadvantage is that such instruments are sensitive to question wording and may misrepresent true public opinion as a result. Thomas recommends such surveys when managers are unclear about public opinion, where options are clearly defined, and where there is a complex public will that only sophisticated polling can accurately reflect (p. 105).

Jeffrey Berry and his colleagues (1993) selected five core cities (Birmingham; Dayton; Portland, Oregon; Saint Paul; and San Antonio) and ten comparison cities to determine the effectiveness of citizen participation efforts. The core cities each had significant citizen participation programs and satisfied criteria for adequate size, heterogeneity, and the broadness and representativeness of the efforts employed, among other things. The efforts in each of the five cities were matched against two similar cities (selected as comparisons on the basis of population size, percentages of black and Hispanic populations, median income, and age). Based on these controls, comparisons were then made (pp. 301–305). These authors suggest that there are three important conditions cities must meet if they are to have effective citizen participation programs.

First, they argue, exclusive powers must be given to the citizen participation structures. In other words, the structures must be able to allocate some goods and services to the community, including control over zoning. This requires that the government cede some of its powers to the citizen organization.

Second, an administrative plan that includes sanctions and rewards for administrators who work with neighborhood groups is important. Berry et al. argue this second condition is needed to avoid administrators acting to prevent neighborhood groups from encroaching on their territory: "Thus, their [administrators'] personal future in city government must be tied to the success of the citizen participation system" (Berry et al., 1993, p. 295).

Third, the citizen participation effort must be citywide: "Each community should have a single, officially recognized neighborhood association that represents an area with well-defined boundaries" (Berry et al., 1993, p. 296). They argue that programs targeted only at disadvantaged neighborhoods will not have the same level of credibility as would citywide programs.

Berry et al. (1993) conclude that if the above three conditions can be met, citizen participation systems stand a good chance of becoming an important part of city government. They further note that citizen participation efforts in general, when conducted as good faith efforts by administrators to involve the public, may have real success (p. 212). None of this suggests, however, that other acts of citizenship, such as voting, improve as a result of such involvement. In this analysis, although citizen involvement provided benefits in service understanding and coordination, the core cities were not different from their two comparison cities in voting patterns and participation (p.284).

Thomas (1995) analyzes published case studies to assess public involvement. He reviews thirty public involvement cases over the past thirty years that involved forty-two distinct decisions, of which 91% required extensive public involvement. He notes that quality requirements and the need for acceptance of the results drive the choice of method selected. Carmine Scavo (1993) recently surveyed 161 U.S. cities with over 100,000 population about their use of citizen participation strategies, categorizing them as open government, information gathering, neighborhood empowerment, or coproduction. Scavo scored these cities on the prevalence of activity in these four categories. The evaluation process was summative, such that cites were scored with a point for each subactivity present under a category. The results, not surprisingly, reveal that overall participation activities vary positively with the size of the city.

All cities reported some use of public hearings (68% broadcast these on television). Information gathering through citizen surveys was prevalent and growing. Of the 60% of cities using citizen surveys, 66% noted that the they had increased this use over the past ten years. These surveys focused on asking citizens about "problems facing the city, city policies, and city services" (Scavo, 1993, p. 98). A breakdown of deliberative opinion strategies or budget queries were not included in this research.

Our experiences resulting from discussing these projects with governments, participants, and students of such efforts as well as from reviewing the results of many of the projects themselves, lead us to concur with Scavo that citizen surveys are growing in popularity and use. This growth appears to be of questionable wisdom, given the lack of rigor applied in many cases. These processes are expensive to conduct and interpret and may represent a form of public opinion folly when assurances cannot be made that the preferences and opinions gathered are stable, represent real choices, and can be applied to real decisions.

Simonsen and colleagues (1996) examine a process employed by the state of Oregon in 1990 to incorporate the public in a "conversation" on that state's budget. Faced with the need to replace school funding lost through a recent tax limitation measure, then-governor Barbara Roberts embarked on an extended citizen participation project. The governor engaged in a two-hour deliberative "conversation" with 10,000 citizens via closed circuit TV. The sessions were facilitated by trained volunteers at locations across the state. Although citizens came to some general consensus about their desired strategies to replace the lost revenues, these were not ultimately employed by the governor in crafting a budget solution, which was developed in secret (p. 19).

These authors develop six lessons about policy sharing with citizens from their analysis of this process and the literature in this area. The lessons are

1. Use a Rigorous Research Design.   The effort is likely to have more legitimacy, both with the public and with decision makers, if the research design is well conceived and implemented. For example, surveys of citizen preferences should be random and generalizable to the target population. This typically requires expert knowledge. Absence of a well-conceived research design could lead to faulty conclusions and cynicism if the effort is seen as mostly a public relations campaign.

2. Provide Adequate Resources.   Sufficient resources need to be allocated to ensure that the research is well conceived, is implemented properly, and represents realistic choices. This may include multiple ways of collecting data (as in Eugene Decisions). This enhances the likelihood the results will be viewed as legitimate. Organizational commitment to the process is also important. For instance, staff time may be needed to cost out various revenue and spending options, explain key services, or run public workshops.

3. Be Inclusive.   Groups that are part of the process are more likely to be stakeholders in the results. Internal groups, including unions, administrators, and elected officials, as well as external constituencies, such as community and business leaders, often have an interest in policy outcomes. Including these groups in the process may vest their interest in the success of the effort.

4. Make the Process Iterative with Active Learning.   Through iterations of public input, decision makers gain a more precise understanding of citizens' preferences and citizens gain a more realistic picture of the choices they face. Because of the complicated and difficult nature of public problems, active learning through iterations is important; otherwise only simplistic solutions are likely to surface, offering little true guidance to officials. An iterative process may require that issues be raised for discussion only in the first round. Subsequent rounds would then build on the results of those discussions until a solution emerges.

5. Open the Process. One of the most important aspects of public participation is a reforging of trust between government and the citizens it serves. If the government undertaking the effort is not open about its findings and decisions are not made in the full light of day, the outcome may be worse than if the public were not included.

6. Cultivate the Media. Positive media response can enhance citizen involvement, validate the process, and increase legitimacy. Exclusion of the media may contribute to cynicism.

Some of these lessons are echoed in the work of Rob Atkinson and Stephen Cope (1995) exploring citizen participation in the City Challenge and Single Regeneration Budget urban renewal strategies in the early 1990s in Great Britain. Both programs stressed the role of citizens in their local communities as part of regeneration strategies. These authors conclude that "citizen participation is time consuming, and as many people as possible need to develop organizational skills and acquire knowledge. There is a very real danger that participation will become too dependent upon a (potentially unrepresentative) few, and if they become exhausted, activity will then collapse" (p. 9).

Some combination of methods that ensure representativeness as well as constraint of choices reflecting the real decision environment appear best suited to carry citizen participation into the decision-making arena. The methods combined in Boulder and Eugene are a good example of how such processes may work well. Kathlene and Martin (1991) note that their design accomplished some specific things, including lowering citizen participation costs, increasing the total number of those having input while increasing the "breadth of issues" considered, and obtaining legitimate representation of the community. This was accomplished by the use of stratified sampling in addition to ongoing deliberative panels of participants.

Lessons from Participation Projects

Much of our work in this chapter has involved reviewing the citizen participation efforts of various local governments. Often, too little information about the outcomes of these processes was available to make fair assessments of their success. We have chosen to describe these efforts by offering descriptive classifications rather than evaluative criteria. We feel that there are certain lessons to be drawn from these projects based on the described experiences of the participating governments and citizens and our own experiences conducting and researching the data surrounding the Eugene Decisions process. A classification of the projects for which we had adequate information appears in Table 2.1. This table indicates

TABLE 2.1   Components of Citizen Surveys and Forums

Location	Representative Sample	Budget Constraint	Deliberation	Open Survey or Forum
Scottsdale, AZ	–	–	–	X
Tempe, AZ	X	–	–	–
Pasadena, CA	–	–	–	X
Sacramento, CA	X	X	X	X
Santa Clarita, CA	–	–	–	X
Ukiah, CA	–	–	–	X
Upland, CA	–	–	–	X
Boulder, CO	X	–	X	–
Fort Collins, CO	X	–	X	–
Longwood, CO	–	–	–	X
Thornton, CO	–	–	–	X
Orlando, FL	–	–	–	X
Sioux City, IA	–	X	X	–
Decatur, IL	–	–	–	X
Lexington, KY	–	–	–	X
Louisville, KY	–	–	X	X
Chelsea, MA	–	X	X	–
Gaithersburg, MD	–	–	–	X
Blue Springs, MO	–	–	–	X
Sparks, NV	–	–	–	X
Eugene, OR	X	X	X	X
Portland, OR	X	–	–	–
Springfield, OR	X	–	X	–
Chattanooga, TN	–	–	–	X
Fort Worth, TX	–	X	–	–
Henrico County, VA	–	–	–	X
Virginia Beach, VA	–	–	–	X

which projects employed representative samples and deliberative elements and which had open ("come one, come all") forums or employed budget constraints. The lessons that we find from reviewing the typically descriptive reports of these efforts may best be summarized by the following statements:

The need for broad-based citizen participation must be compelling enough to outweigh its costs.   It is not reasonable to expect that governments will conduct a formal benefit-cost analysis of each citizen participation opportunity. Yet, such decisions should be made with notions of the relative merits of proceeding (or not) in mind. In addition to the significant money and other resources consumed by such processes, there is the public trust to consider, which may be eroded by a poorly conducted process.

Citizen participation projects should employ rigorous methodologies. The notions of validity described here apply throughout the design and implementation of these projects. Designers should be certain that their methods assess what they think they are assessing. Traditional ways of achieving this involve the extensive use of process review and the pretesting of survey forms and questions. Residents should be selected in a manner that ensures each citizen an equal chance of participating. The structure of the sample should be designed to reflect the composition of the community. The project experiences of the participants should be designed to model the real decision(s) facing decision makers. This may include constraining choices to reflect real budget limitations and presenting participants with the broadest range of concerns being weighed. None of the developers of the methods reviewed here that call on citizens to deliberate, think deeply, and consider complex problems or solutions have found that citizens are not up to the task.

Efforts to include citizens in decision making through surveys, forums, or other methods should be conducted in a manner to move beyond the dominance of interest groups and stakeholders in influencing government decision making. If this is not the intention, governments may hold hearings (at a much reduced cost) where testimony can be gathered from all of those with the most compelling motivations to attend such functions. Citizen participation projects, when conducted with valid and rigorous methods, help governments to identify the real values and judgments *of all of their citizens*. These efforts may serve to build the public trust to the degree that citizens are convinced of this validity and see the corresponding impact of such efforts on the governments around them.

Nonetheless, there has been a veritable explosion of nonrepresentative efforts, including come one, come all public forums; clip-out quickie surveys; and nonrepresentative focus groups, among others. The use of budget constraints, deliberation, and random sampling go a long way to convince us that what is being captured truly represents the judgment of the public. It may be possible to justify a project without these elements on process grounds alone. The process itself may cause participants to feel more civically engaged and thus they may be in a position to help politically when the time comes to implement a proposal. These efforts may feel good to the citizens who attend them and may satisfy some government decision makers, but as a tool to gauge public will such efforts are limited.

The use of casual methods (such as satisfaction surveys) in which the needs for participation are less significant may be a poor use of

resources if the goal is to reveal an informed view of the public.   Many local governments seem to be missing an important point. The use of quickie polls, clip-out surveys, and open idea sessions to assess general satisfaction levels may cost some fraction of a larger effort in dollars, but they have little validity and are simply not designed to provide real guidance to government officials seeking to establish citizen preferences in the face of complex problems. Citizens are sharp and concerned about the use of public resources. Such casual efforts may be very discouraging to a watchful public.

The use of casual methods may serve to reinforce the lowest expectations about the government that employs them, with citizens recognizing how poorly their ideas and preferences are represented. Because of their design, these nonrepresentative efforts do not portray the feelings of the general population. Unless they include a representative method for gauging the opinions of those who did not participate, such projects appear, at least in our view, to be for show alone and not for guidance.

We should also note that elaborate methods employed to involve citizens in decisions may be both costly *and* invalid. Large, iterative, come one, come all efforts may cost a great deal—and at the same time yield an unstable and nonrepresentative result if they fail to employ rigorous methodologies.

Some combination of methods, such as representative sampling, surveying, and deliberation, appear best structured to accurately gauge citizen attitudes and preferences.   Projects that appear to have been particularly successful, such as those in Eugene, in Boulder, and in Illinois (IVP) have employed combinations of methods that give citizens real information and the opportunity to think about or work out a problem alone or in groups and are truly representative. Planning and implementing such efforts is a huge task requiring the commitment of people and money. The usefulness of the results seems to relate to the ability of such processes to learn from themselves, either through various rounds or iterations or through citizen input on the ongoing structure of the activities. Any methodologically rigorous approach may be used, but those that combine approaches may have an advantage for tackling particularly complex or divisive issues.

The media play an important part in the influence of citizen participation projects.   The staff of the IVP, the Jefferson Center, and many of the local officials agree with Simonsen et al. (1996) that the media play an important role in communicating the message of a citizen participation project. They can help potential participants to become aware of such processes and are very important in spreading the results. To gain legitimacy, public trust, and influence over decision making, such efforts need a presence, and that provided by the media is uniquely powerful.

Projects should conclude with a formal assessment of their outcomes. Governments are busy, and resources are tight. The last item on most cities' budgets, and one of the first to come off during a budget shortfall, is evaluation. Given the amount of organizational resources consumed by large-scale participation efforts and the number of governments that appear to be repeating these processes in subsequent years, some assessment of the success of these processes in accomplishing what they set out to do appears important. This is particularly true in light of the culture of local governments that rely on the institutional memories of their staff and the actions of the municipalities around them to guide them in their decisions and innovations.

When carefully done, innovative citizen participation techniques can deliver positive outcomes. It is hard to find the positive outcomes, however, without looking for them. The work done by Kathlene and Martin (1991) in Boulder, Colorado, included an evaluation of their citizen panel. They found that the citizens who participated also overwhelmingly felt good about the process and would participate again. They found as well that the decision makers gave careful attention to the conclusions of the citizens on the panel and used these conclusions to guide them in making their choices.

Evaluations that examine the ultimate outcomes of such processes are probably unrealistic. Although we care about how a citizen deliberation process may make the community that sponsors it better off, there is no clear theoretical, empirical, or popular consensus to gauge what this means. If we allow ourselves to constrain our viewpoint to that of the decision maker, a good process is one that provides a reliable and representative picture of the reasoned and informed judgment of citizens. Ideally, a good process increases the faith of the broader citizenry, beyond the direct participants, that its representatives are making choices that reflect informed citizen preferences. Documenting this requires additional sampling of citizens' opinions and beliefs.

Discussion

Many municipalities are using special projects to give citizens real information about their communities in an attempt to gauge their preferences or satisfaction with services or to gain their input in a particular decision choice. The call for increased and better public participation has not come out of nowhere. A long historical and theoretical tradition exists that has guided the development of citizen participation in the United States.

Much of the background in which citizen participation operates is described by the larger tensions of representation versus participation, politics versus administration, and bureaucracies and expertise versus citizen access. Some trace the roots of these efforts back as far as ancient Greece, but we see a good case for contemporary participation rising out of the social crises of the 1960s and 1970s. It was during this period that mandates for participation through hearings and agencies first appeared. Public hearings and citizen agencies each have their strengths and drawbacks. The drawbacks refer mostly to some compromise between representativeness and efficiency, as characterized by the narrowness of views collected in hearings and the redundancy and accountability issues of the "near-government" CAAs.

Modern citizen participation efforts relating to the resource decisions facing governments are commonly some form of satisfaction survey that may not be conducted in a manner that is representative of the population at large. Of those that do use representative sampling, many do not constrain the choices of respondents in a manner that reflects the real decisions facing decision makers. Operating under these limits, governments may be committing significant resources to efforts that yield little practical result and may even further erode the confidence of citizens. Those projects that have successfully combined representative sampling and real constraints have produced thoughtful, innovative, and interesting results that provide valuable information to decision makers. Getting the commitment of decision makers up front and the cooperation of the media may help these efforts to go even further in influencing decisions. An honest evaluation of these processes following their completion is essential to ensuring that such efforts are carefully designed and executed and that they managed to match the decision need at hand.

Evaluation criteria that focus on voting outcomes miss the point of an information-rich deliberative process, which is to inform. In fact, depending on the level of the information incongruity between participants and the public, the results of a deliberative information process may be the opposite of a popular vote. If this difference is profound, decision makers may need to use the process result to inform the rest of the citizenry.

Notes

1. We attempted to find out about the range of possible citizen involvement techniques by looking at both likely and unlikely sources. These sources included a traditional literature review of appropriate books and journals; use of electronic search tools, including World Wide Web searches, requests for information through topically related list services and news groups, and Nexus searches of news accounts of participation projects; and formal queries to organizations, in-

cluding the International City Managers Association (ICMA) and the National Civic League. We cast as wide a net as possible but cannot claim that the list of citizen involvement techniques we developed is completely exhaustive.

2. A more thorough explanation of the mechanisms and outcomes of Eugene Decisions is presented in Chapter 3.

3. See Neijens, Deridder, and Saris (1992) for a review of survey research in the Netherlands that attempts to gather citizen input on energy strategies. A short discussion of this review appears in Chapter 3.

3

How Do Citizens Balance the Budget?

In Chapter 1, we looked at the historical and theoretical roots of citizen participation in the United States and how certain tensions frame the relationship of the citizen to government administration. In Chapter 2, we cataloged a series of innovative participation projects and looked at the elements that seem best poised to allow decision makers to benefit from such projects. Next, we examine in detail the results of one process that employed deliberation, random sampling, and a budget constraint when querying citizens about their budget preferences. Our analysis allows us to capture some of the complexities inherent in the citizen decision-making process. In this chapter, we examine the determinants of citizen budget-balancing strategies, and in Chapter 4 we will look at how service use and presenting fiscal information tends to alter the expressed support for services. As throughout the book, we seek to give the reader an understanding of the kinds of lessons that can be drawn from careful citizen participation surveys.

How people's characteristics relate to their desire for various budget-balancing strategies is becoming increasingly important as cities across the United States continue to face serious fiscal pressures. Contributing to cities' fiscal stresses are the growing cost of mandates and other expenditure pressures, as well as the popular "Read my lips, no new taxes" credo that has led to legal (and political) limits on property taxes (Ladd and Yinger, 1989; Lemov, 1991; Simonsen, 1994a and 1994b; Yinger, 1990).

Eugene, Oregon, and Eugene Decisions

During 1991 and 1992, the city of Eugene, Oregon, employed an innovative combination of public forums, budget-balancing exercises, and representative surveys to determine public support for a variety of spending and budget-balancing alternatives. The fundamental mission was to provide guidance about how to balance the city's budget in a way that was sustainable over time. The citizen involvement process was known as Eugene Decisions. The key to the Eugene Decisions process was to force respondents into a realistic approximation of the budget problems facing the city.

Eugene is Oregon's second-largest city, with a population of about 120,000. About 93% of the population are white, about 1% are black, and about 3% are Hispanic of any race. The median family income in 1989 was $34,153, compared to the national median of $35,353 (U.S. Bureau of the Census, 1990 and 1992).

The city has a council-manager form of government. In theory, the city council develops policy and legislation and the city manager oversees personnel and operations to carry out the city council's directives. Eugene is a home rule city, so it has all powers not prohibited by its own charter or the state of Oregon. The city charter can be amended by a vote of the people. Charter amendments can be placed on the ballot by a city council referendum or directly by the citizens through a popular initiative.

The Eugene city council has eight members elected by the eight wards in the city. Councilmembers are elected for staggered four-year terms, so that one-half of the council is elected every two years. The council sets city goals, enacts legislation, adopts plans and policies, decides what services to provide, and enacts the city budget (City of Eugene, 1993). The mayor is elected at large and acts as the chairperson of the council. The mayor presides over the council meetings but does not vote except to break a tie. The mayor can veto council decisions, but a two-thirds vote of the council can override a veto. The mayor and the council are elected on a nonpartisan ballot and are unpaid. As with most local governments, the majority of Eugene's revenues come from property taxes. The Table 3.1 illustrates Eugene's revenue and expenditure mix.

The city projected in fiscal year 1991 that by fiscal year 1994 it would face an $8 million (about 10%) shortfall between revenues and expenditures. Revenues had been growing slower than expenditures for several years, due in part to the growth in the major revenue source, property taxes, lagging behind expenditure demand. The amount of property tax that may be levied by cities in Oregon is limited by statute and the Oregon constitution (Oregon Department of Revenue, 1990). Property tax levies are allowed to increase 6% annually without voter approval. This 6% cap can be exceeded if approved by a simple majority of voters. In addition, in November 1990 Oregon voters approved Measure 5, a constitutional amendment further limiting property taxes.[1] Measure 5 limits annual property taxes levied for all local governments other than schools to 1% of real market value (schools have a separate limit). Measure 5 does not void the earlier 6% limit; both limits are in effect since its passage.

TABLE 3.1   Eugene General Fund Revenues and Expenditures

	Percent
Revenues	
Property taxes	49
Other taxes	9
License and permits	3
Intergovernmental revenues	2
Rental income	1
Charges for service	14
Fines and forfeits	3
Miscellaneous revenues	1
Interfund transfers and loans	7
Working capital	12
Expenditures	
Public safety	38
Culture/leisure services	15
Development services	17
Central business functions	16
Net nondepartmental	14

SOURCE: City of Eugene (1993), percentages based on the city of Eugene's General Fund Budget for Fiscal Year 1994.

Other factors contributed to the structural budget problem. Federal funding was reduced by $38 million over the previous eight years. The city's growing population was adding to the demand for public services such as police, fire protection, and cultural and recreational programs. At the same time that the population was growing, its composition was changing toward increasing percentages of elderly and youths—which placed added demands on the city for senior and youth services. These factors—property tax limits, decreases in federal funding, and increasing service demands—led to the city's budget problems. It is in this context—expenditures growing faster than revenues and a new property tax limit—that the Eugene city council decided to undertake Eugene Decisions, an ambitious strategic financial-planning exercise that included substantial citizen involvement.

Eugene Decisions was deliberative, in that there were multiple rounds of citizen input. The Table 3.2 shows the overall Eugene Decisions process. The first phase of the process included citizen forums designed to generate a wide range of ideas about how to solve the city's financial problems. The second phase examined these ideas in greater detail and included three

TABLE 3.2   Eugene Decisions Process

Phase	Description
Phase 1	City council assesses trends and service issues; conducts public meetings and workshops to gather citizen ideas.
Phase 2	Surveys aid city council in refining understanding of citizen preferences for city services and revenue sources.
Phase 3	City council develops preliminary revenue and expense strategies and Eugene residents are asked their preferences.
Decision	City council makes final decisions on budget-balancing strategy.

surveys sent to randomly selected citizens, a survey sent to each household in the city, and a series of in-person budget workshops. The three survey instruments, which fell into a natural hierarchy, were used to gauge citizen budget preferences. One survey (called Ivory after the color of the paper on which it was printed) asked respondents about city services without providing much information about the costs of the services (see Appendix B). Another survey, called BOB for Build Your Own Budget, was a budget template that led respondents though a budget-balancing exercise (see Appendix A). Respondents could increase any of six services; reduce any of forty services; and raise revenues through any combination of nine taxes, three bond measures, and four user fees. This survey provided the most realistic approximation of the choices facing the city council. The third survey (called Blue after the color of its paper) provided substantially more information than the Ivory Survey on the fiscal impact on households (see Appendix C). The response rates to the surveys was outstanding: The lowest was in excess of 50%; the highest surpassed 80%.

The second phase was followed by another round of public input that built on its results. For Phase 3, the city council developed three strategies based on the citizen input data developed in Phase 2. Public opinion about these three strategies was collected through representative surveys, workshops, and a tabloid sent to each household in the city.

Large numbers of citizens were brought into the budget process in a meaningful way, that is, they were engaged in a serious, realistic discussion of a complex budget problem. Multiple survey instruments were used, allowing triangulation of a truer representation of public opinion. During the eighteen-month process, interested groups of citizens, employees, and business leaders were continually updated and informed.

Additionally, the media was constantly advised about the process status and results. The Eugene Decisions effort was an open and public process.

The Eugene city council relied on the results of the citizen input in designing a budget-balancing plan. Because the choices of the participants were constrained to conform to the real limits of the problem, the decision makers were provided with a result that was highly valuable in assessing an informed public will. The preferred strategies identified through Eugene Decisions, including reorganization and consolidation of services, new work procedures, service reductions, new and increased user fees, and the implementation of a restaurant tax, were acted on by the city council (Weeks, Robinette, and Boles, 1993).

The restaurant tax was put to a vote of the people in March 1993. It was defeated by a two to one margin (Wright, 1993b). Several reasons (Weeks et al., 1993) were given for the defeat of the restaurant tax, including

1. The council delayed in putting the measure on the ballot. It was delayed from the previous December when the awareness of the process was at its peak. The reason for the delay was that the council and mayoral election was in November. "The council first decided on a restaurant tax in September, but backed off again when mayoral and council candidates began bad-mouthing the restaurant tax and Eugene Decisions in general" (Wright, 1993b, p.B1).
2. The council expanded the tax to apply to prepared foods purchased in grocery stores.
3. The council decided not to dedicate the tax to a specific service or to indicate which services would be cut if the tax failed.
4. There was no campaign in favor of the restaurant tax. According to the *Eugene Register-Guard* columnist Don Bishoff (1993), "The City Council treated the tax like an orphan skunk on its doorstep. Avoidance was preferred, enthusiasm out of the question" (p. B1).
5. The most expensive, professionally managed campaign in Eugene history was waged against the tax.

The defeat of the restaurant tax raised questions about the predictive validity of Eugene Decisions. According the Editorial Board of the *Eugene Register-Guard* (*Register-Guard,* 1993), "The big question about Eugene Decisions all along has been whether the budget choices made by the participants accurately reflected the views of the majority of voters. The election provided the most concrete answer to date. No" (p. A10). This criticism misses the point of deliberative processes like Eugene Decisions: These processes reflect what an *informed* public *would* choose. Respondents to the Eugene Decisions surveys were faced with the real dilemma facing the city and faced realistic choices. They made the choices that the general public would have made if it had the same level of information and faced the same constrained choices. If the aim was to predict how an uninformed public would vote, then a simple poll would be a more accurate mechanism. The virtue of a process like Eugene Decisions is that it provided decision makers with the guidance of public opinion based on informed judgments.

Eugene Decisions made its mark on Eugene city government. A total of seventy-one program cuts, fee hikes, and other changes resulted from the Eugene Decisions process (Wright, 1993a). The total amount of savings that was estimated to have resulted from Eugene Decisions was $5.4 million (Wright, 1993a). Although less than the $8 million target (no restaurant tax), these savings went a long way toward helping the city achieve a sustainable budget balance.

The Design of the Surveys

Researchers at the University of Oregon worked with city of Eugene staff to administer a series of surveys aimed at determining voter preferences about revenue enhancements and service reductions (Weeks and Simonsen, 1992, Weeks and Weeks, 1992). Weeks and Simonsen (1992) designed a budget survey that attempted to provide a realistic approximation of the budget problems facing the city. This was called the BOB (Build Your Own Budget) Survey.

The data for this chapter are drawn from the BOB Survey (from Eugene Decisions, Phase 2). The survey was a budget template that led respondents through a realistic budget-balancing exercise in which they were provided an opportunity to balance the budget according to their own priorities. The BOB Survey is very similar in concept to budget pies, in that it constrained respondents with real choices and forced trade-offs between different services and revenues. This survey was computationally challenging, requiring respondents to keep track of the amounts of money they were raising and allocating to different government functions such that the budget was balanced. The survey is reproduced in Appendix A.

There are a small family of methodologies that attempt to provide more realistic options for survey respondents, including panel designs and budget pies (see Chapter 2). The key problem with including a budget constraint, à la budget pies, has been cognitive and computational overhead. The worry is that if you make the survey too time consuming or too difficult people will not complete it. Indeed, this worry is most fundamental for respondents with lower socioeconomic status (McIver and Ostrum, 1976). The Eugene Decisions surveys substantially overcame this problem.

Two other surveys, Ivory and Blue, were mailed at the same time as the BOB Survey (these surveys are analyzed in Chapter 4). The Ivory Survey asked respondents about city services without providing much information about the costs of the services. The Blue Survey provided substantially more information than the Ivory Survey on the fiscal impact of budget items on households. Neither of these surveys included budget-balancing requirements such as those used in the BOB template.

The response rates for these mail surveys were unusually high: 83% for Ivory, 76% for Blue, and 52% for the BOB budget-balancing template. The majority of respondents filled out their questionnaires, even the computationally difficult BOB Survey. Perhaps even more important, counter to earlier critiques of budget pies, lower-income respondents filled out and returned their surveys. The percentage of respondents with family incomes under $20,000 was consistent across the three surveys: 24% for Ivory, 26% for Blue, and 22% for BOB. The key message is that including realistic fiscal information—a budget constraint—does not always mean low response rates, even for low-income people. This result was largely accomplished through diligent follow-up procedures and the use of a handsomely designed survey. The BOB Survey was printed in color with attractive clip art.

The population surveyed comprised Eugene registered voters. Care was taken to ensure representative results through use of random sampling and diligent follow-up procedures to produce as high a response rate as possible. The survey was mailed to 400 registered voters selected at random. To enhance the response rate, the selected voters were telephoned prior to being sent the questionnaire to alert them it was coming, and the initial mailing was followed by a reminder postcard, two reminder letters to those who had not yet responded, and finally a follow-up phone call. The sponsorship of Eugene Decisions helped to add authority to the process. Except for the postcard, the mailings included a cover letter signed by the mayor and the respondent's city councilmember, a tabloid describing the city services and revenue options, the questionnaire, and an addressed stamped envelope.

The BOB Survey realistically mirrored the budget-balancing options available to the city. Respondents began the survey facing the projected $8 million gap and were informed of the amount currently spent on each service. Thus, the questionnaire required the budget be balanced in the context of the city's projected $8 million gap between revenues and expenditures. Enhanced services added to the gap and thus required higher revenues or cuts in other areas for the budget to balance.

The BOB budget-balancing survey was designed to determine how the Eugene electorate would fund the projected budget gap. Thus, it was quite different from typical surveys of city services that ask respondents how much they prefer certain services or what is their level of satisfaction with the delivery of these services. The BOB Survey required decisions about funding a real $8 million budget gap and therefore provides a glimpse of the respondents' marginal trade-offs among different services and revenues.

Analysis of the Survey Results

This chapter uses ordinary least squares (OLS) and logistic regression methodology to analyze how factors such as income, age, educational attainment, property ownership, or gender are related to an individual's overall choice of a budget-balancing strategy as well as decisions to cut particular services or enhance specific revenues. The policy ramifications of this analysis are enormous, since it points to possible natural constituencies for service enhancement or budget cutting. First, we present some of the literature about people's preferences for services, followed by the descriptive statistics for the BOB Survey. Next, the framework for analysis and methodology are described. Then, the findings are presented, and finally we conclude this chapter with a discussion of the policy implications.

Stalking the Free Lunch: Determinants of
Citizen Attitudes Toward Public Taxes and Services

Typically, when citizens are asked whether they prefer continuing or enhancing services, lowering taxes, or increasing efficiency they usually choose lower taxes and increased efficiency. Several notions of efficiency may be represented by these responses. In one case, efficiencies are possible where service levels are increased and revenues remain constant. In the other scenario, service levels are maintained while revenues are reduced. Commonly, it is a third and more extreme interpretation of efficiency with which governments are faced. This is the belief that services may be increased or maintained while taxes are substantially decreased. This represents a belief that taxpayers can find and enjoy the elusive free lunch.

A seminal piece of literature in this area comes from Jack Citrin (1979). He examines public opinion surrounding tax limitation measures in California and explores public opinion nationally with respect to attitudes about government spending. One of his findings is that survey respondents generally express satisfaction with current service levels and that fully one-third feel that government could continue these service levels even with a 40% decrease in funding. This suggests that voters are asking for simultaneously lower taxes and increased efficiencies and presents evidence that citizens seek a free lunch from government.

Citrin also demonstrates that people favor spending increases on police, fire protection, mental health services, and education while favoring cuts in welfare, public housing, and administration. The following are some of the specific results:

- Homeowners are more likely than renters to favor budget cutbacks.
- Whites are more likely than nonwhites to favor budget cutbacks.
- Respondents with lower incomes are less opposed to tax increases than those with higher incomes.
- Age is negatively related to spending on public schools.
- High income is negatively related to spending on welfare programs.

Paul Courant and his colleagues (1980) surveyed Michigan residents to assess the determinants of votes on tax limitation measures. Measures limiting state spending and local spending were examined separately. The results of their regression analysis indicate, on average, that individuals in families are more likely to favor public spending, as are females. They also find a weak relationship between increased spending support and education. Specifically, higher education levels are highly associated with support for increased spending on the state level, but not at the local level. This may be a demonstration of preference for equalized education funding in that state.

In a follow-up to this research, Edward Gramlich, Daniel Rubinfeld, and Deborah Swift (1980) seek to predict voter turnout on tax limitation measures. After analyzing the same data set as the previous research, they conclude that "individual attributes and spending preferences are rather poor proxies for the actual vote of an individual, and do not predict votes much better than a random prediction." (p. 123). They also confirm the "alienation hypothesis," finding that those not voting would have had a very low probability of voting yes if they had voted. In their conclusions, they note the implication for those concerned with the burgeoning movement of tax limitation measures: Support for taxes and services may reside with abstaining voters who are alienated for reasons other than dissatisfaction with taxes.

Helen Ladd and Julie Boatwright Wilson (1982) studied why voters supported or opposed the Massachusetts property tax limit, Proposition 2½. Their findings are consistent with other research in this area: The favorable vote was more an attempt to obtain lower taxes and more efficiency in government than to obtain reduced service levels or to substitute other revenues for the property tax.

The free lunch notion that citizens prefer both increased services and decreased taxes is explored further by Susan Welch (1985). She explores this "more for less" paradox in her research on public attitudes toward taxes. She selected 900 households at random to participate in a telephone survey in which respondents were asked if they desire increased spending on eight budget areas across national, state, and local governments. These areas are "energy, health care, the elderly, the poor and unemployed, farm problems, education, crime prevention, and water resources" (p. 311).

Ninety percent of the respondents favored some spending increases, and Welch establishes a willingness-to-pay scale based on their responses. Those favoring some level of spending increase thus were placed in one of four categories along a continuum from "Taxers" to "Free Lunchers." Taxers are those wanting more new taxes, and Free Lunchers those who favor only efficiencies to fill this gap. The categories in between represent those who seek some change in intergovernmental aid or reallocation. At the local government level, only 7% of those choosing increased services are not willing to tax, assess fees, or reallocate local aid. Welch concludes from this data that support for expansion of public services is high and that those truly wanting more for less are a minority. Her work suggests that such a paradox exists, but makes up a small relative portion of the attitude base toward taxes and spending. This work also suggests that citizens respond with more sophistication when presented with the trade-offs for taxes and services.

L. A. Wilson (1983) looks at the more-for-less paradox by composing a measure of sincerity. Sincere spending preferences are defined by this author as a willingness to increase city taxes that corresponds with their preferred budget increases. Wilson surveyed residents in Tempe, Arizona; and Eugene, Oregon, to determine whether preferences for spending occur with a corresponding willingness to pay. Survey recipients were given service descriptions and statements describing the current amount spent on specific services. They were then prompted to choose between spending less, the same, or more for that service. Those choosing a greater level of spending were then asked if they would increase, decrease, or reallocate funding to pay for this service improvement.

Wilson finds that the majority of those requesting service enhancements are sincere. On average, he finds 67% of the Tempe respondents and 73% of the Eugene respondents were making sincere choices about services and taxes. He concludes that citizens are willing to pay more to receive more government services.

Soren Winter and Poul Erik Mouritzen (1997) examined the free lunch concept in Denmark. They surveyed 3,000 randomly selected adults in a Danish municipality with a total population of about 175,000 people (61% of the sample returned completed questionnaires). Winter and Mouritzen find that people demand both more spending, item by item, and a smaller tax. They also find that for several services women are significantly more likely than men to support government spending and that age affects preferences about spending, but the variations (about age) are not consistent and may be interpreted as a self-interest rather than public interest perspective.

Paul Allen Beck and Thomas Dye (1982) asked survey respondents in Florida to rate their level of taxation on a four-level scale from "Much too High" to "Too Low." Using this data, the authors examine public attitudes toward local, state, social security, and federal income taxes. They test many common explanations for opposition to taxes and support for tax limitation measures.

These authors find that nonwhites and those with the lowest levels of education have less favorable attitudes toward local property taxes. They control for general orientations toward government, length of residence, perceptions of tax burden, and race and income. In this way, they are able to assess some of the determinants of tax attitudes.

Their results demonstrate that for state and local taxes, race is the only significant demographic variable related to tax attitudes. Nonwhites are more likely than whites to feel that these taxes are too high (Beck and Dye, 1982, p.180). Another finding is that as incomes increase, so does the perception that social security taxes are too high. This is particularly interesting in light of the relative advantage upper-income individuals have enjoyed, paying a lower proportion of their income in social security taxes compared to others.[2] This finding is explained by the authors as possibly due to the belief of upper-income individuals that they could do a better job investing their own money. Also positively related to the attitude that taxes are too high are distrust of government and beliefs that there is waste in government.

Beck et al. (1987) evaluated the responses of 1,300 citizens in their research into public opinion about taxes in three Florida cities. These residents were surveyed by telephone about their attitudes toward taxes and services and the trade-offs between services. The data collected are used to assess the contributions of self-interest, demographics, and political symbolism (ideological preference) toward these citizen preferences:

> Perceived net benefits, alienation, distrust in city government, disapproval of city leaders, and satisfaction with the community almost always exhibit significant relationships, and these relationships are almost always of substantial magnitude. . . . In general, the demographic variables do rather poorly as correlates of service, tax, or trade-off attitudes. (p. 234)
>
> . . . self-interest variables—financial situation and perceptions of increased taxes or utility costs—displace some of the generalized symbolic attitudes as prime predictors of tax burden attitudes. (p. 235)

Following are some of the specific findings of Beck et al. from their bivariate analysis:

- High voting regularity is negatively associated with service dissatisfaction.
- Nonwhites are positively associated with service dissatisfaction, perception that the tax burden is too high, and the tendency to select less revenue raising in trade-offs between reduced services and increased taxes or cuts versus service maintenance.
- Higher education is negatively associated with the perception that the tax burden is too high.
- Age (older) is negatively associated with service dissatisfaction.
- Middle age (forty-five years) associates positively with the perception that the tax burden is too high.
- The perception of increasing utility fees is positively related to the perception that the tax burden is too high.
- The perception that costs exceed the benefits of government services is positively related to the perception that the tax burden is too high.
- Overall satisfaction with the community is negatively related to service dissatisfaction.

Of these factors, only the last three remain significant in the multivariate analysis, suggesting that age, income, education, and race are only mitigating factors in the larger ideological formulation of tax burden perceptions.

General attitudes toward government are the greatest predictors of service satisfaction in this research, although self-interest variables appear to affect perceived tax burdens. No direct assessment of attitudes for specific taxes and fees is attempted here. Beck et al. (1987) conclude with a "theory of cost-benefit analysis of local government" (p. 240). This theory suggests that taxes and fees have a particular salience compared to government services. This is because monetary concepts are readily observable and concrete, particularly in comparison to the more abstract notions of government services. This effect may be involved in the low levels of knowledge which citizens generally have about local government services.

Further analysis of this data attempts to assess the bases for these attitudes about services and taxes (Beck, Rainey, and Traut, 1990). Here, the authors hypothesize that the costs of government services and programs would have greater salience for respondents than would the services themselves. Their results confirm this hypothesis. They find that economic disadvantage is the primary determinant of attitudes toward taxes, followed by community disaffection and race (nonwhite) (p. 82). All of these variables relate positively to dissatisfaction with taxes.

Neijens et al. (1992) review survey research that attempts to solicit informed opinions from citizens. In the face of growing energy needs and opposition to the use of nuclear power in the Netherlands, these authors designed and analyzed instruments to not only gather the opinions of Dutch citizens, but to be sure that the opinions proffered were based on a real assessment of the issues and trade-offs at hand.

The authors presented a "decision aid" to citizens with information about available energy policy options. This decision aid includes general information about costs to consumers, but primarily focuses on giving respondents information that forces them to fully consider the competing factors involved in their decisions. Completing the survey requires trade-offs between economic, efficiency, and environmental impacts.

This survey asks citizens to indicate their relative support for many different energy strategies. These describe available policy options to deal with the continual growth of energy demands in their country. Each option is presented with its concurrent trade-offs. The survey presents a series of these options, one at a time. Beneath each option is a narrative list of the consequent advantages and disadvantages associated with it. Among these are considerations such as increased reliance on fossil fuels, revenue raising, and greenhouse effects.[3] Respondents indicate whether or not each of these consequences is important and set weights for these relative advantages and disadvantages.

One of the key questions from this research was an assessment of whether the resulting "Choice Questionnaire" was too difficult to ensure an unbiased and representative response. Neijens et al. (1992) examine the extent to which information helped their respondents to successfully develop quality responses. The measure used to indicate successful effects of the decision aid is that of consistent decision making across the questions presented. They define a consistent decision as one where respondents made a choice that agreed with their own judgment of the consequent advantages and disadvantages. Those that rated a policy option high or low on all counts are understood as demonstrating a halo effect and consequently characterized as inconsistent. The authors measure an 11% increase in the consistency of these decisions in the condition where increased information is provided. The authors are so convinced of the usefulness of this approach to solicit informed opinions that they recommend that their government perpetuate its use with all of the elements included (p. 258).

The key lesson from this literature review is that people take a free lunch when it is offered to them. Greater efficiencies and lower taxes while maintaining existing services is the preferred option. But if a free lunch of this type is not offered, people are willing to raise revenues or reallocate among services to get what they want. Also, the literature suggests that age, gender, race, income, and service use (or benefit from it) have been found to relate to preferences for services, but not in consistent ways. How does this study of Eugene, Oregon, add to this literature? We now turn to analysis of the BOB Survey to pursue this question.

Descriptive Statistics

Table 3.3 shows the overall budget-balancing strategies chosen by survey respondents. The table shows that only 13.4% of the respondents chose to solve the budget problem in Eugene solely through service cuts. On the other hand, only 10.8% funded the gap exclusively through revenue enhancements. When faced with a budget gap of at least $8 million (the gap could be higher if the respondent chose to add any of the five possible service enhancements), the vast majority of respondents chose some combination of service cuts and revenue enhancements. *When faced with a realistic look at the options for service reductions, that is, no free lunch, the overwhelming majority of respondents chose to raise at least some revenues.*

The median respondent (50% above and 50% below) funded the budget gap through a combination of 38% service cuts and 62% revenue enhancements. Since this is a survey of Eugene voters, this represents the preferences of the median voter.[4] Under a certain set of assumptions, the budget of the median voter is the one that would be chosen if a vote were taken. Are the choices of the median voter socially optimal? Only by

TABLE 3.3   Percent of the Budget Gap Funded Through Service Cuts

Percent of Budget Gap Funded by Service Cuts	*Percent Choosing This Level of Service Cuts*	*Cumulative Percent*
0	10.8	10.8
1 to 10	9.6	20.4
11 to 20	12.9	33.3
21 to 30	9.7	43.0
31 to 40	10.2	53.2
41 to 50	10.1	63.4
51 to 60	8.1	71.5
61 to 70	4.3	75.8
71 to 80	2.2	78.0
81 to 90	6.9	84.9
91 to 99	1.7	86.6
100	13.4	100.0

NOTE: The median respondent chose to fund the budget gap through a combination of 38% service cuts and 62% increased revenues.

chance! The socially optimal choice is where the marginal social benefit equals the marginal social cost. Providing additional service beyond this point would entail more costs than benefits, whereas producing less would leave potential net benefit gains unrealized. There is nothing that guarantees the median voter will choose the optimum point (O'Sullivan, 1996).

We take a closer look at respondents choices about specific service cuts through the percentage of respondents choosing to cut any amount from the various services (Table 3.4). Some options were combined around thematic categories.[5] The most frequently cut services were planning functions (cut by 72.9% of respondents), recreation programs (61.8%), park maintenance (59.4%), and Hult Center for the Performing Arts (58.5%). These services fit into two broad categories: (1) services where user fees may be available (Hult Center and recreation programs) and (2) services where the impacts of the cuts may not be realized immediately (planning functions and park maintenance). This second category of services is less directly felt by recipients and more collectively consumed, and therefore the impacts may be less well understood.

The services cut by the least number of respondents include fire-EMS (20.8% of respondents), bookmobile (25.6%), specialized recreation for the disabled (27.5%), human services contracts (29.5%), the public library (31.4%), and police (40.6%).[6] These services may have been viewed by respondents as important social goods and public safety needs that ought to be collectively supported. Also, although planning functions were most frequently cut, one planning function—affordable housing—was less fre-

TABLE 3.4   Service Reductions

Service	Percent Choosing to Cut This Service	Average Amount of Cut	Existing Cost of This Service per Household
Planning functions	72.9	$0.96	$4.35
Recreation programs	61.8	0.44	3.20
Park maintenance	59.4	0.61	4.35
Hult Center	58.5	0.37	1.55
Building maintenance	52.2	1.08	4.50
Police	40.6	0.86	14.85
Public library	31.4	0.28	2.75
Human services contracts	29.5	0.07	0.65
Specialized recreation for the disabled	27.5	0.04	0.30
Bookmobile	25.6	0.02	0.10
Fire-EMS	20.8	0.40	9.55

quently cut than the others. This buttresses the notion that social programs represent preferred spending categories.

As mentioned earlier, some of the choices offered to respondents were combined for analysis purposes. It is possible that simply a larger number of available choices would bias upward these percentages. For example, since respondents were offered four different police services as cutting possibilities (patrol teams, investigations, community response teams, and crime prevention), they had more of an opportunity to cut a police service, compared to fire-EMS, for instance, where there is only one option. Table 3.5 shows the average percentage of the total cost of the service that respondents cut. This provides another way of looking at preferences for services. Indeed, looking at preferences in this way shows a slight reordering of priorities. Police and fire-EMS were cut the least, and the Hult Center for the Performing Arts and planning functions were cut the most. The following implications continue to be supported, however:

- Respondents cut services where user fees may be available and where the impacts of the cuts may not be realized immediately or are obscure.
- Social programs and public safety programs were most preferred.

Table 3.6 shows the percent of respondents choosing various taxes. Fully 71.5% of respondents chose at least one of the tax options to balance the budget. There was not a majority consensus on which tax was preferred, however. Here is an analogy: A group of friends agree to go out together on a Saturday evening. One person wants to go bowling, another to the movies, and yet another loves to minigolf. The friends know they want to go out as a group, yet do not agree on where to go. Any one

TABLE 3.5   Percent of Service Cost Cut

Service	Percent of Service Cut
Hult Center	23.9
Planning functions	22.1
Bookmobile	18.2
Park maintenance	14.0
Recreation programs	13.8
Specialized recreation for the disabled	13.3
Human services contracts	10.8
Public library	10.2
Police	5.8
Fire-EMS	4.2

TABLE 3.6   Taxes

Type of Tax	Percent Choosing This Tax	Average Amount (millions of $)
Any tax	71.5	5.68
Corporate income	35.3	0.48
Room	33.3	0.11
Restaurant	30.9	1.43
Entertainment	29.0	0.17
Retail sales tax	21.7	1.20
Gross receipts	19.3	0.94
Utility	12.6	0.22
Personal income	9.7	0.67
Payroll	9.2	0.46

of their individual choices will be easily defeated by the majority of the group, despite their larger agreement. In this case, over 70% of respondents chose at least one of the taxes, but lack of agreement on which one makes voter approval difficult. (An example is the restaurant tax that was put before the voters and defeated.)

The taxes chosen by the least number of respondents were the payroll tax, the personal income tax, and the utility tax. These taxes may have been perceived as the most directly paid, and least avoidable, of the taxes. The two most popular taxes (corporate income and hotel/motel room tax) are not levied directly on the respondents and may have appeared to be the easiest to avoid. These results suggest that the major principle of tax policy elucidated by former Senator Russell Long (D-Louisiana) may still be the guiding norm for Eugene voters: "Don't tax you, don't tax me, tax that fellow behind the tree" (Reese, 1978, p. 199).

Framework for Analysis

Ordinary least squares (OLS) and logistic regression are used to isolate the influence of respondent characteristics on their budget-balancing choices. The response rate was 52% for this survey; after listwise deletion of primarily demographic data, 187 responses (about 47%) were used in the OLS and logistic regressions.

Respondents' budget-balancing choices are hypothesized to be a function of their level of educational attainment, income, and household and respondent characteristics.[7] The independent variables in the regressions reflect these postulated determinants of budget-balancing preferences.

The first category includes educational attainment variables. Educational attainment may reflect individual tastes and preferences and is measured by two variables: whether the respondent completed a college degree or more or is a high school graduate or less.

The next set of independent variables measures respondents' household income. If one assumes that public goods are normal goods, higher incomes should lead to increased demand for public services (see, e.g., Vernez, 1976). Income is measured by two variables: respondents with household incomes below $20,000 and those with incomes over $50,000.

The next category reflects various household characteristics. Larger households potentially have increased needs for both public and private goods, at any given level of income. Whether the respondents rent or own their home may influence budget-balancing preferences. Renters do not directly pay property taxes and may not view the burden of the tax as falling completely on their household, compared to homeowners, who pay the tax directly. Therefore, a dummy variable (1 if household rents a home, 0 if not) is included. Whether or not respondents use city services may influence their perception of the city government, either positively or negatively. The survey asked respondents whether they, or a member of their household, often, sometimes, or never use eleven different city services for which a user fee exists or may potentially be instituted.[8] The first service use variable is a count of the number of services respondents answered they or a household member often or sometimes use. Whether respondents or a household member often or sometimes use the service is included for those services where the data were available.

The fourth set of independent variables includes respondent characteristics. Respondents' gender may influence their budget-balancing strategy. Therefore, a dummy variable reflecting the respondents' gender (1 if female, 0 if male) is included. Respondents' age may also influence their fiscal choices. Some researchers have argued that the elderly may represent a gray peril—supporting taxes for services important to them while opposing taxes for other programs (Aday and Miles, 1982; Swan, Estes, and Wood, 1983). The evidence supporting this contention is mixed, however (Mullins and Rosentraub, 1992; Simonsen, 1994a).

The final category includes the amount of the budget gap to be closed and an interaction of household size and low income variables. The size of the budget gap may influence respondents' budget-balancing choices. The budget gap grows as respondents add enhanced services, and as the gap increases, additional service cuts or revenues are needed to balance the budget. Individuals who enhance services may be systematically more likely to be sympathetic to city services and therefore more likely to use revenues to fund the budget gap rather than make cuts in other services. Low income and household size interaction reflects the increased pressure that additional household members may place on a low-income household's finances. Several OLS regressions were estimated based on the above-hypothesized determinants budget-balancing preferences as follows:

CUTPCT = f(EDUCATIONAL ATTAINMENT, INCOME, HOUSEHOLD CHARACTERISTICS, RESPONDENT CHARACTERISTICS, OTHER);

TOTLCUT = f (EDUCATIONAL ATTAINMENT, INCOME, HOUSEHOLD CHARACTERISTICS, RESPONDENT CHARACTERISTICS, OTHER);

TOTLREV = f (EDUCATIONAL ATTAINMENT, INCOME, HOUSEHOLD CHARACTERISTICS, RESPONDENT CHARACTERISTICS, OTHER);

SERVICE CUTS = f (EDUCATIONAL ATTAINMENT, INCOME, HOUSEHOLD CHARACTERISTICS, RESPONDENT CHARACTERISTICS, OTHER);

REVENUES = f (EDUCATIONAL ATTAINMENT, INCOME, HOUSEHOLD CHARACTERISTICS, RESPONDENT CHARACTERISTICS, OTHER);

where

CUTPCT is the percent of the budget gap funded by service cuts;

TOTLCUT is the cumulative dollar amount (in millions) of all the services cut;

TOTLREV is the cumulative dollar amount (in millions) of all the revenues raised;

SERVICE CUTS includes the dollar amount cut (in millions) for specific services;

REVENUES includes the dollar amount raised (in millions) for specific revenue sources;

EDUCATIONAL ATTAINMENT includes variables for whether the respondent completed a college degree or more or is a high school graduate or less;

INCOME includes variables for household incomes over $50,000 and under $20,000;

HOUSEHOLD CHARACTERISTICS is a vector of variables including household size, whether the respondent owns or rents his or her home, the number of services (out of eleven) often or sometimes used by the respondent or other household members, and whether the respondent or a household member often uses the service (if applicable).

RESPONDENT CHARACTERISTICS includes the respondent's gender (coded as 1 if the respondent is female and 0 if male) and age;

OTHER includes the size of the budget gap and an interaction of low income variable and household size.

In addition to the OLS regressions, several logistic regressions were estimated. The SERVICE CUTS and REVENUES dependent variables were coded as 1 if the respondent cut the service any amount (or raised any amount of revenue), 0 if not. This provides a different view of the respondent's decision by focusing on the probability of cutting a service (or raising a revenue) rather than the actual amount. Table 3.7 provides some descriptive statistics for the independent variables used in the regressions.

Findings

We calculated three sets of OLS regression estimates for models with dependent variables that represent the percent of the gap funded through cuts (CUTPCT), the total amount of service cuts (TOTLCUT), and the total amount of revenues raised (TOTLREV) (see Table 3.8).

TABLE 3.7   Descriptive Statistics

Variables	Percent in Category	Mean
Education		
BAORMORE (Bachelors degree or higher)	51	–
HSORLESS (High school diploma or less)	16	–
Income		
HIINC (Household income $50,000 and over)	28	–
LOWINC (Household income under $20,000)	22	–
Household Characteristics		
HSHLD (Household size)	–	2.47 people
RENT (Respondent rents home)	24	–
USE (Use of city services)	–	2.26 services used
Respondent Characteristics		
FEMALE (Respondent's gender is female)	53	–
AGE (Respondent's age)	–	48.42 years old
Other		
GAPCLOSE (Amount of the budget gap)	–	$11.46 million

TABLE 3.8   OLS Regression Coefficients

Independent Variables	CUTPCT	TOTLCUT	TOTLREV
Education			
BAORMORE	−0.1482***	−2.6388**	1.1831
(Bachelor's degree or higher)	(−2.877)	(−2.452)	(1.160)
HSORLESS	−0.0409	−0.0811	1.7343
(High school diploma or less)	(−0.549)	(−0.055)	(1.232)
Income			
HIINC	−0.0021	0.5151	0.1696
(Household income $50,000 and over)	(0.039)	(0.459)	(0.159)
LOWINC	−0.0538	−5.2761**	−0.3687
(Household income under $20,000)	(0.460)	(−2.191)	(−0.162)
Household Characteristics			
HSHLD	−0.0032	−0.3133	0.0685
(Household size)	(−0.139)	(−0.648)	(0.150)
RENT	−0.1134*	−0.7033	1.7105
(Respondent rents home)	(1.828)	(−0.571)	(1.464)
USE	−0.0160	0.3038	0.1007
(Use of city services)	(−0.891)	(0.824)	(0.288)
Respondent Characteristics			
FEMALE	−0.0194	−0.2303	0.0617
(Respondent's gender is female)	0.433	(0.249)	(−0.070)
AGE	−0.0015	−0.0131	0.0419
(Respondent's age)	(−0.889)	(0.380)	(1.287)
Other			
GAPCLOSE	−0.0384***	0.0525	1.3804***
(Amount of the budget gap)	(5.723)	(0.383)	(10.618)
HSHLD * LOWINC	0.0819*	3.5531***	0.0328
	(1.750)	(3.652)	(0.036)
CONSTANT	1.099***	5.2339	−11.5032***
	(7.283)	(1.645)	(−3.815)
R²	.26	.12	.40
Adj. R²	.21	.07	.36

*** Significant at the .01 level, ** significant at the .05 level, * significant at the .10 level.

Numbers in parentheses are t-values.

CUTPCT = percent of the budget gap closed through cuts, TOTLCUT = aggregate amount of service cuts in millions of dollars, TOTLREV = aggregate amount of revenue raised in millions of dollars.

First, we look at the results for the CUTPCT variable. One striking result is that respondents with the highest level of education, a bachelor's degree or higher, had significantly (at the .01 level) lower percentage of cuts to revenues. *On average and all else being equal, individuals with a college degree or higher balanced the budget with a percentage of cuts almost 15% lower than those not finishing college.* Also, the coefficient for the size of the budget gap (GAPCLOSE) variable was positive and statistically significant at the .01 level. A $1 million increase to the budget gap resulted, all else being equal, in about a 4 percentage point reduction in the cuts to revenues ratio.

The interaction of household size and low income was positive and significant at the .10 level. This suggests, all else being equal, that for lower-income households, the larger the household size the larger the percentage of cuts. *For each additional household member, a low-income family will on average have a 7.9 percentage point higher ratio of cuts to revenues.* This supports the hypothesis that the larger the household, the more pressure is put on a low-income household's finances. Thus, as household size increases, low-income households seem to more highly value private consumption and are less supportive of using revenues to fund the budget gap. Also, the coefficient for RENT was negative and significant at the .10 level, suggesting that renters balanced the budget with 11 percentage points less in cuts than did home owners, all else being equal.

The results for TOTLCUT and TOTLREV provide some additional insights. The higher education variable is significant (at the .05 level) for TOTLCUT but not for TOTLREV. *This indicates, all else being equal, that individuals with a bachelor's degree or higher are less likely to cut services but are not significantly different from other education groups in their preferences for revenues.* The GAPCLOSE coefficient, on the other hand, was positively related (significant at the .01 level) to TOTLREV but not significantly related to TOTLCUT. This suggests that all else being equal, the larger the gap to close, the higher the revenues raised, but the gap size does not seem to be related to the amount of dollars cut. This finding supports the earlier hypothesis that respondents who increased the budget gap though the addition of service enhancements may be more sympathetic to government and therefore more likely to raise revenues to balance the budget.

The coefficient for the household size and low income interaction variable is significant and positive (at the .01 level) for TOTLCUT but not significant for TOTLREV. In other words, all else being equal, increases in household size for low income respondents increase the amount of service cuts but do not appear to significantly affect revenues raised. Also, the coefficient for the low income variable is negative and significant at the .05 level. *A low-income household with only one household member, all else being equal, can be expected to cut about $1.7 million less than middle-income groups. An increase in the household size to two results in $1.8 million higher in cuts, all else being equal, and a household size of four would be expected to have $8.9 million of additional cuts.*

The OLS regression results for specific expenditure areas appear in Appendix D. The low income household size interaction coefficient is positive for all of the services and significant at the .10 level or higher for nine of ten service categories (planning functions is the exception). The positive relationship between low-income household size and the amount of cuts is robust across the different services. Those with a college degree cut significantly less from park maintenance, recreation programs, planning functions, and the Hult Center for the Performing Arts. Interestingly, these were the four most frequently cut services. Renters cut significantly less from the Hult Center for the Performing Arts, recreation programs, and specialized recreation for the disabled than did home owners, all else being equal.

Appendix E shows the OLS regression coefficients for the nine different taxes and for all taxes combined. The GAPCLOSE coefficient is significant at the .01 level for combined tax variable and at the .10 level or higher for seven of the nine specific taxes. Renters raised significantly more (at the .10 level) in overall taxes compared to home owners, but the payroll tax was the only specific tax where there was a significant difference. Also, although the corporate income tax was the most popular tax overall, respondents with high household incomes did not favor this tax—the coefficient was negative and significant at the .01 level.

The logistic regressions for service cuts presented in Appendix F provide additional insights. The logistic regressions focus on the choice of whether or not to cut the service, regardless of how much is cut. The coefficient for the low income household size interaction variable is no longer significant across a wide range of services—only the Hult Center, human services contracts, and the bookmobile show significant positive relationships, all at the .10 level. The likelihood of choosing specific services for cutting does not appear to be strongly related to increases in low-income household sizes, although, on the other hand, the amount cut from the services is seemingly robustly related. The BAORMORE variable also shows an interesting trend. Respondents with a college degree or higher were significantly less likely to choose to cut police and fire-EMS services at the .05 level, all else being equal. The OLS regressions did not show the amounts, however, to be significantly different.

A very interesting result is shown by the age variable. Respondents' age is significantly (at the .05 level or better) negatively related the choice of cutting five of the ten services. *This provides some evidence contrary to the gray peril hypotheses: Older individuals are less likely to choose to cut some services.*

The logistic regressions for taxes are shown in Appendix G. The GAPCLOSE variable is again significantly positively related across a wide range of taxes. An interesting story is suggested by the gender variable. Women were significantly more likely than men to choose the restaurant tax and hotel/motel room taxes, and significantly less likely to choose the utility tax. The hotel/motel room tax and the restaurant tax are the tax options presented that are most easily avoided, whereas the utility tax could have been perceived as excessively burdensome to that group. *This provides some evidence, although clearly not conclusive, that women view the choice of taxes differently from men and may be more likely to choose a tax that is less onerous to society's disadvantaged or more easily exported to nonresidents.* The coefficient for the rent variable was positive for all nine taxes, and significant at the .10 level or higher for four taxes.

Discussion

The BOB Survey was designed to provide a realistic budget-balancing exercise in which the respondents were faced with an $8 million budget gap between revenues and expenses. The realistic nature of this survey sets it apart from typical questionnaires that stop short of providing the respondents with the genuine constraints facing decision makers. Because the respondents are forced to make the marginal trade-offs between various services and revenues, the results give meaningful guidance to elected officials. This chapter looks at how citizen characteristics relate to budget-balancing strategies. The analysis reveals a number of interesting relationships.

When faced with realistic options for service reductions, the overwhelming majority of respondents chose at least some revenue increases. Conversely, only a few balanced the budget exclusively by revenue enhancements. This result is consistent with the outcome of the Jefferson Center's Citizens Jury on the federal budget deficit, where participants supported greater tax increases than the Democrats and larger service reductions than the Republicans (Jefferson Center, 1993), as well as with the telephone interviewing conducted by the Americans Talk Issues Foundation (Kay et al., 1992).

The median voter chose a combination of 38% cuts and 62% additional revenues. This suggests the majority of respondents were willing to have higher taxes rather than continue to cut services. Indeed, through choosing higher taxes, respondents were willing to trade private consumption for public goods. It is not correct, however, to assume that this spending reduction/revenue split would result if an actual vote were taken. The respondents who completed the BOB Survey have a clearer picture about the budget trade-offs than does the public at large. BOB Survey results represent how an *informed* citizen would vote. Thus, the results point to an interesting paradox. The more realistic the instrument, such as the BOB Survey, the better guidance it provides decision makers about complex and difficult issues. On the other hand, the more realistic the instrument, the less that respondents are representative of a less informed general public. Therefore, there is apt to be a lower likelihood that an uninformed public will think—and vote—in accordance with how respondents fill out a complex and realistic survey like BOB.

The services cut by the largest number of respondents included those where the impacts of the cuts would not be immediately realized (planning functions, park maintenance, and building maintenance). These services are less directly felt, and therefore the impacts may be less well understood. Other services cut by large numbers of respondents were those where user fees could possibly be instituted to stave off the impacts of the service reductions (recreation programs and the Hult Center for the Performing Arts). It is possible that these services are more highly valued than the survey indicates, but respondents were reluctant to fund them through taxes or by cutting other services when other alternatives are possible. On the other hand, the least popular taxes were the ones that may have been perceived as the least avoidable.

Our conclusions based on a descriptive examination of the BOB data resonate with those of Welch (1985). Those absolutely unwilling to include any service cuts—or only willing to use them to balance the budget—represent a small minority of citizens surveyed. The results of the regression analysis suggest that a key determinant of budget-balancing strategy is the level of education—respondents with a college degree or higher cut less overall and were less likely to reduce several services (similar to the bivariate findings of Beck et al., 1987). This group has a taste for publicly provided goods for which they are willing to pay higher taxes.

The regressions also show that for low-income respondents, as household size increases, so does the propensity to choose cuts over increased revenues—they seemingly place a higher value on private consumption compared to public goods. This most likely reflects the increasing strain put on the personal finances of low-income households by additional household members. In general, as household size increases low-income respondents were no more likely to choose a service to cut, but the amount of their cuts were significantly deeper. The logistic regressions also suggest that age was negatively related to the choice of cutting several services—providing some evidence countering the gray peril hypothesis.

The size of the budget gap was robustly related to the choice of several taxes. This may suggest that as the budget gap grew, it became harder to find acceptable service cuts. Or perhaps respondents who chose to enhance services, and thus increase the gap, were systematically more likely to be supportive of government services generally. When faced with the marginal trade-offs between cuts and revenues, these respondents were more likely to tax themselves more rather than choose additional service reductions.

This research supports the notion that a natural constituency for those favoring higher spending are the more highly educated individuals. This is particularly true for services where the benefits may be more obscure, less well understood, and less immediate, such as planning functions, park maintenance, recreation, and performing arts. Fiscal conservatives, oddly, may be most closely aligned with low-income families, who may not have a philosophical aversion to government spending, but for whom tax payments compete with the most essential household purchases.

We have looked at the budget-balancing strategies of citizens in this chapter, finding certain differences between different groups of respondents. In the next chapter, we explore the effect of information on citizens considering budget decisions. We also look at the relationship between citizen service use patterns and support for government services.

Notes

1. Measure 5 was superseded in 1997 by Measure 50, which further limits property taxes.

2. At the time this article (Beck and Dye, 1982) was published, the social security tax was 0% for all earnings over $50,000.

3. The Dutch government is the primary recipient of revenues from natural gas sales in the Netherlands (Neijens et al., 1992, p. 248).

4. The survey sample actually comprised registered, not persistent or actual, voters.

5. Planning functions includes twelve different planning services, recreation programs includes five recreation activities, park maintenance has six different parks, and police includes four different police functions. Certain services are omitted from this analysis primarily because of their small size (convention and visitors bureau, cultural/visual arts, special events, sister cities, animal control, and tree pruning) or because they are administrative/support services (public building maintenance). The bookmobile and human services contracts were included despite their small size because they are social service–type programs.

6. User fees were available for the library and for fire-EMS and were chosen by 20.8% and 24.2% of respondents, respectively. The fee option may have reduced the number of respondents choosing to cut these services.

7. In addition to work cited earlier, there has been substantial research into the determinants of local government spending, including Berne and Scramm (1986): Borscheding and Deacon (1972); Gabler (1971); Hirsch (1970 and 1973); Ladd (1990); Ladd. and Yinger (1989); Levine (1980); Morgan and Pammer (1988); Perkins (1977); Vernez (1976); and Weicher (1970).

8. These services include (1) concerts in the park, (2) senior centers, (3) specialized recreation for the disabled, (4) public library, (5) library bookmobile, (6) swimming pools, (7) adult athletics, (8) community centers, (9) outdoor activities, (10) building permits, and (11) Hult Center for the Performing Arts.

4

How Fiscal Information and Service Use Influence Citizen Preferences

The first two chapters of this book introduced some of the historical and theoretical roots of citizen participation and reviewed the design of some specific new and innovative processes. The third chapter introduced a novel budget-balancing survey methodology and explored how citizens in Eugene, Oregon, responded to this task. One fundamental assumption of these new processes is that they present information that allows citizens to make judgments that are qualitatively different and, it is to be hoped, better than those made without such processes. If citizens are given opportunities to make decisions with relevant information that in some way reflects the real problems facing their government, they may appreciate more fully the issues involved. We expect the resulting decisions to be more stable and perhaps even to be more or less sympathetic to government, depending on the issue. In any event, we would expect these decisions to be *different*. If there is no difference, why bother with these elaborate and resource-consuming citizen participation processes? If there is a difference, we want to know how large it is, what kind of difference it is, and how it might affect citizen choices. These differences are empirically testable. We can measure the size and direction of these effects. One aim of this chapter is to test whether fiscal information influences support for services. The other aim is to see if service use affects support for services. We analyze two of the Eugene Decision surveys to test these ideas,[1] but first we step back to frame this analysis in terms of our ideas of citizenship and citizen motivation.

Notions of Citizenship and Responses to Fiscal Information

The "good citizen" is invoked daily in the political and administrative rhetoric of city councilmembers, mayors, and managers across thousands of governments. We know the good citizen. This person votes, pays taxes, and participates in the life of the community in a significant and tangible manner. This citizen is well informed and philanthropic. This citizen understands and appreciates what government does. This citizen attends hearings. This citizen recycles. The good citizen cares about government and government cares about the nurture and propagation of the good citizen.

Reforms that move to eliminate or separate functions from government provision might be construed as responding to a "private citizen" desire for smaller and more economically efficient government.[2] Providing cheaper services without a government face rewards citizens of this view by costing them less. The stain of government association is eliminated by the invocation of the unblemished ideal of privateness. This idealized form of private government is one in which citizens only pay for what they individually use, what they use costs little, and it is delivered tidily and efficiently. When providing public services, the less that government, with its associations of bloat and bathos, is invoked, the better.

Efforts taken to change the face of government so that it looks less governmental assume that the private citizen and the good citizen are the same person. We assume that as we reduce the identification of services as *government* services that the good citizen is well pleased. We assume that less is more. There are, of course, some fundamental collective, administrative, and public functions for which citizens must pay if any services are to be provided. This is where tensions between the good citizen and the private citizen become apparent. It seems illogical to expect that citizens who decreasingly view themselves as government service users will increasingly support such collective actions. If we are right, then service elimination, privatization, contracting out, and other strategies that reduce the self-identification of the citizen as a government service user may result in decreases in the support (for the taxes) necessary to carry out some of the basic functions of government.

Is it possible that support for collectively consumed services varies with the use of individually consumed services? If so, then decisions about what services to provide or eliminate may affect more than their recipient constituencies. Their effects may reach beyond immediate revenue impacts and influence the long-term fiscal support for broader sets of public services. The data from Eugene, Oregon, do not provide any direct insight into how citizens view their relationship with government or what their motivations look like. We must likewise leave it to other research to observe the effects where services have been moved from public to private provision (more about these possibilities are discussed in Chapter 5). What we can observe—and empirically examine—here are relationships between service use and fiscal support.

In this chapter, we also look to see if fiscal information influences expressed levels of support for taxes to pay for government services. The vast majority of all government surveys that we found that probe citizen service support do so on the basis of satisfaction or service interest. The implicit assumption of such surveys, when they are used to guide resource allocation decisions, is that the level of satisfaction relates to the expenditure preferences of the citizens. Citizens, however, actually select a level of public expenditure by voting on tax referenda or selecting the community with the particular service and tax mix that they desire. In other words, their actual expressions of tax and fee support are made in the presence of information about the cost of services (reflected in tax rates and housing prices) that they will receive. It makes sense, then, that preference surveys include this information about the cost of services when querying residents about how much they support, enjoy, or intend to consume these services.

Does information about the amount that households pay for services influence support for these services? If so, does information affect groups differently, such as older versus younger people, or lower- versus higher-income people? An understanding of the impacts of providing fiscal information may influence the amount and type of such information provided to citizens. Therefore, this chapter has two key foci as we attempt to address the following two research questions:

1. What are the effects of fiscal information on citizen preferences for revenues to support city services?
2. Does service use influence support for services?

Knowledge of how fiscal information changes support for services could influence how much and what type of information is provided to citizens. That is, less principled individuals could rig the game by withholding or providing fiscal information to affect citizen responses in certain ways. If service use is related to support for government services generally, then privatization or the downsizing of government could negatively affect the core financial support for collectively consumed services.

Research on Effects of Fiscal Information and Service Use

Issues in Determining the Value of Government Services

Much of the theory development that underlies notions of service provision and consumption and of preference revelation comes from public finance economics. This work explains these questions through the definition and application of the theory of public goods. The principal characteristics of public goods are the fact that they are nonrival in consumption and exclusion is difficult (Rosen, 1992). In other words, additional people can consume the public good without adding additional costs, and excluding people from such consumption may be hard (Raimondo, 1992). Public goods are distinguished from private goods that may be allocated efficiently through markets. It is difficult for the private market to provide public goods, because of nonrival consumption and the fact that people are not easily excluded from their benefits. This contributes to a conundrum facing those who decide how much of such goods to provide.

People have an incentive to understate their demand for a public or collectively consumed service because they may hope to enjoy the benefits made possible by the contributions of others. In the language of public finance, citizens have an incentive to become free riders. A free rider is someone who expects to benefit from a service for which others pay without personally contributing anything to the financing (Hyman, 1993). Public goods present an allocation problem because the cues for how much to produce do not proceed from the individual directly to the government but are expressed in individuals' choices about where to live and how to vote. The decision makers choosing how much of a public good to produce are typically elected officials (or, in the case of initiatives or referenda, the citizens themselves) and have little citizen information to rely on when seeking to identify appropriate spending levels. Citizen surveys provide a mechanism for gauging the demand for public or collectively consumed goods and services. Such surveys can help to match service provision and expenditure levels to citizen preference and willingness to pay.[3]

The benefit equity principle suggests that the payment for a public good or service should equal the value of the benefit received by the individual who consumes the service (Hyman, 1993; Mikesell 1991; Raimondo, 1992). It is difficult to implement the benefit equity principle for collectively consumed services, since it requires an understanding of how benefits are distributed across individuals.

The benefit equity principle is one of the generally accepted criteria for evaluating tax systems (Holcombe, 1996; Hyman, 1993; Mikesell, 1991; Raimondo, 1992). A strict benefits principle provides a rationale for collecting taxes in proportion to the benefits received. Gasoline taxes that are used to maintain roads are said to satisfy a strict benefits test since (1) increased driving uses more gasoline, (2) using more gasoline means paying higher gasoline taxes, (3) increasing driving contributes to maintenance costs for roads, and therefore (4) gasoline taxes are directly related to the rate of use, and benefit derived, from streets and roads. A general benefit equity standard is also clearly associated with user fees for services, in that those using a service pay for it. Although the benefit equity principle is a widely accepted criterion for evaluating tax and revenue systems, the relationship between service use and willingness to pay for fees and taxes has rarely been empirically tested.

The public sector provides many services that are not pure public goods in the sense of nonrivalness and nonexclusion. This occurs because as a society we have other values besides efficiency that we seek to promote in the distribution of goods and services, such as fairness, democratic ideals, and health and safety. Despite movements to privatize and transfer more services from government to private provision, many governments retain responsibility for services that could be allocated through market mechanisms. These individually consumed services are often paid for through some combination of general taxes and user fees.

Information Effects

As described in Chapters 1 through 3, when citizens are asked whether they prefer continuing or enhancing services, lowering taxes, or increasing government efficiencies, they typically favor lowered taxes and more efficient government to a smaller public sector. This appears to change somewhat in the presence of a budget constraint, as with Eugene citizens who indicated a preference for some combination of service cuts and tax increases when completing the surveys analyzed in Chapter 3. Government efficiency is a popular choice, since it allows the respondent to gain a free lunch—lower taxes while maintaining or enhancing services. Much of the related work in this area focuses on process and looks at the following question: How can citizens be brought into the workings of government decisions? There are several types of these processes: Crosby's Citizens Jury, Kathlene and Martin's citizen panels, Watson et al.'s (1991) institutionalized citizen surveys for the city of Auburn, Alabama, and others. The key lesson from this literature is that greater efficiencies and/or lower taxes while maintaining existing services is the preferred option when it is offered.

There has been one earlier study that tried to determine the effects of fiscal information on support for public services. Thomas Arrington and David Jordan (1982) used data from a survey of registered voters in Mecklenburg County, North Carolina, to determine the influence of fiscal information on citizens' willingness to pay for the costs of government services. The results, which do not control for demographic variables or service use, reveal that "for virtually every [government service] activity the support was less when respondents were asked whether they would pay the costs directly" (p. 169). Arrington and Jordan's work suggests that the effects of fiscal information on citizen decision makers are ubiquitous and profound.

Service Use and Service Support

Our work seeks to contribute to our understanding of willingness to pay by examining the relationship between use and tax and fee support for a wide variety of local services. This relationship is analyzed for evidence of consonance with benefit equity principles. This includes exploring how the overall support for government varies with the number of services that individuals use (Does support transfer across services?). Our findings provide insight for those interested in understanding the underlying structure of the support for individual and collective services.

Additionally, our research has implications for privatization and the reduction of the government scope of provision and production. Collective services rely on collective public support for their existence. At the same time, such services include vital but unnoticed functions such as financial administration or, in the case of Eugene, land use planning and public buildings maintenance: functions with which citizens have limited direct contact. Based on the survey conducted in Eugene, we cannot view the result of a shift toward privatization or contracts and observe their effects on support for collective services. We can, however, begin to look for patterns that suggest that changes in the identification of citizens as users of government services may have effects on citizens' financial support for basic government functions.

An important dimension of this research is how resource shifts emphasizing the private citizen customer affect government support. We choose two scholars in particular to represent this concern. Hindy Lauer Schacter (1995) distinguishes the citizen-owner model of service provision from the citizen-consumer model promoted in reinvention. The former emphasizes bidirectional responsibility and demands information and education. The latter possesses a unidirectional responsibility and demands responsiveness. Jon Pierre (1995) warns that the reconceptualization of citizens as customers distorts the mutual entitlements and obligations between the state and the individual. The customers' source of individual resources comes from individual purchasing power as opposed to legal right. Customers have no responsibilities, compared to the variety of civic and political responsibilities of citizens. The policy objectives of the customer system differ as well, focusing on individual empowerment, as opposed to the larger social welfare (Pierre, 1995, p. 65).

Douglas Morgan and his colleagues (1996, pp. 362–363) note that eliminating layers of management by shifts to private provision removes a decisive role in the provision of goods and services that may negatively impact the public trust. Desmond King and Jon Pierre (1990) cite Graham Mather's concern that the increased use of local service contractors will transform local government "out of recognition" (p. 10). Donald Kettl

(1993) writes that contracting out and privatization create important partnerships that require a great deal of attention and expertise to manage. Using the private sector for public goals creates problems:

> In seeking to solve these problems, government faces a sometimes sharp tension between seeking accommodation through market-based compromise with its agents and pursuing without compromise the public interest that the law demands. Critical issues cascade in uncommon complexity from the ideological and pragmatic imperatives that brought government into these growing relations with the private sector. (p. 40)

As a basis for his discussion of privatization, E. S. Savas (1987) classifies goods and services into four types: private goods, toll goods, common pool goods, and collective goods. Of these, private and collective goods correspond with public and private goods as discussed by Rosen (1992) and others. Like private goods, common pool goods are individually consumed, but unlike private goods they are nonexcludable in consumption. Like public goods, toll goods are collectively consumed, but unlike pure public goods they are excludable. Savas indicates that although market provision is possible for private or toll goods, collective and common pool goods require provision through voluntary, contractual, or intergovernmental agreement. In other words, there is room for policy discretion in selecting the means of provision of many services.

We refer to individual services (private and common pool) and collective services (public and toll goods) in this chapter. The individual services are those for which the notion of frequent use and the ability to charge fees are the most reasonable in concept and practice. The collective services are those for which use is more abstract and fees less tenable. In the case of the survey effort described below, the classification is based on whether the government of the city of Eugene was using or considering fees for these services.

Among the uncommon complexities associated with downsizing and privatization, we would include the possibility of unintended consequences for long-term fiscal stability. Citizens' desire for services and their commitment to support them are complex and difficult to gauge. Mark A. Glaser and W. Bartley Hildreth (1996) relate willingness to pay taxes to demand for (use of) park and recreation services and find evidence of discontinuity. In their study, respondents were asked about their willingness to pay for the services about which their use was also queried. Many of their respondents were traditionalists (those whose willingness to pay generally corresponded to service use), but they also found many free riders (heavy users with low levels of willingness to pay) and philanthropists (low service users with higher levels of willingness to pay).

Alan Lewis (1979) was interested in whether tax attitudes are based on altruism or self-interest. His research into some of the determinants of general attitudes toward taxes uses a sample of 200 male taxpayers in Bath (United Kingdom). Respondents noted their relative levels of agreement with a variety of statements about the fairness and ethical considerations of taxation plans. Responses were also gathered about satisfaction with current levels of taxation. Lewis concludes that attitudes toward income taxation are in part dependent on earnings. He observes that antipathy toward taxation increases with income. Of income, age, social class, and party, only income has a consistently significant effect. The fact that his sample population is principally composed of middle-class males may contribute to this finding.

Lewis also notes that responses change based on whether survey questions point out the connection between taxes and services: "There is much greater agreement that progressive taxation is fair when it is stated that this provides services for the lower paid they would not normally be able to afford . . . than when no mention is made of these services" (p. 253). Absent such explanatory information, respondents' primary motivation is to reduce their taxes. Lewis concludes that the need exists for broad education about these issues in the United Kingdom.

Debate in the area of service delivery reform has focused on efficiency and equity concerns. Proponents of private service delivery argue that private sector involvement can lead to more efficient production due to increased competition (Boycko et al., 1996; Butler, 1991; Savas, 1987). Others contend that even if efficiencies exist initially, they often diminish or disappear over time as the system becomes captive to business interests, and competition wanes (Bradford, Malt, and Oates, 1969; Pack, 1991; Peters and Savoie, 1996; Pierre, 1995). Still others argue that private sector production cannot guarantee equitable service delivery (Kettl, 1993; Starr, 1991). Nonetheless, contracting out has increased to become a significant part of the delivery of government services.

Does the elimination and contracting out of some individual services erode support for other general government services? If citizens' support depends in part on their use of government services, then discontinuation or privatization of services that touch people may result in reduced support for government generally. If true, this relationship has profound implications for service elimination and contracting out. There is considerable pressure to make such changes, given the context of suspicion and distrust in which most local governments presently operate.[4] Is it possible that local governments' attempts to demonstrate to the citizenry that they can reduce, downsize, and privatize could result in an ultimate inability to pay for essential but less visible and attractive functions of government such as maintenance, planning, and administration? Conclusive answers to these questions require longitudinal study employing panel or time series data. The cross-sectional data examined here allow us to take the first step. Here, we may establish whether an underlying relationship between individual service use and more general service support actually exists.

Methodology

As mentioned in Chapters 2 and 3, in 1991 and 1992 the city of Eugene, Oregon, completed a citizen participation process to ascertain public sentiment for a variety of spending and budget balancing alternatives called Eugene Decisions. Eugene Decisions employed an innovative combination of public forums, clip-out budget-balancing exercises, and representative surveys.

Eugene Decisions sought to bring citizens together to render public judgment about alternative strategies for addressing the city's budget deficit. Through the provision of real information about the actual amounts of fees, taxes, and the budget shortfall, participants gained a clearer picture of the true dilemma facing policy makers. As described earlier, three random sample surveys provided the city council with a realistic picture of how citizens viewed city services and revenues. One survey was a budget template that led respondents through a realistic budget-balancing exercise in which they were provided an opportunity to balance the budget according to their own priorities but constrained by real choices. The analysis of that survey is reported in Chapter 3. Two other surveys were used to gauge citizen support for services and taxes. The Blue Survey asked respondents to express their support for taxes for a variety of government services; it also presented the *amount* of the taxes paid by an average household (see Appendix C). The Ivory Survey was similar to the Blue Survey except it did not present the tax amounts (see Appendix B). In this way, decision makers at the city of Eugene were presented with surveys that ranged from no fiscal information, to the presentation of the household tax amounts, to a budget-balancing exercise that forced trade-offs among and between services and revenues.

Individually Consumed Services and
Collectively Consumed Services

The three surveys provided the city of Eugene with a wealth of information to help solve its budget problems. Although they were not originally designed for this purpose, the Ivory and Blue Surveys also provide the opportunity to test whether fiscal information (in the form of household tax amounts) and service use influences support for services. Questions were asked about twenty-three different services. They have been separated for analysis here into two distinct groups: those services for which fees are in place or could conceivably be charged (eleven) and those for which fees could not be as easily imagined (twelve). Throughout this discussion, these will be referred to as individually consumed services (library, book-mobile, swimming pools, adult athletics, community centers, outdoor programs, Hult Center (for the Performing Arts), specialized recreation for the disabled, building permits, senior citizen centers, concerts in the park) and collectively consumed services (police, fire-EMS, special events [e.g., street festivals], sister cities, business assistance, Metropolitan Partnership, downtown development, affordable housing and neighborhood development, land use planning, neighborhood groups, human services, public buildings and facilities [repair and maintenance]). See Table 4.1 for a full description of these services.[5]

For the purpose of this analysis, the two surveys (Ivory and Blue) were combined and analyzed collectively. The influence of information and service use on respondents' preferences for services and taxes are examined through analyses of the pooled Ivory and Blue Surveys using logistic regression.

There are two possible approaches for comparing these surveys: pooling the surveys together or leaving them separate. Pooling is not appropriate unless a strong case can be made for equivalent groups. In the case of the Eugene Decisions data, the instruments used were sent to city residents selected through the same random process (voter registration rolls) at the same time. Each registered voter in the city had an equal chance of being selected for *either* survey. Both questionnaires asked questions about the same set of services, and both asked respondents whether they strongly support, somewhat support, somewhat oppose, or strongly oppose the use of taxes for the services. The survey response rates for these mail surveys were extraordinarily high: 83% for Ivory and 76% for Blue.[6] Furthermore, aside from the information presented, the surveys ask the same questions in approximately the same order. Apart from individually consumed services (described below) the questions were of similar construction.

The two survey instruments have several sections. Four of these sections are matched together to form one data set for this analysis. Both surveys have variables for each of the questions in each section. These variables are combined by matching the corresponding responses from each instrument. This is done in such a way that one variable is created by combining all of the observations from both surveys. The sections combined are

Support for taxes
Service use
Demographic variables

TABLE 4.1   Individual and Collective Services

Individual Services (Fee Services)	Collective Services (Tax Services)
1. *Public Library.* Public library services for the city	1. *Police.* Responds to police calls, enforcement of laws, and investigation of criminal cases
2. *Library Bookmobile.* Library services to those who have difficulty getting to the library on their own	2. *Fire and Emergency Medical Services.* Fire protection, emergency medical, ambulance, and other rescue operations.
3. *Swimming Pools.* Recreational opportunities, water safety instruction, and fitness activities	3. *Special Events.* Promotion of events for the community
4. *Adult Athletics.* Adult recreational programs, such as softball and soccer	4. *Sister Cities.* Cultural exchange for Eugene's sister cities in Korea, Nepal, Japan, and Russia
5. *Community Centers.* Four community centers providing year-round recreational classes (such as aerobic dancing) and meeting places for a wide range of community groups	5. *Business Assistance.* Assistance to new and existing small businesses
6. *Outdoor Programs.* Instruction in various outdoor activities, such as rock climbing and skiing	6. *Metro Partnership.* Work to attract new business to the Eugene area
7. *Hult Center.* Two performing arts theaters that provide a place for local, national, and international artists to perform	7. *Downtown Development.* Promotion of private development of downtown Eugene
8. *Specialized Recreation.* Recreational opportunities for people with disabilities	8. *Affordable Housing and Neighborhood Development.* New low-cost and low-rent housing and emergency shelter for homeless families
9. *Building Permits.* Checking plans and issuing permits for residential construction	9. *Land Use Planning.* Management of the city's land use rules, including the historic preservation program
10. *Senior Centers.* Recreational and social activities for city residents over 55 years old	10. *Neighborhood Groups.* Opportunities for citizens to participate in decision making with the city
11. *Concerts in the Park.* Throughout the summer, concerts at various parks	11. *Human Services.* Contracts with nonprofits to assist homeless and low-income people with food, shelter, and medical attention
	12. *Public Buildings and Facilities.* Renovation and repair of city-owned buildings and equipment

Support for Taxes. Support for taxes is measured in both the Ivory and Blue Surveys along a four-point continuum following a brief service description. In the Blue Survey, the tax per household is included in the description.[7]

Service Use. People who use services regularly may have structurally different attitudes about taxes and fees than those who do not. Those who use a specific service may make choices that represent their constituency for that service, and those who use government services generally may also view them differently. Both surveys asked respondents how often they use a series of city services. These lists are identical and offer a three-point continuum from "often use" to "never use." All of the services described in the questions about individually consumed services have use variables that correspond directly to them.

The questions about collectively consumed services do not have service use variables that correspond directly to them. Fire-EMS and police, public buildings, downtown development, and others in the tax section of the surveys are services that respondents are unlikely to use frequently or in some cases ever. Some indication of the quality of a respondent's contact with these services would be preferable but is not possible with these data. As a surrogate, we counted the responses for the fee-supportable activities (a continuous variable with a range from 0 to 11). This provides a measure of respondents' contact with city government.

Demographic Variables. Demographic variables appear at the end of each survey. Respondents are asked to indicate their age, gender, household size in number of persons, number of household members under age eighteen, number of household members over age sixty-five, whether they rent or own their home, if a home owner the amount of property
tax expected to be paid that year, highest level of education, and approximate household income. The questions asking about the proportional ages of household members and the amount of property taxes contain numerous missing or miscoded entries and are discarded from this analysis.

The demographic information helps in answering whether different demographic groups are likely to be influenced by fiscal information in different ways. The logistic regression model predicts support for the various services as a function of the characteristics of the survey respondents, their use of services, and whether or not they received information about the specific tax amounts.

Tax Support = *f*(Fiscal Information, Service Use, Respondent
    Characteristics)

Logistic regressions are estimated for each of the eleven individually consumed and twelve collectively consumed services. Three different dependent variables are used: whether the respondent (1) strongly supports taxes for the service, (2) either somewhat or strongly supports taxes for the service, or (3) strongly opposes taxes for the service. The logistic regressions include the following independent variables:

Information—1 if respondent had fiscal information, 0 if not

Often Use—1 if respondent (or household member) often uses the service, 0 if not (individually consumed only)

Never Use—1 if respondent (or household member) never use the service, 0 if not (individually consumed only)

Use Often—Number of individually consumed (0–11) which respondents report using often (tax services only)

Use Never—Number of individually consumed (0–11) which respondents report using never (tax services only)

Age—expressed as natural logarithms

Gender—1 if female, 0 if male

Home ownership—1 if renter, 0 if home owner

Low Income—1 if household income under $20,000, 0 if not

High Income—1 if income over $50,000, 0 if not

Household Size—Number of people in the household

Higher Education—1 if respondent had a bachelor's degree or higher, 0 if not

Less Education—1 if respondent has high school diploma or less education, 0 if not

Research Questions

We seek to answer several research questions about fiscal information and service use.

Research Question 1. *What are the effects of fiscal information on citizen preferences for revenues to support city services?*

1a. Does information effect different groups of people differently? For example, how do women with fiscal information differ from women without this information?

1b. How does the information effect on one group contrast with that of converse groups. For example, what is the effect of information on those over sixty-five compared to those under sixty-five?

Based on the literature, we expect that presenting fiscal information will reduce support for (increase opposition to) government services. If knowledge of the tax amounts erodes support, we would expect significant negative coefficients for the information variable for strong support or for somewhat or strong support. Conversely, significant positive coefficients for strong opposition would also indicate tax aversion.

Are one or two groups of respondents with strong antitax or antifee sentiments driving this effect, or are all groups equally deterred in the face of actual taxes? In addition to the general effects, we also test the differential effects of information among groups of individuals. If the influence of information is ubiquitous, we would expect it to show up across demographic groups.

We tested this general information effect using the variable reflecting whether fiscal information was available (1 if the respondent had fiscal information, 0 if not). We test for differences in information effects across demographic groups by employing a series of dummy variables. Each set of analysis required the creation of a different set of dummy variables based on the questions being asked. When comparing information effects between groups, for instance, each group has at least two variables associated with it. In the case of seniors with information, variables were created for seniors with information, and seniors without information were the comparison case. Logistic regressions were run, controlling for all other factors, for each level of support for each service for this group, and the entire process was repeated for each of the subsequent groups (e.g., women, men, high income, low income, etc.).

Research Question 2.   *Does service use influence support for services?*

2a. Is support for individually consumed services influenced by service use?
2b. Is support for collectively consumed services influenced by the use of government services generally?
2c. Is support for the user fee/tax combination to finance services influenced by service use?

We would expect to find that willingness to pay increases with service use for individually consumed services, based on the findings of Alan Lewis (1979) that support for taxes increases when the taxes are associated with specific services and Mark Glaser and W. Bartley Hildreth

(1996), who find that increased use corresponds with increased willingness to pay. We test for the connection between individual service use and willingness to pay for collective services in order to be able to say something about the complexity of the relationship between citizens and services. Although a relationship between individual service use and support for collective services does not directly demonstrate that the elimination of services would erode the willingness to pay for services, it should be enough to justify some retrenchment of thought and theory development in this area.

The following are the independent variables used for the first research question (individually consumed services):

Often Use—1 if respondent (or household member) often uses the service, 0 if not

Never Use—1 if respondent (or household member) never uses the service, 0 if not

For research question 2b (collectively consumed services):

Use Often—Number of individually consumed services (0–11) which respondents report often using

Use Never—Number of individually consumed services (0–11) which respondents report never using

We measured the intensity of respondents' perceived use of government services by counting their responses about using the individual services. Respondents were asked about their use of eleven individual services, so up to eleven services could be indicated for each observation. If use enhances support for services, we would expect positive coefficients for the strong support and somewhat or strong support variables. Negative coefficients for the strong opposition variables indicates service use reduces opposition to taxes for services.

We also look at whether willingness to pay user fees for individually consumed services are influenced by service use through using responses from the Blue Survey. The Blue Survey asks about support for user fees by querying respondents about the combination of fees and taxes they prefer to fund the service, holding service delivery constant. The questions were set up as follows:

The Hult Center provides a place for local, national, and international artists to perform. The Hult Center operations are now paid for by a combination of user fees (tickets) and taxes. Ticket prices now average $13, and the average household contributes about $22 in taxes. What combination of ticket price and taxes would you prefer?

Ticket Price	$13	$14.50	$16	$17.50	$19
Annual Tax	$22	$16.50	$11	$5.50	$0
	[ ]	[ ]	[ ]	[ ]	[ ]

The questions were constructed so that the choices ran from the existing tax/fee situation up to 100% fee financing. In the case of the Hult Center, for example, the starting fee was the average ticket price. The three in-between choices are the fee/tax combinations that represent fees increasing to cover 25%, 50%, and 75% of the difference between the existing tax/fee split and 100% fee financing. In several cases, such as the bookmobile, there was no existing fee.

Logistic regressions were estimated for two separate dependent variables: (1) whether the respondent chose the existing tax/fee split, and (2) whether the respondent preferred the 100% fee option. The service use variables are the same as for Research Question 1, as are the control variables.[8]

A positive relationship between the often use variable and fee support suggests that those who use a service support the use of user fees to fund that service. Conversely, a negative relationship would suggest a desire to have services supported by taxes levied on the collective regardless of use. In other words, such respondents would prefer that others pay for the services they use—they would like to be free riders.

Details of Survey Methodology

The survey methodology used in our analysis is different from, but motivationally related to, *contingent valuation,* a complex system of citizen inquiry by which each respondent's personal willingness to pay is revealed. With contingent valuation, citizens are taken through a series of nested decision trees designed to elicit the direct dollar value that they attach to certain public resources. The method was originally developed in the 1960s in the realm of natural resources (Mitchell and Carson, 1989; see Note 3 for further references). The surveys used by the city of Eugene were designed to elicit levels of support and willingness to pay for services—some of which at least conceivably possessed privately provided analogs. Contingent valuation was developed to establish the benefit levels derived from purely public and intangible goods such as the aesthetic benefits derived from the existence of a wilderness area.

Examining the results of surveys used in a decision process not designed with theory tests in mind is several steps removed from the world of pure experiments but has the advantage of capturing responses to a real dilemma facing a government and its members at a discrete point in time. The design of the instruments used in this process was informed by the lessons learned through contingent valuation research and more generally through that for mail surveys (Dillman, 1978). Close attention was paid to wording the questions to avoid vague or leading language. For example, concerns about the upward bias in assessing willingness to pay in mail surveys (Mitchell and Carson, 1989) were alleviated by including the full scope of government services as opposed to focusing on one or two areas of the budget.[9]

Guided by the lessons of work that has demonstrated that public opinion can be intransitive and transitory, the present surveys provide additional information about the costs of services to mitigate these effects as they relate to prices, measure their magnitude, and increase the predictive validity of the project.

Findings — Information Effects

We find that when the tax amount is known respondents are significantly less likely to support, and more likely to oppose, these services. The general effects of information are presented based on simple descriptive statistics. The percentages listed in Table 4.2 show the base rates for service support (Ivory Survey) and the support in the presence of information (Blue Survey). The percentage of respondents indicating that they strongly support taxes for the services decreases for the Blue Survey compared to the Ivory Survey for nineteen of the twenty-three services. The percentage of respondents indicating that they strongly oppose taxes for the services increases for the Blue Survey for all twenty-three of the services presented! The relative amounts of support vary for each of these services, but the pattern remains clear: *Whatever the initial level of support, it drops in the face of fiscal information.* These differences are visible even in the absence of controls for other factors.

The effect of information is measured by the logistic regressions. How much does fiscal information matter to respondent preferences? The short answer is *a lot*. For the vast majority of services, *presenting the tax amount results in reduced support*. Table 4.3 shows that knowing the amount of the tax makes it significantly more likely that respondents will strongly oppose taxes for eleven out of twelve collectively consumed services (all at least at the .01 level of significance). Fiscal information also makes it significantly less likely that respondents will strongly support taxes for eight of twelve collectively consumed services. Somewhat or strong support is decreased for eleven of the twelve services. The sole service that does not show this effect, sister cities, bears a tax amount of only $1.

Among the individually consumed services, the information effect is equally stunning. Strong opposition significantly increases for every

TABLE 4.2 Percent Supporting or Opposing Services

	Strongly Oppose		Somewhat Oppose		Somewhat Support		Strongly Support	
	Blue Survey	Ivory Survey	Blue Survey	Ivory Survey	Blue Survey	Ivory Survey	Blue Survey	Ivory Survey
Collective Services								
Police	13.9	0.6	9.6	2.4	27.2	14.8	49.0	82.2
Fire-EMS	8.3	0.3	10.0	0.3	27.2	8.0	54.2	91.4
Special events	41.9	21.4	20.1	23.3	21.1	37.1	13.4	18.2
Sister cities	45.3	33.8	18.1	28.0	20.1	31.2	12.4	7.1
Business assistance	32.1	13.4	19.7	22.0	31.4	42.5	14.0	22.0
Metro Partnership	29.9	15.0	18.8	17.6	28.5	35.1	20.1	32.3
Downtown dev.	47.0	30.0	27.0	24.3	17.0	28.1	7.0	17.7
Affordable housing	14.3	7.6	13.0	13.0	24.9	33.5	47.2	45.9
Land use planning	53.7	12.0	23.5	25.9	11.4	45.3	7.7	16.8
Neigh. groups	27.0	15.8	23.0	26.0	29.4	42.1	17.9	16.1
Human services	17.5	4.3	16.2	10.5	30.1	37.2	35.1	48.0
Public bldg.	36.9	3.7	23.2	7.8	24.8	43.0	11.7	45.5
Individual Services								
Library	17.6	5.1	12.5	10.6	25.3	33.8	43.6	50.5
Bookmobile	20.3	10.4	10.0	23.6	27.1	43.3	40.2	22.7
Swimming pools	18.5	2.7	20.5	12.9	33.2	44.4	25.7	39.9
Adult athletics	34.4	20.7	23.8	30.7	24.8	34.7	14.6	13.9
Community centers	24.0	8.5	25.3	13.1	31.8	42.4	17.8	36.0
Outdoor programs	36.6	26.6	29.7	25.9	20.3	31.6	10.7	15.8
Hult Center	37.2	20.5	25.3	23.2	24.6	32.1	12.6	24.2
Specialized rec.	21.8	4.9	12.8	9.5	28.4	44.0	33.6	41.6
Bldg. permits	36.6	12.0	30.0	25.9	20.7	45.3	9.7	16.8
Senior centers	14.2	4.8	15.9	8.1	34.9	41.4	33.2	45.6
Park concerts	34.7	25.7	16.3	26.3	22.4	32.6	25.5	15.4

Blue survey contains fiscal information, Ivory survey has no fiscal information.

TABLE 4.3   Information Effects

	Strongly Support		Somewhat or Strongly Support		Strongly Oppose	
	B	Sig.	B	Sig.	B	Sig.
Collective Services						
Police	−1.6322	***	−2.5236	***	3.9679	***
Fire-EMS	−2.1942	***	−4.2004	***	−	−
Special events	−	−	−0.8213	***	1.1601	***
Sister cities	0.9033	***	−	−	0.5719	***
Business assistance	−0.4465	**	−0.7088	***	1.2544	***
Metro Partnership	−0.4991	**	−0.6605	***	0.8876	***
Downtown dev.	−0.9730	***	−0.9309	***	0.7246	***
Affordable housing	−	−	−0.5182	**	0.8654	***
Land use planning	−0.7491	***	−1.9736	***	2.5480	***
Neighborhood grps.	−	−	−0.5031	***	0.8665	***
Human services	−0.5513	***	−1.2711	***	1.6367	***
Public bldg.	−1.7938	***	−2.5504	***	2.8588	***
Individual Services						
Library	−	−	−0.9646	***	1.5015	***
Bookmobile	1.0528	***	−	−	0.9105	***
Swimming pools	−0.5615	***	−1.3081	***	2.6227	***
Adult athletics	0.1217	***	−0.3900	**	0.7386	***
Community ctrs.	−0.8866	***	−1.2829	***	1.2480	***
Outdoor programs	−0.4562	*	−0.7682	***	0.5150	***
Hult Center	−0.7742	***	−0.8539	***	0.9701	***
Specialized rec.	−	−	−1.4230	***	1.1960	***
Bldg. permits	−0.5130	**	−1.3599	***	1.6918	***
Senior centers	−0.4386	**	−1.3131	***	1.5766	***
Park concerts	1.0396	***	−	−	0.3978	*

*** Significant at the .01 level, ** significant at the .05 level, * significant at the .10 level.
B is the logistic regression coefficient.

service when respondents know the tax amount. Strong support wanes once the tax amount is known for seven of eleven services.

Table 4.4 shows the change in the predicted probability of support for (or opposition to) services when fiscal information is provided. In many cases, the changes in support are huge. The logistic regression coefficients do not relate directly to the probability of choosing support for taxes for services. The coefficients represent the change in the log of the odds of choosing tax support (or opposition) based on a one-unit change in the independent variable. This figure is not straightforward to interpret. An-

TABLE 4.4 Information Effects and Change in Probability

	Strongly Support			Somewhat or Strongly Support			Strongly Oppose		
	B	Sig.	Change from .5	B	Sig.	Change from .5	B	Sig.	Change from .5
Collective Services									
Police	-1.6322	***	-0.3365	-2.5236	***	-0.4258	3.9679	***	0.4814
Fire-EMS	-2.1942	***	-0.3997	-4.2004	***	-0.4852	10.0333		0.5000
Special events	-0.1265		-0.0316	-0.8213	***	-0.1945	1.1601	***	0.2614
Sister cities	0.9033	***	0.2116	-0.0944		-0.0236	0.5719	***	0.1392
Business assistance	-0.4465	**	-0.1098	-0.7088	***	-0.1701	1.2544	***	0.2781
Metro Partnership	-0.4991	**	-0.1222	-0.6605	***	-0.1594	0.8876	***	0.2084
Downtown dev.	-0.9730	***	-0.2257	-0.9309	***	-0.2173	0.7246	***	0.1736
Affordable housing	0.0891		0.0223	-0.5182	**	-0.1267	0.8654	***	0.2038
Land use planning	-0.7491	***	-0.1790	-1.9736	***	-0.3780	2.5480	***	0.4274
Neigh. grps.	0.1645		0.0410	-0.5031	***	-0.1232	0.8665	***	0.2040
Human services	-0.5513	***	-0.1344	-1.2711	***	-0.2809	1.6367	***	0.3371
Public bldg.	-1.7938	***	-0.3574	-2.5504	***	-0.4276	2.8588	***	0.4458
Individual Services									
Library	-0.1331		-0.0332	-0.9646	***	-0.2240	1.5015	***	0.3178
Bookmobile	1.0528	***	0.2413	0.1197		0.0299	0.9105	***	0.2131
Swimming pools	-0.5615	***	-0.1368	-1.3081	***	-0.2872	2.6227	***	0.4323
Adult athletics	0.1217	***	0.0304	-0.3900	**	-0.0963	0.7386	***	0.1767
Community ctrs.	-0.8866	***	-0.2082	-1.2829	***	-0.2829	1.2480	***	0.2770
Outdoor programs	-0.4562	*	-0.1121	-0.7682	***	-0.1831	0.5150	***	0.1260
Hult Center	-0.7742	***	-0.1844	-0.8539	***	-0.2014	0.9701	***	0.2251
Specialized rec.	-0.2957		-0.0734	-1.4230	***	-0.3058	1.1960	***	0.3721
Bldg. permits	-0.5130	**	-0.1255	-1.3599	***	-0.2957	1.6918	***	0.3445
Senior centers	-0.4386	**	-0.1079	-1.3131	***	-0.2880	1.5766	***	0.3287
Park concerts	1.0396	***	0.2388	0.2538		0.0631	0.3978	*	0.0982

*** Significant at the .01 level, ** significant at the .05 level, * significant at the .10 level.

B is the logistic regression coefficient.

Change from .5 denotes the predicted change from .5 due to the respondent having fiscal information.

other way to measure the influence of the variables is to calculate the change in the probability resulting from fiscal information. The columns marked "Change from .5" show the logistic regression models' predicted change from a starting value of .5. For example, provision of fiscal information is predicted to increase opposition to taxes for land use planning by 43% (based on a starting probability of opposition of 50%).[10] Or stated another way, the logistic regression model predicts a probability of 93% that respondents with fiscal information will strongly oppose taxes for land use planning (50% + 43%), compared to 50% if they did not have fiscal information.[11] The predicted probability change due to fiscal information can be extremely large, ranging from a low of 3% to a high of 49% (for the significant coefficients).

The information effect is so strong that it cries out for further analysis. We can see clearly that once the amounts of taxes are known, citizens are far less supportive. This finding is consistent with our common understandings of human behavior as well as the empirical research that has preceded this work. We all recognize the person who supports a variety of causes and efforts without hesitation—until it becomes time to do the work or to pay the bill. It seems to make sense that people might support generally what they would not like to pay for specifically.

Influence of Fiscal Information on Sociodemographic Groups

We again use logistic regression to assess the influence of information on different groups of individuals. In this portion of the analysis, respondents are compared among their own group. Women with fiscal information, for instance, are compared to women without information, and those over sixty-five with fiscal information are compared to those over sixty-five without it, and so forth. Tables 4.5 and 4.6 show that all groups are affected, but some slightly more than others. Regardless of group, knowing the tax amount generally decreases the support for (increases opposition to) services. Therefore, for the vast majority of services, we reject our null hypothesis and conclude that fiscal information generally lowers support for services (or increases opposition to services) regardless of demographic group.

These results speak to the ubiquity and power of tax information's influence on citizens. Those who know the tax amounts are significantly more likely to oppose the service than other members of their sociodemographic cohort, regardless of whether that group is women, men, seniors, home owners, those from low- or middle-income households, or college graduates. Some groups are more consistently affected than others, however. The elderly, women, and men seem particularly affected by fiscal information. Fiscal information has somewhat less of an effect on those

TABLE 4.5 Information Effects Within Sociodemographic Group—Collective Services Logistic Regression Significant Coefficients

Service	HS Diploma with Information			College or More with Information		
	Strong Support	Strong and Somewhat Support	Strong Opposition	Strong Support	Strong and Somewhat Support	Strong Opposition
Police	-***	-***	-	-***	-***	+***
Fire-EMS	-***	-**	-	-***	-***	-
Special events	-	-**	+**	-	-***	+***
Sister cities	-	-	-	-	-	+***
Business assistance	-	-***	+***	-*	-**	+***
Metro Partnership	-	-	-	-*	-**	+**
Downtown dev.	-	-**	+***	-***	-***	-
Affordable housing	-*	-*	+*	-	-**	+*
Land use	-	-***	+***	-**	-***	+***
Neighborhood grps.	-	-*	+***	-	-***	+***
Human services	-***	-**	+***	-**	-***	+***
Public buildings	-**	-***	+***	-***	-***	+***

Service	65 or Over with Information			Men with Information		
	Strong Support	Strong and Somewhat Support	Strong Opposition	Strong Support	Strong and Somewhat Support	Strong Opposition
Police	-***	-***	+***	-***	-***	+***
Fire-EMS	-***	-***	+***	-***	-	-
Special events	-	-**	+***	+**	-**	+***
Sister cities	-	-**	+***	-	-	+***
Business assistance	-**	-***	+***	-	-***	+***
Metro Partnership	-**	-***	+***	-*	-***	+***
Downtown dev.	-**	-***	+**	-**	-**	+*
Affordable housing	-	-***	+***	-	-	+*
Land use	-*	-***	+***	-	-***	+***
Neighborhood grps.	-	-**	+***	-	-**	+***
Human services	-	-***	+***	-*	-***	+***
Public buildings	-***	-***	+***	-***	-***	+***

93

Homeowners with Information

Service	Strong Support	Strong and Somewhat Support	Strong Opposition
Police	+***	–***	–
Fire-EMS	+***	–***	–
Special events	–	–***	+***
Sister cities		–	+***
Business assistance	–***	–***	+***
Metro Partnership	–**	–***	+***
Downtown dev.	–***	–***	+***
Affordable housing		–**	+**
Land use	–***	–***	+***
Neighborhood grps.		–***	+***
Human services	–***	–***	+***
Public buildings	–***	–***	+***

Renters with Information

Service	Strong Support	Strong and Somewhat Support	Strong Opposition
Police	–***	–***	+**
Fire-EMS	–***	–	–
Special events	–	–	–
Sister cities	–***	–	–
Business assistance	–	–	–
Metro Partnership	–	–	–
Downtown dev.	–	–*	–
Affordable housing	–	–	–
Land use	–	+***	+***
Neighborhood grps.	–	–	–
Human services	–	–***	+*
Public buildings	–***	+***	+***

Women with Information

Service	Strong Support	Strong and Somewhat Support	Strong Opposition
Police	–***	–***	–
Fire-EMS	–***	–***	–
Special events	–	–***	+***
Sister cities	–**	–	–
Business assistance	–*	–**	+***
Metro Partnership	–*	–**	+***
Downtown dev.	–**	–***	+**
Affordable housing	–	–***	+***
Land use	–***	–***	+***
Neighborhood grps.	–	–	+**
Human services	–**	–***	+***
Public buildings	–***	–***	+***

Low Income with Information

Service	Strong Support	Strong and Somewhat Support	Strong Opposition
Police	–***	–***	+***
Fire-EMS	–***	–***	+***
Special events	–	–	+***
Sister cities	–**	–	–
Business assistance	–	–	+**
Metro Partnership	–*	–***	+***
Downtown dev.	–	–	+*
Affordable housing	–	–	–
Land use	–	–***	+***
Neighborhood grps.	+**	–	–
Human services	–	–	–
Public buildings	–***	–***	+***

(continues)

TABLE 4.5 (continued)

Service	High Income with Information		
	Strong Support	Strong and Somewhat Support	Strong Opposition
Police	–***	–**	+**
Fire-EMS	–***	–**	+*
Special events	–	–	–
Sister cities	–	–	–
Business assistance	–	–	–
Metro Partnership	–	–	–
Downtown dev.	–	–*	–
Affordable housing	–	–**	+*
Land use	–	–***	+***
Neighborhood grps.	–	–	+**
Human services	–	–**	+***
Public buildings	–***	–***	+**

*** Significant at the .01 level, ** significant at the .05 level, * significant at the .10 level.

TABLE 4.6 Information Effects Within Sociodemographic Group—Individual Services Logistic Regression Significant Coefficients

Service	HS Diploma with Information			College or More with Information		
	Strong Support	Strong or Somewhat Support	Strong Opposition	Strong Support	Strong or Somewhat Support	Strong Opposition
Library	–	–	+*	–	–***	+***
Bookmobile	–	–	–	+***	–	+**
Swimming pools	–	–	–	–***	–***	+***
Adult athletics	–	–	–	–	–*	+***
Community ctrs.	–	–	–	+***	–***	+*
Outdoor prog.	–	–	–	–	–***	+***
Hult Center	–	–	–	+***	–***	+***
Specialized rec.	–	–	–	–*	–***	+***
Bldg. permits	–	–	–	–	–***	+***
Senior centers	–	–	–	–	–***	+***
Park concerts	–	–	–	+***	–	+***

Service	65 or Over with Information			Men with Information		
	Strong Support	Strong or Somewhat Support	Strong Opposition	Strong Support	Strong or Somewhat Support	Strong Opposition
Library	–**	–*	+***	–	–***	+***
Bookmobile	–	–	–	+*	–	+**
Swimming pools	–***	–***	+***	–*	–***	+***
Adult athletics	–	–	+**	–	–***	+***
Comunity ctrs.	–***	–***	+***	–**	–***	+***
Outdoor prog.	–	–***	+*	–**	–***	+***
Hult Center	–**	–***	+***	–***	–***	+**
Specialized rec.	–***	–***	+***	–*	–***	+***
Bldg. permits	–	–***	+***	–	–***	+***
Senior centers	–	–**	+**	–	–***	+***
Park concerts	–	–	–	+**	–	+**

(continues)

TABLE 4.6 (continued)

Service	Homeowners with Information			Renters with Information		
	Strong Support	Strong or Somewhat Support	Strong Opposition	Strong Support	Strong or Somewhat Support	Strong Opposition
Library	–	–***	+***	–	–**	–
Bookmobile	+***	–	+***	+**	–	+**
Swimming pools	–***	–***	+***	–	–	+**
Adult athletics	–***	–***	+***	–	–	–
Community ctrs.	–***	–***	+***	–**	–***	–
Outdoor prog.	–	–***	+**	–	–*	–
Hult Center	–***	–***	+***	–*	–**	–
Specialized rec.	–	–***	+***	–	–	+***
Bldg. permits	–**	–***	+***	–	–***	–
Senior centers	–**	–***	+***	–	–	+***
Park concerts	+***	–	+**	+***	+**	–

Service	Women with Information			Low Income with Information		
	Strong Support	Strong or Somewhat Support	Strong Opposition	Strong Support	Strong or Somewhat Support	Strong Opposition
Library	–	+**	+***	–	–**	+**
Bookmobile	+***	–	+***	–	–	+*
Swimming pools	–**	–***	+***	–	+**	+*
Adult athletics	–	–	–	–	–	+*
Community ctrs.	–***	–***	+***	–*	–***	–
Outdoor prog.	–	–*	–	–	–*	–
Hult Center	–*	–***	+***	–	–***	+***
Specialized rec.	–	–***	+***	–*	–***	+***
Bldg. permits	–	–***	+***	–	–***	+***
Senior centers	–**	–***	+***	–	–	–
Park concerts	+***	–	–	+***	+*	–

High Income with Information

Service	Strong Support	Strong or Somewhat Support	Strong Opposition
Library	–	–	–
Bookmobile	+*	–	–
Swimming pools	–	–	–
Adult athletics	–	–	–
Community ctrs.	–	–	–
Outdoor prog.	–	–**	+**
Hult Center	–	–	–
Specialized rec.	–	–	+*
Bldg. permits	–	–*	+***
Senior centers	–	–**	+*
Park concerts	–	–	–

*** Significant at the .01+ level, ** significant at the .05 level, * significant at the .10 level.

who have a high school degree or less (individually consumed services), renters, and high-income respondents. The power behind this finding is simple: We are all the same, even with our differences, when it comes to how the amount of taxes affects our decisions.[12]

Does Fiscal Information Matter in the Ordering of Preferences?

We find that for the city services presented, providing fiscal information lowers support and increases opposition. But does the presence of fiscal information change the ordering of preferences? That is, we now know that fiscal information lowers the level of support, but do the services that enjoy the greatest (or least) amount of support remain the same? Table 4.7 presents the rank ordering of the services from highest to lowest. Generally speaking, the popular services remain popular in the presence of fiscal information. The same is true of the least popular services. Table 4.8 shows the correlation coefficients for the percent strongly supporting, somewhat or strongly supporting, or strongly opposing the services. The significant and high correlations indicate that although fiscal information typically reduces levels of support, the ordering of the preferences is not significantly changed.

Findings — Service Use

Service Use and Individual Services

For each service presented in this survey, respondents were asked to indicate their level of use. The response options were "often," "sometimes," or "never". Table 4.9 shows the percentage of individuals who responded often, sometimes, or never to questions about each service. The Hult Center for the Performing Arts, the library, concerts in the park, community centers, and swimming pools are the services most used by respondents (or members of their households).

Reported in Table 4.10 are the coefficients of Often Use or Never Use related to the listed service across sixty-six different logistic regressions where level of support for the indicated service is the dependent variable. Many of the relationships between service use and strong support, somewhat or strong support, or opposition to individual services are statistically significant. The relationship between service use and strong support for individual services is astonishingly strong. Respondents who often use a service are significantly more likely to strongly support that service for eight of the eleven services, the exceptions being outdoor programs, specialized recreation for the disabled, and building permits. Respondents who never use the service are significantly less likely to somewhat

TABLE 4.7   Service Rankings

Strongly Support

Collective Services	Ivory Survey	Blue Survey
Fire-EMS	1	1
Police	2	2
Human services	3	4
Affordable housing	4	3
Public buildings	5	10
Metro Partnership	6	5
Business assistance	7	7
Special events	8	8
Downtown development	9	12
Land use	10	11
Neighborhood groups	11	6
Sister cities	12	9

Individual Services	Ivory Survey	Blue Survey
Library	1	1
Senior centers	2	4
Specialized recreation	3	3
Swimming pools	4	5
Community centers	5	7
Hult Center	6	9
Bookmobile	7	2
Building permits	8	11
Outdoor programs	9	10
Park concerts	10	6
Adult athletics	11	8

Somewhat and Strongly Support

Collective Services	Ivory Survey	Blue Survey
Fire-EMS	1	1
Police	2	2
Public buildings	3	8
Human services	4	4
Affordable housing	5	3
Metro Partnership	6	5
Business assistance	7	7
Land use	8	12
Neighborhood groups	9	6
Special events	10	9
Downtown development	11	11
Sister cities	12	10

(continues)

TABLE 4.7   (Continued)

Individual Services	Ivory Survey	Blue Survey
Senior centers	1	2
Specialized recreation	2	4
Library[a]	3	1
Swimming pools[a]	3	5
Community centers	5	6
Bookmobile	6	3
Building permits	7	11
Hult Center	8	9
Adult athletics	9	8
Park concerts	10	7
Outdoor programs	11	10

Strongly Oppose

Collective Services	Ivory Survey	Blue Survey
Fire-EMS	1	1
Police	2	2
Public buildings	3	8
Human services	4	4
Affordable housing	5	3
Land use	6	12
Business assistance	7	7
Metro Partnership	8	6
Neighborhood groups	9	5
Special events	10	9
Downtown development	11	11
Sister cities	12	10

Individual Services	Ivory Survey	Blue Survey
Swimming pools	1	3
Senior centers	2	1
Specialized recreation	3	5
Library	4	2
Community centers	5	6
Bookmobile	6	4
Building permits[b]	7	9
Hult Center	8	11
Adult athletics	9	7
Park concerts	10	8
Outdoor programs[b]	11	9

NOTE: 1—lowest percent, 12 (or 11 for Fee Services)—highest percent.

Ivory survey contains no fiscal information, Blue Survey contains fiscal information.

[a] Library and Swimming pools both had 84.3% Somewhat or Strongly Support for the Ivory survey.

[b] Building permits and Outdoor programs both had 36.6% Strongly Oppose for the Blue survey.

TABLE 4.8   Correlations

(Ivory and Blue)	*Correlations*
Tax Services (n=12)	
Strongly support	.88***
Strongly or somewhat support	.78***
Strongly oppose	.72***
Fee Services (n=11)	
Strongly support	.66**
Strongly or somewhat support	.77***
Strongly oppose	.87***

** One-tailed significance at the .05 level, *** one-tailed significance at the .01 level.

Correlations are based on the percent strongly supporting, somewhat or strongly supporting, or strongly opposing each service.

or strongly support nine of the eleven services (the exceptions are specialized recreation for the disabled and building permits). Indeed, for seven of the eleven services, respondents who do not use the service are more likely to strongly oppose taxes for the service.

Just as for information effects, the predicted probability change from .5 resulting from service use can be very large, ranging from a low of 18% to a high of 42% (significant coefficients only). These results clearly indicate that an individual's use builds personal support for that service, whereas those who do not use services are significantly less likely to back the taxes to pay for them.

TABLE 4.9   Service Use

Service	*Percent That Often Use the Service*	*Percent That Sometimes Use the Service*	*Percent That Never Use the Service*
Library	25.1	49.7	25.1
Bookmobile	1.6	5.2	93.2
Swimming pools	7.0	35.0	58.0
Adult athletics	7.0	22.0	71.0
Community centers	7.0	44.2	48.6
Outdoor programs	1.3	14.5	84.2
Hult Center	19.4	64.4	16.2
Specialized rec.	0.6	7.5	91.9
Building permits	1.1	25.6	73.3
Senior centers	1.9	13.3	84.8
Park concerts	9.6	42.5	47.9

TABLE 4.10 Individual Service Use and Willingness to Pay Taxes

	Strongly Support			Somewhat or Strongly Support			Strongly Oppose		
	B	Sig.	Change from .5	B	Sig.	Change from .5	B	Sig.	Change from .5
Often Use									
Library	1.2944	***	0.2849	0.8600	**	0.2027	−0.2934		−0.0728
Bookmobile	2.4347	**	0.4194	3.5569		0.4723	0.0292		0.0073
Swimming pools	0.7511	***	0.1794	0.4284		0.1055	0.8976		0.2105
Adult athletics	1.7931	***	0.3573	1.2385	***	0.2753	−1.0479	*	−0.2404
Community ctrs.	1.2476	***	0.2769	1.1148	*	0.2530	−6.4985		−0.4985
Outdoor athletics	1.1651		0.2623	−0.1364		−0.0340	0.5600		0.1365
Hult Center	1.2969	***	0.2853	1.0813	***	0.2467	−1.0742	***	−0.2454
Specialized rec.	1.4268		0.3064	3.6586		0.4749	−1.9082		−0.3708
Bldg. permits	0.7921		0.1883	−0.2737		−0.0680	1.1726		0.2636
Senior centers	2.2544	**	0.4050	5.0268		0.4935	−3.3890		−0.4674
Park concerts	1.3257	***	0.2901	1.2366	***	0.2750	−1.1087	*	−0.2519
Never Use									
Library	−1.2004	***	−0.2686	−1.3669	***	−0.2969	1.5751	***	0.3285
Bookmobile	−0.2883		−0.0716	−1.8546	**	−0.3647	6.4944	***	0.4985
Swimming pools	−0.7297	***	−0.1747	−0.9546	***	−0.2220	1.1889	***	0.2665
Adult athletics	−0.4869		−0.1194	−0.7752	***	−0.1846	0.3026		0.0751
Community ctrs.	−1.3101	***	−0.2875	−1.0985	***	−0.2500	1.0462	***	0.2400
Outdoor athletics	−1.0384	***	−0.2385	−1.6634	***	−0.3407	1.5673	***	0.3274
Hult Center	−1.9380	***	−0.3741	−0.8505	***	−0.2007	1.1248	***	0.2549
Specialized rec.	−0.2059		−0.0513	−0.7131		−0.1711	0.9075		0.2125
Bldg. permits	−0.4257		−0.1048	0.1352		0.0337	−0.1170		−0.0292
Senior centers	−0.2874		−0.0714	−0.9295	**	−0.2169	1.9570	**	0.3762
Park concerts	−1.8257	***	−0.3632	−1.3933	***	−0.3011	1.3807	***	0.2991

*** Significant at the .01 level, ** significant at the .05 level, * significant at the .10 level.

B is the logistic regression coefficient.

Change from .5 denotes the predicted change from .5 due to respondent indicating they often use (never use) that service (compared to the base case of sometimes using the service). Strongly Support indicates the respondents chose Strongly Support for taxes for the service. Somewhat or Strongly Support indicates the respondent chose either Strongly Support or Somewhat Support for the service. Strongly Oppose indicates the respondent chose Strongly Oppose for the service.

Service Use and Collective Services

Many of the services government provides are collectively consumed, such as police protection, fire fighting and prevention, land use planning, or maintenance of public buildings. Other services provide help to the economically disadvantaged, such as affordable housing or human services. These are not services that typical citizens frequently use.[13] They represent the less visible, less attractive, but in some cases essential functions of government. The next set of logistic regressions we review here demonstrate the degree to which use of individual services translates into support for more general and collectively consumed services.

Table 4.11 shows the relationship between the number of individual services used and support for the collective services. In this table, the responses to the "often use" option are tallied. Responses are broken down into those indicating "often use" for zero services, those indicating this for one service, those indicating it for two, and those indicating that they often use three or more of the individual services. Eight of the twelve collective services show a steady increase in strong support as the number of services often used increases. For several of these services, the pattern is remarkable. Affordable housing and human services are strongly supported by about one-third of respondents who do not use any services. But they are strongly supported by *three-quarters* of respondents using three or more services. Fire-EMS, special events, and public buildings and facilities also show sharp increases in support as service use increases. The exceptions are police, sister cities, business assistance, and the Metro Partnership. For

TABLE 4.11   Number of Individual Services Used and the Percent of Respondents Strongly Supporting Collective Services

	Number of Individual Services Used by Respondent			
Service	Zero	One	Two	Three or More
Police	64	68	72	69
Fire-EMS	70	74	82	88
Special events	9	18	25	41
Sister cities	7	12	16	15
Business assistance	17	17	26	20
Metro Partnership	28	27	20	32
Downtown development	10	13	17	23
Affordable housing	36	49	64	77
Land use planning	9	15	17	21
Neighborhood groups	15	14	27	29
Human services	33	43	55	77
Public buildings/maint.	23	33	37	56

police, sister cities, and business assistance, support fell slightly for users of three or more services, whereas for the Metro Partnership support fell for users of two services.

Table 4.12 shows the logistic regression results. The results do not refer to the use level of the specific service (e.g., police) but to the respondents' indication of use of the individual services as a whole. The table presents results across seventy-two different logistic regressions where level of support for the indicated service is the dependent variable and the independent variables are the controls given in the variables table above (coefficients on the control variables are not reported). For eight of the twelve services, the likelihood that respondents will either strongly or somewhat or strongly support taxes *increases significantly* as the number of services for which people identified themselves as often using increases. The only exceptions are police, sister cities, the Metro Partnership, and neighborhood groups. Strong opposition significantly decreases as the number of services used increases for special events, business assistance, and downtown development.

On the other hand, as the number of individual services respondents claim they never use increases, seven of the twelve services show *significant decreases* in the likelihood of strongly supporting or somewhat or strongly supporting the services. For five of the twelve, as the number of services respondents say they never use increases, strong opposition also *significantly increases*.

The predicted probability change reflects respondents reporting that they often use (never use) one additional service across the range of eleven individual services. The predicted probability change runs from a low of 2.6% to a high of 12.01% across the significant coefficients. The results demonstrate that for these respondents, increased support for the taxes necessary to pay for the collective services of government are associated with individual service use. Indeed, the association is strongest for redistributive services, including affordable housing and human services and for the less obvious, more obscure services such as land use planning services and public buildings and facilities.

Service Use and Support for User Fees

Table 4.13 shows the percent choosing each of the user fee/tax combinations for the eleven individually consumed services. For only four of the eleven services (public library, bookmobile, swimming pools, and specialized recreation for the disabled) did a majority of the respondents favor the existing tax/fee split. In no case did a majority support the 100% fee option. For each service presented in the surveys, respondents were asked to indicate their level of use. Table 4.14 shows the results of the

TABLE 4.12 Individual Service Use and Willingness to Pay Taxes for Collective Services

	Strongly Support			Somewhat or Strongly Support			Strongly Oppose		
	B	Sig.	Change from .5	B	Sig.	Change from .5	B	Sig.	Change from .5
Often Use									
Police	0.0277		0.0069	0.0904		0.0226	0.0012		0.0003
Fire-EMS	0.2179	*	0.0543	0.4901	*	0.1201	-0.3454		-0.0855
Special events	0.3227	***	0.0800	0.2240	**	0.0558	-0.2792	**	-0.0694
Sister cities	0.1048		0.0262	0.0624		0.0156	-0.1056		-0.0264
Business assistance	0.0001		0.0000	0.3189	***	0.0791	-0.2781	*	-0.0691
Metro Partnership	-0.0774		-0.0193	0.0498		0.0124	-0.0200		-0.0050
Downtown dev.	0.2736	**	0.0680	0.3237	***	0.0802	-0.2071	*	-0.0516
Affordable housing	0.3375	***	0.0836	0.1598		0.0399	-0.2135		-0.0532
Land use planning	0.1466		0.0366	0.2067	*	0.0515	-0.1761		-0.0439
Neighborhood grps.	0.1654	***	0.0413	0.1432		0.0357	0.0235		0.0059
Human services	0.3072	***	0.0762	0.1221		0.0305	-0.2027		-0.0505
Public bldg.	0.1998	*	0.0498	0.0970		0.0242	-0.0662		-0.0165
Never Use									
Police	-0.0069		-0.0017	-0.0988		-0.0247	0.0403		0.0101
Fire-EMS	0.0003		0.0001	-0.1113		-0.0278	-0.0847		-0.0212
Special events	-0.1402	**	-0.0350	-0.2019	***	-0.0503	0.1986	***	0.0495
Sister cities	-0.0748		-0.0187	-0.2060	***	-0.0513	0.1372	***	0.0342
Business assistance	-0.0601		-0.0150	-0.0391		-0.0098	0.0738		0.0184
Metro Partnership	-0.0666		-0.0166	-0.0041		-0.0010	-0.0097		-0.0024
Downtown dev.	-0.0840		-0.0210	0.0159		0.0040	0.0144		0.0036
Affordable housing	-0.1272	**	-0.0318	-0.0909		-0.0227	0.0874		0.0218
Land use planning	-0.1385	**	-0.0346	-0.0519		-0.0130	0.1162	*	0.0290
Neighborhood grps.	-0.0952		-0.0238	-0.1042	**	-0.0260	0.1412	**	0.0352
Human services	-0.0609		-0.0152	-0.1600	***	-0.0399	0.0671		0.0168
Public bldg.	-0.1575	***	-0.0393	-0.0398		-0.0099	0.1301	*	0.0325

*** Significant at the .01 level, ** significant at the .05 level, * significant at the .10 level.

B is the logistic regression coefficient.

Change from .5 denotes the predicted change from .5 due to the respondents indicating they often use (never use) an additional service. Strongly Support indicates the respondent chose Strongly Support for taxes for the service. Somewhat or Strongly Support indicates the respondent chose either Strongly Support or Somewhat Support for the service. Strongly Oppose indicates the respondent chose Strongly Oppose for the service.

TABLE 4.13   Percent Choosing User Fee/Tax Combinations

Service	No Fee or Existing Fee and Existing Taxes	Fees Increased To Cover 25% of the Difference Between Existing Fee and All Fee	Fees Increased To Cover 50% of the Difference Between Existing Fee and All Fee	Fees Increased To Cover 75% of the Difference Between Existing Fee and All Fee	All Fee and No Taxes
Library	51.6	25.6	7.8	4.3	10.7
Bookmobile	70.0	9.7	3.1	1.0	16.2
Hult Center	16.6	9.7	22.8	9.3	41.5
Swimming pools	55.2	18.8	5.9	2.8	17.4
Adult athletics	29.2	14.6	12.8	3.1	40.3
Community centers	36.2	16.0	19.2	4.5	24.0
Outdoor programs	27.0	11.8	16.3	3.1	41.9
Specialized recreation	76.4	8.2	4.5	1.7	9.2
Building permits	24.5	10.0	19.0	7.9	38.6
Senior centers	48.4	23.2	11.8	3.1	13.5
Park concerts	37.5	10.1	16.3	3.5	32.6

TABLE 4.14 Logistic Regression Results—Fee/Tax Split: Predicted Change in the Probability of Choosing Tax and Fee Options

Service	No Fee or Existing Fee And Existing Taxes						All Fee and No Taxes					
	Often Use	Sig.	Change from .5	Never Use	Sig.	Change from .5	Often Use	Sig.	Change from .5	Never Use	Sig.	Change from .5
Library	0.7137	**	0.1712	-1.7497	***	-0.3519	-0.4600		-0.1130	1.0472	**	0.2402
Bookmobile	4.2018	*	0.4853	-1.8736	*	-0.3669	0.6082		0.1475	7.4719		0.4994
Swimming pools	1.1508	*	0.2597	-0.6991	**	-0.1680	-0.6426		-0.1553	1.1420	**	0.2580
Adult athletics	1.2022	**	0.2689	-0.5348		-0.1306	-2.4386	**	-0.4197	0.5679	*	0.1383
Community ctrs.	1.9800	**	0.3787	-0.6539	**	-0.1579	-6.1478		-0.4979	1.2389	***	0.2754
Outdoor programs	0.0564		0.0141	-0.9705	**	-0.2252	1.1434		0.2583	1.0748	**	0.2455
Hult Center	1.6276	***	0.3358	-0.8218		-0.1946	-1.2184	***	-0.2718	0.9857	**	0.2282
Specialized rec.	—		—	0.0495		0.0124	—		—	-0.1231		0.0307
Bldg. permits	-0.2449		-0.0608	-3.8079		-0.4783	6.1580		0.4986	0.2736		0.0680
Senior centers	6.0258		0.4976	-0.2874		-0.0714	-5.2169		-0.4946	0.7752		0.1846
Park concerts	1.1874	**	0.2663	-0.9658	***	-0.2243	-1.5797		-0.3292	1.2450	***	0.2764

*** Significant at the .01 level, ** significant at the .05 level, * significant at the .10 level.

B is the logistic regression coefficient for Often Use and Never Use.

Change from .5 denotes the predicted change from .5 due to the respondents indicating they often use (never use) that service (compared to the base case of sometimes using the service). No Fee or Existing Fee represents the choice that maintains the existing fee and tax structure. All Fee and No Taxes represents the option that eliminates taxes in favor of 100% fee financing.

tax/fee logistic regressions. For six of ten services, those who often use the services were significantly more likely to support the existing tax/fee split (there were not enough respondents who often used specialized recreation for the disabled to model it). Conversely, for six of eleven services, those who never use the services were significantly more likely to support an increase in fees. In addition, for seven of eleven services, those who never use the services were significantly more likely to choose 100% fee support (and consequently no taxes).

In some cases, the predicted change in probabilities due to service use can be quite high. For those who never use community centers, the model predicts a 15.79% reduced chance of picking the no fee/existing fee option, ranging to a 41.97% reduction in the predicted probability of choosing the all fee option for those often using the adult athletics program.

The results suggest that those who often use a service are less likely to support the all fee option. Individuals who never use a service appear more likely to support the all fee approach and less likely to want the no fee (or existing fee) choice.

In terms of our research questions, the logistic regressions provide strong evidence that

- Service use increases support for individually consumed services.
- Increasing use of individually consumed services is positively associated with support for collectively consumed services.
- Service use has a negative influence on preferences for fees and a positive association with taxes and the means to fund individually consumed services.

Discussion

Fiscal information is ubiquitous in its effect on the tax and service preferences of citizens. The implications are profound: The very indication of the amount of a tax will, all else being equal, decrease the likely support and increase the likely opposition for a service. The effect stands for citizens generally and also in comparisons among groups. The policy implications are important. Fiscal conservatives who wish to stymie government spending would be well served in this aim by publicizing the true costs of government services. On the other hand, it appears that fiscal liberals wishing to increase spending would do better with their program if the citizenry remained in financial ignorance.

What does this tell us about what to expect from citizens in the polling booth or responding to opinion surveys? The decision about whether to include fiscal information is crucial to the level of support expressed for a service. This does not mean that fiscal conservatives can expect to prevail in bond referenda or other tax measures simply by including fiscal information. We could reasonably expect more no votes, however, particularly from those on the margin. These findings also suggest that an information campaign geared to influence voters' opinions about services would not need to be sophisticatedly designed or narrowly targeted to be effective in eroding support for public services.

In a small number of instances, the coefficients for both strong support and strong opposition are positive for the same service. An example of this is the sister cities program, where knowledge about the $1 tax actually leads to an increased likelihood of both strong support and strong opposition. One explanation may lie in the distinction between two possible reactions from citizens faced with the amount of a tax. One sentiment is absolute tax aversion. The other resembles "sticker shock."

Those who are absolute in their aversion to taxes are affected minimally, if at all, by the amount of a particular tax because for them any tax is unacceptable. Knowing that some specific amount of tax will be charged, regardless of its size, makes these individuals more likely to oppose a service. At the same time, other citizens seem to have a threshold for tax support. For these individuals, the acceptability of a tax is assessed relative to some standard of reasonableness. Citizens may use a heuristic model, or mental shortcut, to compare such amounts with other payments that they routinely make. If the tax is within some common limits of their spending patterns or expectations for a service, they support it. If they are startled by how large a tax is, they do not support it, just as potential car buyers may shake their heads and walk out of the showroom after seeing the price of a new vehicle.

Where this gets interesting is when both groups are responding differently to the same service. Faced with a $1 tax to continue the sister cities program, some citizens responded with aversion despite the minimal size of the tax. These people may drive the increased likelihood of strong opposition to this tax. At the same time, some portion of the citizenry was more likely to strongly support this tax only after knowing how much (or little) it cost. You can imagine that for these people $1 was not a shock, but a comfortable (if unusually low) amount to pay for something.

This effect surfaces for three services in this research. An increased likelihood of support as well as opposition is seen for one of the tax services (sister cities with a $1 tax) and two of the individually consumed (bookmobile with a $1 tax, concerts in the park with a $2 tax). Further explanation for the level of support of these individually consumed services may lie in the fact that information-receiving respondents were presented elsewhere with the amount of fees necessary to eliminate the tax ($100 for the bookmobile and $4 for concerts in the park). To some, the tax may have seemed a far more acceptable amount of money than the fee necessary to supplant it, particularly in the case of the bookmobile.

Therefore, our findings also suggest that citizen surveys often are methodologically flawed. The typical survey asks respondents how much they favor government services such as police. The methodological flaw is the absence of a budget constraint—the link between service level and how much it costs. Or, stated another way, citizen surveys without a budget constraint often systematically overstate how much respondents support a service. The lesson for survey researchers is that the surveys that systematically overstate support for services because of the lack of fiscal information do not provide a realistic view of support for government services. But it may be that the ordering, or ranking, of services is not greatly affected by the typical surveys' systematic overstatement of support.

Our findings provide support for the notion of the free lunch. Citizens may or may not always want more for less, but they surely prefer more when it is offered for free. All else being equal, as consumers we prefer more of a service as opposed to less of it.

The tax/fee split logistic regressions show that those who never use services are, for most services, significantly more likely to prefer user fees as compared to taxes. Indeed, for the majority of services, those who never use them are likely to prefer no tax support at all. The magnitude of this effect is also quite large. This supports the benefit equity principle in reverse: Those who do not use the service would rather leave it to those who do to pay for it. For the majority of services, those who report often using them do not support increased fees (or instituting a fee if none existed). Indeed, it appears that service use leads to a preference for others to pay for the service through taxes. This is consistent with the free rider notion. Why pay more individually if others in the collective will support the service?

This research demonstrates a strong association between individual service use and citizen support for taxes to fund both individual and more general or collective services. Our findings, therefore, provide evidence that the notion of benefit equity is alive and operational as citizens gauge their willingness to pay for public services. Those who benefit from a service are more likely to support taxes for it. Respondents to the Eugene Decisions surveys are increasingly more willing to support taxes for services as their individual use of them increases. This supports the benefit principle that individuals should pay for services in relation to the benefits that they receive.

Thus, the analysis of the surveys is consistent with both the notion of benefit equity and the notion of free riders. This outcome is not necessarily inconsistent. It may be that people prefer a free ride when it is made available, as in the choice respondents were given between fees and taxes.

But when this option is unavailable, respondents who use services are more likely to support the taxes to pay for them, consistent with the idea of benefit equity.

Another way to interpret these results is as evidence of customer behavior. Customers pay more as they consume more, and the respondents here demonstrated increased willingness to pay as their use of services increased. Customers, however, pay only for what they consume. Although we see that consumers of fewer services appear to want to pay less for government activities, we also see that those consuming more are willing to pay for more than they alone consume. This suggests that there are at least two kinds of respondents. One is a group of private citizens or customers who may seek to minimize their contributions by consuming fewer services and paying for only those that they consume. The other group are the good citizens, those whose philanthropic natures may be stimulated by the recognition of the amount of government services they receive.

Bill Clinton and Al Gore (1992), Gore (1992), David Osborne and Ted Gaebler (1992), and many others advocate that government be reinvented with emphasis on citizens as customers deserving of good service. It would be hard to argue that government could not do a better job providing some of these services. The findings presented here suggest, however, that we should beware of possible consequences when citizens perceive themselves as customers.

It may be that as government is identified in the minds of the citizen as a consumable, people begin to define government as that which they use personally rather than that which they support as a community. If the public good comes to be defined out of deference to individual consumers alone, only those actions of government for which customers are personally willing to pay will be well supported. Indeed, social programs, with relatively few constituent users, could be the most deeply affected. We find a very strong relationship between service use and social programs, for example, affordable housing and human services. In fact, these services, which support the neediest members of society, are the most affected by this phenomenon. Support for taxes to pay for affordable housing and human services programs more than doubles as service use increases from none to three or more. This suggests that such services could be the first casualties of "privatized government."

Those who consider themselves users of government services are more likely to support taxes for services than those who believe they do not use them. This demonstrates an apparent halo effect and transfer of support *across services*. Those who consider themselves users of government services will support taxes not only for those services but for other services as well. This support increases with the number of services for which respondents identify themselves as users.

Notes

1. Portions of this chapter draw on "The Benefit Equity Principle and Willingness to Pay for City Services" by William Simonsen and Mark D. Robbins (forthcoming, *Public Budgeting and Finance*) and "The Influence of Fiscal Information on Preferences for City Services" by William Simonsen and Mark D. Robbins (forthcoming, *Social Science Journal;* used with permission of Elsevier Science).

2. We deliberately set aside here any evaluation of the circumstances under which such reforms might possibly increase economic or technical efficiency.

3. A separate literature exists surrounding one particular method of benefit estimation called *contingent valuation.* Contingent valuation methodologies have been used to attempt to attach monetary benefits to public goods or to resources for which consumption has been deferred. This method, employing a complex series of linked conditional responses, was first used in identifying the benefit value to be placed on environmental resources when conducting benefit-cost analysis. See Bjornstad and Kahn (1996); and Kopp, Pommerehne, and Schwarz (1997) for additional information about this method.

4. Only 6% of respondents to a survey conducted by the Advisory Commission on Intergovernmental Relations (1992) said they had a great deal of confidence that local government does a good job in carrying out its responsibilities, and this percentage has fallen over time.

5. As a practical matter, the tax services are the ones for which the city of Eugene was not considering the possibility of a user fee. We understand that the distinction between collective (tax) and individual (fee) services is open to interpretation.

6. This resulted in 333 completed survey instruments for the Ivory Survey and 304 completed instruments for the Blue Survey.

7. The surveys, because of their structure, provide an interesting opportunity to see if providing information on the cost of public services influences public support. The surveys were designed to help solve a real-time fiscal problem, not as an experiment. Thus, the questions are not exactly symmetrical, although they are extremely close. The difference is that in the Ivory Survey (the one without information) the questions are neutral whereas in the Blue Survey (which includes information) the questions are framed to maintain current levels (avoid reduction). Implicit in the neutral questions is the current level of service. Also, Kahneman and Tversky (1982) demonstrate that the value function for losses is steeper than for gains. In other words, if a question is presented as a loss avoidance it may be responded to more favorably than the same question presented as a gain. The effect of this for our analysis is that if a bias did exist, it would be toward a higher level of approval for the Blue Survey, which is framed as loss avoidance, and would make it more difficult to find statistical significance. Also, in the Blue Survey, questions about what users individually consume do not include a description of the service. The preceding section of the survey included descriptions.

8. Information is not included in the support for user fee logistic regressions, since only the Blue Survey is used.

9. Smith (1980) notes, "It is always appropriate to ask whether particular experimental results are due to artifacts unrelated to the theory one purports to test" (p. 597). Although this is not an experiment, we may still scrutinize our findings

for artifacts. These are the results from a survey conducted to assess registered voters' desired strategies for solving a real fiscal problem facing their government. It was a survey, however, and not a referendum or a ballot (many of which arguably bear significant artifacts of human design). The possibility exists that respondents used gamesmanship or responded to different sets of influences from what they would do if displaying voting behavior or if serving in the seats of their elected officials. For better or worse, and with potential bias and artifact intact, this information is what was used to guide elected officials in their course of action.

10. The table presents the change in decimal form.

11. The logistic regression model predicts the strongest effects when the starting probability is at .5. Therefore, the predicted change in probabilities are top-end estimates.

12. But what about the differential effects of information *between* groups? Are there different patterns of influence when comparing, for instance, men with information versus women with information or seniors with information versus nonseniors with information? If the mere presence of information is powerful enough to dissuade those within most demographic groups, we might expect to see only a small effect when comparing different groups (such as men and women, those sixty-five and over and those younger than sixty-five, etc.). This is largely true (results not shown). The only group that is consistently more likely to strongly oppose taxes for these services (and less likely to strongly support them) across both the individually and collectively consumed services, is the senior set. Those sixty-five and over with information are significantly more likely than those under sixty-five with the same information to strongly oppose taxes for five of the tax-supported and eight of the individually consumed services. They are also significantly more influenced in their decisions to strongly or strongly or somewhat support services for eight of the tax services and nine of the individually consumed services. Interestingly, one of the nine is concerts in the park, which seniors with information are more likely to support than nonseniors. (We can only surmise that this particular effect may vary from place to place with the type of music being played!)

For individually consumed services, men with information are consistently different from women with information in this analysis. For those with fiscal information, men are less likely than women to support (strongly or somewhat strongly) taxes for the bookmobile, outdoor programs, Hult Center for the Performing Arts, specialized recreation for the disabled, and concerts in the park. Men are significantly more likely than women to strongly oppose these programs and services: bookmobile, swimming pools, community centers, outdoor programs, specialized recreation for the disabled and concerts in the park. These data suggest that men (with or without information) are distinctly less supportive and more opposed to services. An interesting observation about gender differences is that in no instances are there services that men are more likely to support than women.

13. Again, as a practical matter, these services are those where the city of Eugene was not considering the possibility of a user fee, and therefore questions about direct service use were not asked.

5

Conclusions: Lessons for Governments

Where We Have Been

The purpose of this book is to explore citizen participation in government resource allocation decisions. Citizens view government with distrust. This distrust is fueled by campaign finance scandals and stories of government waste and bloat. At the same time, elected officials may dismiss citizens as uninformed, whining special pleaders. Growing mutual distrust between government officials and the citizenry, coupled with increased local government responsibilities and increasing revenue constraints, have increased the pressure on governments to align themselves with the citizen will. How that will is discovered and acted on may influence outcomes that we care about. Assessments of the public will that are not representative and demand little of respondents in terms of deliberation and judgment will be different from those that carefully gauge the informed considerations of the citizenry. This lends added salience to attempts to systematically examine the issues and methods of citizen participation in resource allocation decisions.

We set the framework for a historical and theoretical understanding of citizen participation in Chapter 1. In that chapter, we describe how three classic tensions in public administration—politics versus administration, bureaucratic expertise versus administrative access, and representation versus participation—frame the ways in which government functions in the United States. We assert that the call for and use of participation varies as these tensions are balanced in different ways.

Those advocating the ideas of representative democracy and a reliance on administrative expertise circumscribe the role of the citizen mainly to voting—the basic tenet being that people are typically uninformed and if given the chance to make decisions would often make bad ones. In this

115

view of the relationship between the citizen and the government, citizens give their assent to have their public choices made without their contributing further to that decision-making process. We note that trust in representatives has declined, and with it the acceptance of the ideal that the citizen may rely solely on representatives to make the case for government change. The ability of citizens to directly access government balances against the reliance on bureaucratic expertise in the administration of government tasks. Across time and despite the creation of some citizen participation experiments, there has developed a citizen gap. That is, citizens are largely left out of the decision-making arena. Many governments, seeking citizen assent, have taken to designing and implementing citizen participation projects. These projects operate within the same tensions that frame government administration.

In Chapter 2, we discuss some of the innovative ideas and methods designed to involve citizens meaningfully in decision-making processes. Ways of involving citizens range from public hearings to complicated and costly processes that include multiple rounds of input from a variety of sources. These more complicated techniques have as their basic premise that citizens are able and willing to grapple with the complex problems of the public service if given the proper opportunity. None of the examples we examined suggested that citizens were not up to the task. On the contrary, we find that fairly complex survey instruments based on the real problems facing the city of Eugene enjoyed remarkably high response rates (over 50% for a complex budget-balancing exercise and over 70% for a survey with real fiscal information). The question of method boils down to one of the goals of the sponsoring decision makers. If decision makers are looking for a device to improve their predictions of voting outcomes, complex deliberative processes are a waste of resources. If they seek a more thorough understanding of public reasoning and trade-offs in the face of very real budget constraints, then a more sophisticated process is indicated.

The use of sophisticated citizen input processes must be matched to the presenting dilemma. Each municipality has its own decision needs, and its citizens have a corresponding need for representation and inclusion in the making of such decisions. The decision about when to use citizen participation projects of the sort described here is as much a question of when and where as of the selection of the method to employ. Hearings and committee involvement may be adequate for much of what local governments do. Methods to broadly sample the public should be confined to situations where decision makers themselves are at an impasse or where the public will seems particularly hard to define. These circumstances describe the most controversial decisions that governments face. If they wish to avoid further erosion of public trust, decision makers should be sure to avoid the use of citizen participation simply to abdicate their own responsibility for making difficult choices. Moreover, if a broad public involvement process is employed, decision makers must be willing to *listen*, even if the public is saying things they do not want to hear. The public trust is much too fragile to withstand the strain of governments building a hope of meaningful involvement and then dashing that hope by ignoring information that citizens have provided.

In Chapter 3, we look at the budget-balancing exercise completed by a representative sample of voters in Eugene, Oregon. This analysis presents some surprising findings. First, we find little evidence to demonstrate a widespread "something for nothing" mentality on the part of citizens. When choosing a budget-balancing strategy, the overwhelming majority of respondents selected at least some additional revenues. We find an education effect related to budget cuts, with the most educated selecting a lower percentage of cuts in relation to revenue increases. We also find that those with the greatest household budget constraints (low-income households with increasing family size) suggest the highest level of cuts to revenue. The services cut by the largest number of respondents were those for which the effects would not be immediately felt (planning functions, park maintenance, and building maintenance). Thus, although the something for nothing mentality does not fairly describe our respondents, deferring until later the effects of decisions to cut now appears to be a preferred strategy (at least for some indirect, collectively consumed services without an obvious constituency). Policy makers should note that the preferred strategies for budget balancing depend to some degree on which constituency is being queried about its preferences. Our findings from Eugene suggest that citizens with higher levels of education appear to increasingly favor revenue strategies to achieve budget balance. Those with the strictest household budget constraints, however, appear not to share this view, perhaps because of their affordability concerns. Guided by this kind of information, decision makers could design a policy and accompanying public education campaign that address these citizen concerns.

In Chapter 4, we consider a question of general relevance to much related government survey work: Does information matter to citizen decision makers when they are deciding how much they are willing to support a service? We find that it matters enormously and that support erodes even in the presence of nominal costs. We further find that these effects are ubiquitous both among and between groups of individuals. This knowledge could be used in two ways. Cynical officials could rig the game, providing fiscal information on ballot measures that they seek to defeat and withholding such information on measures that they seek to pass. Such knowledge can also be used to improve the decision-making process by gauging the responsiveness of citizens to the price of public services. Surveys providing information about taxes, fees, and services, such as those analyzed here, can be used to inform decision makers who wish to find the service and cost structure most likely to be supported by the citizens. Representation that employs these techniques results in greater citizen input. It also bases decision making on a more sophisticated set of citizen judgments than simple preference polling allows.

Citizen preference surveys, absent some specific constraints, will overstate support for government programs and services. Citizens may or may not want more for less, but surely they prefer more when it is offered for free. We are reminded of the pizza commercials in which focus groups of chimpanzees are asked whether they prefer one pizza for $9.95 or two pizzas for $9.95. We as citizens are no different from these chimps. All else being equal, we as consumers prefer more of a service as opposed to less of it. Absent the reductions in one service, we prefer increasing another. Without the comparative information and demands that decision makers face, we will likely express global satisfaction for almost everything that does not offend us. Given that we know this already, it does not seem useful for governments and citizen groups to spend money to document it further.

Also in Chapter 4, we make the distinction between individually versus collectively consumed services and between the good citizen and the private citizen. Individually consumed services, in this manifestation, are those for which fees may conceptually be charged (this suggests some rivalry in consumption). For our collectively consumed services, fees were not considered (primarily nonrival in consumption). The good citizen is the civic-minded person who is willing to pay for services that are not individually consumed but that provide a public service. The private citizen is more concerned about gaining the lowest price for individually consumed services and less concerned about preserving those collectively consumed. The fact that some services are essential for collective life does not ensure their popularity among a public asked to make hasty judgments. We believe that the erosion of some essential services will ultimately result in a cost that society will face later on, perhaps at a greater price than if such services were better understood and accepted now. Democratic societies need enough good citizens to ensure that the basic functions of collective life continue unimpeded.

We were able to measure service use for individually consumed services and count how many government services each individual used. With this information, we analyzed support for those individual services specifically and for the collective services generally. Remarkably, the relationships were strong in both cases. We found that not only does service use predict support for individually consumed services, but it predicts support for the general collective functions of government. The implications of this cannot be fully tested here but give us pause in the face of service elimination and contracting out.

Citizen consumers may see a distinction between public and private service provision (privatization) or public versus private service production (contracting out) that affects their support for collective services (for instance, they may no longer consider these to be government services that they use). Where this occurs, attempts to move individual services out of the government sphere may have real impacts on the ability of governments to obtain the citizen support necessary to pay for the collective services that remain.

This work on service use intersects that of Glaser and Hildreth (1996) in an interesting way. These authors investigated citizen support for parks and recreation programs. The citizens whom government seeks to maintain might be what they describe as philanthropists. In other words, governments rely on more than the finite set of users of given services to pay for them. In fact, some services are not directly "used" by individuals at all. We have evidence based on this research to suggest that tax support for services is *transferable* from individually to collectively consumed services. We find that as the reported use of individually consumed services increases, so also does support for the taxes necessary to pay for both those specific services and for the more general, less visible and collectively consumed functions of government. We do not know much about the underlying behavior or how much of what we see is attributable to some combination of good citizenship, philanthropy, customer attitudes, and free-ridership. It appears that the support for some of the services for which user fees are plausible likely rely on citizens' perceived use of *other* services that could possibly be removed from government to be fee supported.

The promoters of privatization, entrepreneurial government, and "downsizing" of services that touch large numbers of people, regardless of motive, may be eroding the financial support that makes the broadest functions of government possible. Ubiquity is the enemy of fiscal conservatism. Those seeking to reduce or abolish government services may be well served as any such functions are reduced in scope or eliminated from governmental purview. If the effect we observed generalizes, then when such services are removed from government through austerity acts or the transfer to other providers, some degree of general support for taxes may also erode. As the types of services from which citizens can see results made manifest in their daily lives begin to be delivered privately, the functions that remain with government may be those that are the most difficult to explain and justify. Furthermore, moving individual services out of the government sphere might have real impacts on the ability of governments to pay for the collective services that remain.

Glaser and Hildreth (1996) conclude that "public agencies must not only enhance performance but must do a much better job of keeping the public informed about government actions and activities" (p. 111). Our research leads us to echo that remark. In addition, we conclude that governments seeking to maintain tax support for a central core of general government functions might use caution when removing or reducing other services to please the public. The leanest government that seeks to satisfy a customer looking to pay the least in taxes could possibly find itself without the support necessary to pay for basic general government services.

Reflections on Citizen Participation Efforts

The implicit premise behind the citizen participation techniques discussed in this book is that the public will is important and should help guide choices made by government decision makers. Thus, the point of view of the processes we reviewed reflect the ways that public input is being structured to provide guidance to decision makers. A key question becomes, what are the goals of these citizen participation processes?

Deliberative citizen involvement techniques involve informing a representative group of citizens about real costs and benefits, as in Lyn Kathlene and John A. Martin's work in Boulder, Ned Crosby's Citizens Jury, Eugene Decisions, and other processes described in Chapter 2. These techniques seem to us best suited for helping decision makers understand the choices citizens at large would make if they were informed about the complexities of the issues. Of course, this can be of significant value to decision makers beyond simply understanding the public will, such as adding to the perceived legitimacy of their choices by the general public. In this way, these deliberative approaches balance nicely some of the tensions we describe in Chapter 1. Representation and participation are in effect balanced when a process uses citizen participants to inform representatives. The political and administrative realms work together to create citizen processes. Their competition for the execution of the citizen will is likewise guided by its direct expression. Similarly, the bureaucratic expertise of the administrator is granted some citizen access, even as citizens are provided with a richness of understanding about the factual decision elements facing administrators. The best of these deliberative and informative techniques, if implemented properly, provide a place for the citizen—or at least an informed representative group of citizens—to shape governance in meaningful ways.

These techniques seem most appropriate when decision makers face difficult choices and are willing to listen seriously to public opinion. Also, given the significantly higher cost of these deliberative techniques, they are more appropriate when there is a relatively large amount of money at stake. For instance, when all was said and done, Eugene Decisions cost over $300,000. This is a relatively small amount, however, when viewed in the context and controversy of decisions surrounding an $80 million budget.

The irony is that the more that a representative group of citizens is exposed to information about complex and difficult decisions not typically available to the general population, the more they become changed and fail to represent the general population. In essence, they stand for what uninformed citizens would choose if they possessed that same information. Therefore, if the goal of the process is to predict voting outcomes, then sophisticated deliberative techniques are not the answer. A public relations campaign touting the results of such a process may help to convince voters to defer to their informed citizen representatives, if the general population is convinced of the legitimacy of the technique. Typical public opinion polling should provide a better gauge of voting outcomes but will do little to provide citizens with an appreciation of the crisis at hand or to build confidence in the remedy ultimately reached.

Call for Research

The findings presented here are evidence that the good citizen behavior that governments seek to augment may be related to the degree to which individuals identify themselves as service users. It may also be the case that service use corresponds with strong support for taxes, regardless of where the services are provided (by a government or a vendor). It may be that it is *positive* contact with government that is the underlying causal relationship that results in increased support and that the number of services used is its proxy. This suggests that increasing negative contacts with government, such as traffic tickets or long delays due to road construction, may have a similar halo effect and erode support for government generally. Future research to test the influence of service visibility, sector of provision, and quality of contact with government on support for government services would be a welcome addition to the literature.

Notions of citizenship also deserve further theoretical exploration. One could hypothesize that those agreeing with the following statement:

I believe my relationship to government is as a customer to a store.

will have systematically different attitudes about taxes and government services as compared to those who might strongly agree with this statement:

I believe that my relationship to government is as a member of a cooperative.

Shifting resources to emphasize the more limited customer relationship might actually result in the diminution of other important citizen behaviors (voting, volunteering, giving, etc.). As the shift toward customer emphasis perpetuates, some research attention should be given to this phenomenon.

Last Words

Should a local government use a rigorous and complex citizen participation process? We have avoided such normative conclusions because there are judgments—and trade-offs—that must be made. Governments in some locations may not experience a citizen gap. They may not face the budget constraints of many other jurisdictions. The trust of their citizens may rest unfettered by the conflict and scandal that have touched so many others. Governments operating in less idyllic environments will be forced to reconcile the resource needs of their communities with the citizen support necessary to meet them. These environments become more complex in places with frequently used ballot initiatives, which may be employed to alter a course of events already begun by decision makers. Even then, the best-designed process will not in and of itself solve the problems of government. To overcome problems requires the presence of able leadership, good management, and sufficient resources.

Good citizen participation will not solve a crisis. It will not buy a new copier. It will not fix the roads. It will not by itself convince citizens that government is relevant or even helpful. Such accomplishments rely on the people inhabiting government: employees, elected officials, and citizens. The participation mechanisms we discuss are tools. The fact that such tools exist does not make them appropriate for every job.

Recall the story of the man without a voice. As a child, he had stopped speaking abruptly and without explanation. Although no laryngeal abnormalities were found, he continued not to speak into adulthood. Despite this silence, he formed a happy and successful life. He worked. He had a family. Things progressed in the usual manner until one autumn when a storm brought down power lines directly behind his son's favorite playground. As the toddler, fascinated with the wires, reached to pick them up, his father suddenly shouted for him to stop. Startled and curious, the boy returned to his father directly. Questioned later about this apparently miraculous cure, the man replied that he had always been able to speak but that he had waited to do so until someone had needed to listen.

There are times—particularly in light of the scarcity of comity and resources in the management of local government—when citizen participation projects are well poised to be the startling voice to which government needs to listen. Good deliberative participation projects ought to be sophisticated, revealing, and rare. The speech of citizens to the administrators of their government comes at the greatest discount when it becomes the regularized pleading and lobbying characteristic of our interest group coalitions, be they neighborhood groups, action collectives, or businesses. The speech of citizens is likewise diminished by popularity polls and happiness indexes. Decision makers need to know the kinds of solutions that citizens will support, and citizens must be able to trust that their judgments are meaningfully captured and then listened to. Citizen participation projects that employ rigorous methodologies with representativeness, realistic constraints, and deliberation are best poised to activate the citizen voice in this way. Opinion and satisfaction surveys and feel-good seminars often simply add to the noise.

Our efforts here have been to describe one tool for governance. We have examined its roots and its relationship to government and searched for some of the lessons resulting from its implementation. As with any tool, its use to craft something useful relies for its satisfactory expression on those who use it.

Appendices

TAKE A LOOK INSIDE
TO HELP DECIDE
OUR CITY'S FUTURE

(continues)

126

November, 1991

This is a survey about City services and taxes. The City of Eugene no longer has enough money to continue offering all current services. If nothing is done to close the gap between the cost of services and the money available to pay for them, the City of Eugene will face an $8 million shortfall by 1994.

Should services be cut? If so, what services? Should taxes be raised or new taxes introduced? If so, how much should they be raised and/or what new taxes should we adopt? Should more of the cost of offering a service be paid directly by the people who use them? If so, for what services should fees be charged? This survey seeks your advice on these very difficult decisions.

With this survey we are sending along a copy of a newspaper tabloid that is also being sent to every household in Eugene. The tabloid will tell you more about the Eugene Decisions process and contains background information on City services, user fees, and taxes. You may find the tabloid helpful as you complete this questionnaire. In any case, do not feel that you need to be an expert in city government to answer these questions.

We deeply appreciate the time you are taking to complete this questionaire. The questions may be about city services and city taxes, but in a larger sense, the survey is about the future of Eugene.

(continues)

APPENDIX A   *(continued)*

HOW WOULD YOU BALANCE THE CITY BUDGET?

The City of Eugene is $8 million short of the money needed just to maintain *current* services. The shortfall would be even bigger if the City were to *increase* services — such as increasing the level of police or fire services, building a new library, or increasing the supply of affordable housing.

How would *you* balance the City budget? Would you reduce services? Would you create user fees, such as a library fee? Would you increase the money available to pay for current and new services by levying a tax — say, a local retail sales tax? Or some combination of these strategies? These are tough choices.

1.

THE BUDGET "SHORTFALL"

Directions: First, *use a pencil with an eraser.* We start with the $8 million budget shortfall.

The Budget "Shortfall" =
Box A | 8.0 Million |

2.

SERVICE IMPROVEMENTS

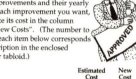

Directions: Next, we have listed service improvements and their yearly cost. For each improvement you want, please write its cost in the column labeled "New Costs". (The number to the left of each item below corresponds to its description in the enclosed newspaper tabloid.)

		Estimated Cost	New Cost
		(in millions)	
41	Affordable Housing Construction	.30	
42	Community Policing	4.00	
43	Fire Redeployment	1.50	
44	New Library	2.30	
45	Tourism/Arts	.70	

Add the "new costs" of the service improvements =
Box B | |

Parks Services

8	Buildings & Park Amenities	1.55	
9	Turf & Grounds	.85	
10	Riverside Parks /Owen Rose Garden	.80	
11	Landscaping/Park Trees/ Hendricks Park	.65	
12	Downtown Mall Maintenance	.25	
13	Planning & Property Management	.25	

Recreation Services

14	Community Centers	1.25	
15	Swimming Pools	.80	
16	Senior Centers	.65	
17	Athletics Programs	.35	
18	Specialized Recreation (for the disabled)	.30	
19	Outdoor/Environmental	.15	

Add the savings from Cultural, Library, Parks & Recreation Services reductions = Box 1 | |

Development Services

20	Building Permits/Plan Checking	1.05	
21	Code Compliance	.40	
22	Business Licensing	.20	
23	Community Information/ Parking Permits	.10	
24	Business Assistance Team	.40	
25	Downtown Development	.20	
26	Affordable Housing/ Neighborhood Development	.15	
27	Metropolitan Partnership Contract	.15	
28	Land Use Permits	.65	
29	Community Planning	.50	
30	Metro Area Planning	.40	
31	Citizen Involvement/ Neighborhood Groups	.15	
32	Transportation: Street Trees	.45	

Add the savings from Development Services reductions= Box 2 | |

(continues)

APPENDIX A   *(continued)*

Add the cost of "service improvements" (Box B) to the $8 million "shortfall" (Box A). The result is the size of the "budget gap" that needs to be closed by cutting budgets and/or raising revenue through fees or taxes.

Current shortfall (Box A) *8.0 Million*
Annual cost of service improvements (Box B)_____

Budget Gap= Box C [   ]

3.
BUDGET CUTTING

Directions: The number in Box C is the "budget gap" that needs to be closed either by cutting services or raising additional money through taxes or user fees. Below is a list of City services. Which services do you want to reduce? Please put the amount of money you want to *cut* on the line in the "budget reduction" column. For example, if you want to reduce the budget for "Hult Center" by $200,000, write that number (or .2) on the "Hult Center" line under "budget reduction".

		Annual Cost	Budget Reductions
	Cultural Services		
1	Hult Center	1.55	_____
2	Convention & Visitors Bureau Contract	.30	_____
3	Special Events /Eugene Celebration	.25	_____
4	Cultural/Visual Arts	.15	_____
5	Sister Cities	.05	_____
	Library Services		
6	Downtown Library	2.75	_____
7	Bookmobile	.10	_____

Public Safety Services

33	Fire/Emergency Medical Services	9.55	_____
	(Master Station=$1.7 million)		
	(Sub-Station=$1.15 million)		
	(Satellite Station=$0.7 million)		
34	Human Services Contracts	.65	_____
35	Police: Patrol Teams	10.10	_____
	(Average team cost=$ .8 million)		
36	Police: Investigations	3.25	_____
37	Police: Community Response Team	1.00	_____
38	Police: Crime Prevention/Education	.50	_____
39	Animal Control Services	.65	_____

Add the savings from Public Safety Services reductions = Box 3 [   ]

Support Services

40	Public Buildings and Facilities	4.50	_____

Savings from Support Services reductions= Box 4 [   ]

Enter the savings from each area of budget reductions:

☞ Cultural, Library, Parks & Recreation Services reductions
(Box 1)_____

☞ Development Services reductions
(Box 2)_____

☞ Public Safety Services reductions
(Box 3)_____

☞ Support Services reductions
(Box 4)_____

Add the savings from the budget reductions
(Box 1 + Box 2 + Box 3 + Box 4)=
Box D [   ]

YOU'RE ALREADY HALFWAY THERE

(continues)

APPENDIX A *(continued)*

Subtract the total budget reductions (box D) from the "budget gap" (box C). If the result is less than or equal to "0" you have balanced the budget. If the result is greater than "0", you will need to make further budget cuts or raise more money through increased taxes or user fees.

Budget Gap   (Box C)_____

Total budget reductions (Box D)_____

> **Money needed from taxes or fees**
> (Box C - Box D)
> **Box E** _____

4.
ADDITIONAL REVENUE

Directions: If the number in Box E is greater than "0" you will need to raise additional money through taxes or fees. The number in Box E is the amount of money you will need to raise. Below is a list of some fees and taxes that can be considered and the amount of money that each fee or tax could yield. For each additional fee or tax you select, please write the amount of revenue to be collected on the line under the "New Revenue" column.

		Estimated Annual Revenue	New Revenue
General Taxes			
50	Corporate Income Tax (1.0%)	1.50	_____
51	Gross Receipts Tax (0.1%)	7.20	_____
52	Local Retail Sales Tax (0.5%)	5.60	_____
	Local Retail Sales Tax (1.0%)	11.20	
53	Payroll Tax (0.25%)	4.70	_____
	Payroll Tax (0.5%)	9.40	
54	Personal Income Tax (0.25%)	6.70	_____
	Personal Income Tax (0.5%)	13.40	
	Designated Industry Taxes		
55	Entertainment Tax (5.0%)	.50	_____
56	Restaurant Tax (3.0%)	4.70	_____
	Restaurant Tax (6.0%)	9.40	
57	Room Tax (1.0%)	.15	_____
58	Utility Tax (1.0%)	2.30	_____

> **Add the revenue from General Taxes=**
> **Box 5** _____

If the result in Box G is greater than "0" you need to reduce the number of service improvements you selected, do some more budget cutting, or raise some more revenue.

If you have raised more money than you needed to (that is, if the number in Box F is larger than the number in Box E), then you can reduce the additional revenues raised, add back some of the budget cuts you made, or add service improvements.

It's okay to have some budget surpluses (or even a small shortfall). Don't worry about making the budget balance exactly to "0".

5.
JUST ONE MORE THING

Finally, some questions about yourself so that we can better tabulate results. All information, of course, is strictly confidential.

1. First, please tell us your age.
   _____ years old
2. Your sex:
   ❑ male
   ❑ female
3. How many persons are there in your household?
   _____ person(s)
4. How many persons under the age of 18 are there in your household?
   _____ person(s)
5. How many persons over the age of 65 are there in your household?
   _____ person(s)
6. Do you rent or own your home?
   ❑ rent
   ❑ own
7. If you own your home, please indicate the approximate amount of property tax you expect to pay this year.
   $_____   ❑ don't know
8. What is your highest level of education completed?
   ❑ K-6 years (elementary school)
   ❑ 7-11 (some high school)
   ❑ 12 years (high school diploma)
   ❑ 13-15 years (some college or post-high school training)
   ❑ 16 years (Bachelor's degree)
   ❑ 17 or more (graduate school)

(continues)

130

APPENDIX A   *(continued)*

Add the revenue from General Taxes=
Box 5

Property Tax (to pay for construction bonds)
61 Housing General Obligation Bond
   (available only if Affordable Housing
   improvement was selected)   .30 _____
62 Fire General Obligation Bond
   (available only if Fire Service
   improvement was selected)   1.00 _____
63 Library General Obligation Bond
   (available only if Library
   improvement was selected)   1.50 _____

Add the revenue from Property Taxes=
Box 6

User Fees
64 Building Permit Fees
   (only if permit services not cut) 1.05 _____
65 Fire Service Standby Fee   5.40 _____
66 Library Fee (only if library is not cut) .50 _____
67 Recreation Fee   1.00 _____

Add the revenue from "User Fees"=
Box 7

Enter the total additional revenue:
☞ Revenue raised through general taxes
                    (Box 5)_____
☞ Revenue raised through property taxes
                    (Box 6)_____
☞ Revenue raised through user fees
                    (Box 7)_____

Add the revenues from each source
(Box 5 + Box 6 + Box 7)=
Box F

Subtract the total new revenues raised (Box F)
from the amount needed to be raised from taxes or fees
(Box E).
        Revenues needed (Box E)_____

        New revenue raised (Box F)_____

NEW BUDGET BALANCE
Box G

9. What is your annual household income?
   ❏ under $20,000
   ❏ $20,000-$29,999
   ❏ $30,000-$39,999
   ❏ $40,000-$49,999
   ❏ $50,000-$74,999
   ❏ $75,000 or over
10. How often do you or someone in your household use
    these city services--often, sometimes, or never?

	often use	sometimes use	never use
a) city library	❏	❏	❏
b) library bookmobile	❏	❏	❏
c) city swimming pools	❏	❏	❏
d) city athletic programs (such as softball or soccer)	❏	❏	❏
e) city community centers	❏	❏	❏
f) city outdoor activity instruction (such as skiing or rock climbing)	❏	❏	❏
g) Hult Center	❏	❏	❏
h) specialized recreation (for the disabled)	❏	❏	❏
i) building permits	❏	❏	❏
j) senior centers	❏	❏	❏
k) concerts in the park	❏	❏	❏

Is there anything else you want to tell us
about City services, user fees, or taxes? Also,
are there any other comments you wish to
make about the **Eugene Decisions** process? If
so, please use the back of this questionnaire
for that purpose ✐

PLEASE RETURN IN THE ENCLOSED ENVELOPE BY
NOVEMBER 30, 1991
EUGENE DECISIONS
P.O. BOX 3318
EUGENE, OREGON
97403

APPENDIX B   Ivory Survey

EUGENE DECISIONS **Our City. . .**   **. . . Our Future**

November, 1991

This is a survey about city services and city taxes. The City of Eugene no longer has enough money to continue offering all current services. If nothing is done to close the gap between the cost of services and the money available to pay for them, the City of Eugene will face an $8 million shortfall by 1994.

Should services be cut? If so, what services? Should taxes be raised or new taxes introduced? If so, how much should they be raised and/or what new taxes should we adopt? Should more of the cost of offering a service be paid directly by the people who use them? If so, for what services should user fees be charged? This survey seeks your advice on these very difficult decisions. While these are tough decisions, you do not need to be an expert in city government to give us your opinion and suggestions.

With this survey we are sending along a copy of a newspaper tabloid that is also being sent to every household in Eugene. The tabloid will tell you more about the Eugene Decisions process and contains background information on city services, user fees, and taxes. You may find the tabloid helpful as you complete this questionnaire.

We deeply appreciate the time you are taking to complete this questionnaire. The questions may be about city services and city taxes, but in a larger sense, the survey is about the future of Eugene.

We have included a stamped, pre-addressed return envelope. If, however, that envelope becomes misplaced, please return this questionnaire to :

Eugene Decisions
P.O. Box 3318
Eugene, Oregon 97403

1

(continues)

APPENDIX B   *(continued)*

Where the Money Goes
Eugene General Fund Expenditures

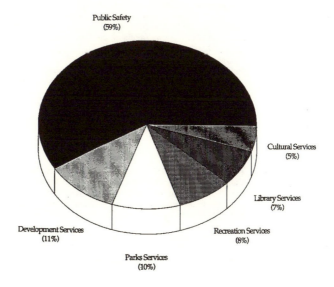

Public Safety
(59%)

Cultural Services
(5%)

Library Services
(7%)

Development Services
(11%)

Recreation Services
(8%)

Parks Services
(10%)

Source: Eugene Decisions

2

(continues)

APPENDIX B   *(continued)*

Part I.   How Much Do You Support Using <u>Taxes</u> For City Services

The city of Eugene provides many services, such as libraries, parks and recreation, cultural services, police and fire safety. For the services listed below, do you strongly support, somewhat support, somewhat oppose, or strongly oppose using taxes to pay for these services. Please check the box that best fits your opinion. If you don't know, or are just not sure, check "no opinion".

How much do you support or oppose using taxes to pay for...

1. **Police Services.** Police respond to calls for services, enforce traffic laws, investigate criminal cases, and support neighborhood watch and block home programs.

Strongly Support	Somewhat Support	Somewhat Oppose	Strongly Oppose	No Opinion
[ ]	[ ]	[ ]	[ ]	[ ]

2. **Fire and Emergency Medical Services.** This includes fire protection, emergency medical, ambulance, and other rescue operations.

Strongly Support	Somewhat Support	Somewhat Oppose	Strongly Oppose	No Opinion
[ ]	[ ]	[ ]	[ ]	[ ]

3. **Library Bookmobile Services.** The bookmobile provides service to people who have difficulty getting to the library on their own, such as senior citizens.

Strongly Support	Somewhat Support	Somewhat Oppose	Strongly Oppose	No Opinion
[ ]	[ ]	[ ]	[ ]	[ ]

4. **All other Library Services.** Mainly the public library downtown at 13th and Olive streets.

Strongly Support	Somewhat Support	Somewhat Oppose	Strongly Oppose	No Opinion
[ ]	[ ]	[ ]	[ ]	[ ]

5. **The Hult Center for the Performing Arts.** The Hult Center is a place for local, national, and international artists to perform.

Strongly Support	Somewhat Support	Somewhat Oppose	Strongly Oppose	No Opinion
[ ]	[ ]	[ ]	[ ]	[ ]

3

(continues)

APPENDIX B   *(continued)*

Using Taxes For City Services

Continued. . .

7. **Convention and Visitors Bureau Contract.** The Visitors Bureau tries to attract conventions and other large meetings to the area and provides information to visitors.

Strongly Support	Somewhat Support	Somewhat Oppose	Strongly Oppose	No Opinion
[ ]	[ ]	[ ]	[ ]	[ ]

8. **Special Events.** Special events include a variety of sporting, arts, children and other community events, most notably the Eugene Celebration.

Strongly Support	Somewhat Support	Somewhat Oppose	Strongly Oppose	No Opinion
[ ]	[ ]	[ ]	[ ]	[ ]

9. **Cultural Arts Program.** The Cultural Arts program primarily provides support for summer concerts in the parks and the Arts in the Vineyard at Alton Baker Park.

Strongly Support	Somewhat Support	Somewhat Oppose	Strongly Oppose	No Opinion
[ ]	[ ]	[ ]	[ ]	[ ]

10. **Sister Cities Program.** This program provides for cultural exchanges with Eugene's sister cities in Korea, Nepal, Japan, and the Soviet Union.

Strongly Support	Somewhat Support	Somewhat Oppose	Strongly Oppose	No Opinion
[ ]	[ ]	[ ]	[ ]	[ ]

11. **Swimming Pools.** The city's swimming pools provide recreational opportunities, water safety instruction, and fitness activities.

Strongly Support	Somewhat Support	Somewhat Oppose	Strongly Oppose	No Opinion
[ ]	[ ]	[ ]	[ ]	[ ]

12. **Athletic Program.** Mainly provides for adult recreational activities, such as softball and soccer.

Strongly Support	Somewhat Support	Somewhat Oppose	Strongly Oppose	No Opinion
[ ]	[ ]	[ ]	[ ]	[ ]

13. **Community Centers.** Four community centers offer year-round recreational classes and provide meeting places for a wide range of community groups.

Strongly Support	Somewhat Support	Somewhat Oppose	Strongly Oppose	No Opinion
[ ]	[ ]	[ ]	[ ]	[ ]

4

(continues)

APPENDIX B   *(continued)*

Using Taxes For City Services

Continued...

14. **Outdoor/Environmental Program.** Primarily instruction in outdoor activities such as skiing and rock climbing, as well as maintenance of the community gardens.

Strongly Support	Somewhat Support	Somewhat Oppose	Strongly Oppose	No Opinion
[ ]	[ ]	[ ]	[ ]	[ ]

15. **Senior Centers.** Provides recreational/social activities for Eugene's residents over 55.

Strongly Support	Somewhat Support	Somewhat Oppose	Strongly Oppose	No Opinion
[ ]	[ ]	[ ]	[ ]	[ ]

16. **Specialized Recreation.** Provides recreational services for people with disabilities, primarily at the Hilyard Center.

Strongly Support	Somewhat Support	Somewhat Oppose	Strongly Oppose	No Opinion
[ ]	[ ]	[ ]	[ ]	[ ]

17. **Business Assistance Team.** The Business Assistance Team provides aid to local small businesses to help them survive and grow.

Strongly Support	Somewhat Support	Somewhat Oppose	Strongly Oppose	No Opinion
[ ]	[ ]	[ ]	[ ]	[ ]

18. **Metro Partnership Contract.** The Metro Partnership helps attract outside industries to relocate or expand in the area.

Strongly Support	Somewhat Support	Somewhat Oppose	Strongly Oppose	No Opinion
[ ]	[ ]	[ ]	[ ]	[ ]

19. **Downtown Development.** This program promotes the private development of downtown Eugene and manages the mall.

Strongly Support	Somewhat Support	Somewhat Oppose	Strongly Oppose	No Opinion
[ ]	[ ]	[ ]	[ ]	[ ]

20. **Affordable Housing and Neighborhood Development.** These programs develop new low-cost/low-rent housing, loan money to low income residents for rehabilitation of their own homes, and provide emergency shelter for homeless families.

Strongly Support	Somewhat Support	Somewhat Oppose	Strongly Oppose	No Opinion
[ ]	[ ]	[ ]	[ ]	[ ]

5

(continues)

136

Using Taxes For City Services

Continued...

21. **Land Use Planning Services.** These services manage the city's land use rules including the historic preservation program.

Strongly Support	Somewhat Support	Somewhat Oppose	Strongly Oppose	No Opinion
[ ]	[ ]	[ ]	[ ]	[ ]

22. **Citizen Involvement/Neighborhood Groups.** This program helps fund and support Eugene's 21 chartered neighborhood groups.

Strongly Support	Somewhat Support	Somewhat Oppose	Strongly Oppose	No Opinion
[ ]	[ ]	[ ]	[ ]	[ ]

23. **Intergovernmental Human Services Contracts.** This program contracts with non-profit agencies to assist the homeless and low income with food, shelter, and medical attention.

Strongly Support	Somewhat Support	Somewhat Oppose	Strongly Oppose	No Opinion
[ ]	[ ]	[ ]	[ ]	[ ]

24. **Public Buildings and Facilities.** This includes maintenance and major repair of city-owned buildings and equipment.

Strongly Support	Somewhat Support	Somewhat Oppose	Strongly Oppose	No Opinion
[ ]	[ ]	[ ]	[ ]	[ ]

6

(continues)

APPENDIX B   *(continued)*

Part II. How Much Do You Support Paying <u>User Fees</u> for City Services

Some government services can be paid for by people who use the service, such as paying a fee for every use of a city swimming pool. For the services listed below, do you strongly support, somewhat support, somewhat oppose, or strongly oppose charging user fees to help pay for the service? Please check the box that best fits your opinion. If you don't know, or are not sure, check "no opinion".

How much do you support ....

1. Charging yearly library user fees to help pay for **library services**.

Strongly Support	Somewhat Support	Somewhat Oppose	Strongly Oppose	No Opinion
[ ]	[ ]	[ ]	[ ]	[ ]

2. Charging yearly fees for using the **library bookmobile**.

Strongly Support	Somewhat Support	Somewhat Oppose	Strongly Oppose	No Opinion
[ ]	[ ]	[ ]	[ ]	[ ]

3. Increasing admission fees for the use of city **swimming pools**.

Strongly Support	Somewhat Support	Somewhat Oppose	Strongly Oppose	No Opinion
[ ]	[ ]	[ ]	[ ]	[ ]

4. Increasing fees for enrolling a team in the city's **adult athletic** programs (such as softball or soccer).

Strongly Support	Somewhat Support	Somewhat Oppose	Strongly Oppose	No Opinion
[ ]	[ ]	[ ]	[ ]	[ ]

5. Increasing fees for recreation programs at Eugene's four **community centers**.

Strongly Support	Somewhat Support	Somewhat Oppose	Strongly Oppose	No Opinion
[ ]	[ ]	[ ]	[ ]	[ ]

6. Increasing fees for instruction in **outdoor activities**, such as rock climbing and skiing.

Strongly Support	Somewhat Support	Somewhat Oppose	Strongly Oppose	No Opinion
[ ]	[ ]	[ ]	[ ]	[ ]

7. Increasing fees for using the **specialized recreation** program for the disabled.

Strongly Support	Somewhat Support	Somewhat Oppose	Strongly Oppose	No Opinion
[ ]	[ ]	[ ]	[ ]	[ ]

7

(continues)

138

User Fees For City Services

Continued...

8. Increasing fees for checking plans and issuing **permits** for residential construction to begin.

| Strongly
Support
[ ] | Somewhat
Support
[ ] | Somewhat
Oppose
[ ] | Strongly
Oppose
[ ] | No
Opinion
[ ] |

9. Increasing fees to use **senior centers**.

| Strongly
Support
[ ] | Somewhat
Support
[ ] | Somewhat
Oppose
[ ] | Strongly
Oppose
[ ] | No
Opinion
[ ] |

10. Charging fees for attending **summer concerts in the park**.

| Strongly
Support
[ ] | Somewhat
Support
[ ] | Somewhat
Oppose
[ ] | Strongly
Oppose
[ ] | No
Opinion
[ ] |

8

(continues)

APPENDIX B   *(continued)*

Part III. How Much Do You Support <u>Additional Taxes</u> for City Services

*One way to balance the city's budget is to raise taxes. Below, seven different ways of increasing taxes are described. **Each one would raise about $8 million in revenue for the city, which is roughly the amount the city needs to fill the expected "budget gap".** Please check whether you strongly support, somewhat support, somewhat oppose, or strongly oppose each proposal. If you don't know, or are just not sure, check "no opinion".*

1. **A retail sales tax of 7 cents for every $10 you spend?** This tax would apply to the purchase of goods and services within the city. Purchase of food, medicine, and the payment of utility bills would not be taxed.

Strongly Support	Somewhat Support	Somewhat Oppose	Strongly Oppose	No Opinion
[ ]	[ ]	[ ]	[ ]	[ ]

2. **A restaurant tax of 50 cents for every $10 you spend?** This tax would cover the sale of food and non-alcoholic beverages by restaurants.

Strongly Support	Somewhat Support	Somewhat Oppose	Strongly Oppose	No Opinion
[ ]	[ ]	[ ]	[ ]	[ ]

3. **A business gross receipts tax of 1 cent for every $10 of business sales?** Businesses within the city pay a tax on their sales revenues.

Strongly Support	Somewhat Support	Somewhat Oppose	Strongly Oppose	No Opinion
[ ]	[ ]	[ ]	[ ]	[ ]

4. **A payroll tax of 4 cents for every $10 earned?** This is a tax on wages and salaries earned within the city, whether the employee is a resident of the city or not.

Strongly Support	Somewhat Support	Somewhat Oppose	Strongly Oppose	No Opinion
[ ]	[ ]	[ ]	[ ]	[ ]

5. **A personal income tax of 3 cents for every $10 of income.** This is a tax on all kinds of income — wages and salaries as well as bank interest, stock dividends, and tips.

Strongly Support	Somewhat Support	Somewhat Oppose	Strongly Oppose	No Opinion
[ ]	[ ]	[ ]	[ ]	[ ]

9

(continues)

APPENDIX B   *(continued)*

Additional Taxes for City Services

Continued. . .

6. **A corporate income tax of about 50 cents for every $10 of profit.** This tax would apply to corporations located or doing business in Eugene, but would not include businesses that are not corporations, such as partnerships.

Strongly Support	Somewhat Support	Somewhat Oppose	Strongly Oppose	No Opinion
[ ]	[ ]	[ ]	[ ]	[ ]

7. **A utility tax of 35 cents for every $10 spent on utilities.** This tax would be added to the monthly billing for electric, water, sewer, gas, telephone, and cable television.

Strongly Support	Somewhat Support	Somewhat Oppose	Strongly Oppose	No Opinion
[ ]	[ ]	[ ]	[ ]	[ ]

8. Assume for a moment that the city must choose between the tax options listed above. Which one or two would you prefer the most, and which one or two would you prefer the least?

Prefer Most: _____

_____

Prefer Least: _____

9. Combining two or more of the tax options would reduce the rate of each specific tax, and still reach the $8 million in needed revenues. If additional revenues were to be raised through taxes, would you prefer...

a) using two or more taxes rather than only one of the tax options above.

Strongly Support	Somewhat Support	Somewhat Oppose	Strongly Oppose	No Opinion
[ ]	[ ]	[ ]	[ ]	[ ]

b) using a single tax option.

Strongly Support	Somewhat Support	Somewhat Oppose	Strongly Oppose	No Opinion
[ ]	[ ]	[ ]	[ ]	[ ]

If you prefer combining taxes, which ones would you combine? (check the taxes you would prefer to be used in combination)

[ ] Retail Sales Tax   [ ] Corporate Income Tax
[ ] Restaurant Tax   [ ] Utility Tax
[ ] Business Gross Receipts Tax   [ ] Payroll Tax
[ ] Personal Income Tax

10

(continues)

APPENDIX B   *(continued)*

Part IV. Some Questions About Yourself

Finally, some questions about yourself so that we can better tabulate and interpret the results. All information, of course, is confidential.

1. Please tell us your age.
    _____ years old

2. Your sex:
    ☐   male
    ☐   female

3. How may persons are there in your household?

    _____ person(s)

4. How may persons under the age of 18 are in your household?

    _____ persons(s)

5. How many persons over the age of 65 are in your household?

    _____ persons(s)

6. Do you rent or own your home?

    ☐   rent
    ☐   own

7. If you own your home, please indicate the approximate amount of property tax you expect to pay this year?

    $_____   ☐ don't know

8. What is your highest level of education completed?

    ☐   K-6 years (elementary school)
    ☐   7-11 (some high school)
    ☐   12 years (high school diploma)
    ☐   13-15 (some college or post-high school training)
    ☐   16 years (Bachelor's degree)
    ☐   17 or more (graduate school)

11

(continues)

142

More Questions.

Continued. . .

9. What is your approximate annual household income?

- ❑ under $20,000
- ❑ $20,000-$29,999
- ❑ $30,000-$39,999
- ❑ $40,000-$49,999
- ❑ $50,000-$74,999
- ❑ $75,000 and over

10. How often do you or someone in your household use these city services –
often, sometimes, or never.

	often use	sometime use	never use
a) city library	❑	❑	❑
b) library bookmobile	❑	❑	❑
c) city swimming pools	❑	❑	❑
d) city athlectic programs (such as softball or soccer)	❑	❑	❑
e) city community centers	❑	❑	❑
f) city outdoor activity instruction (such as skiing or rock climbing)	❑	❑	❑
g) Hult Center	❑	❑	❑
h) specialized recreation	❑	❑	❑
i) building permits	❑	❑	❑
j) senior centers	❑	❑	❑
k) concerts in the park	❑	❑	❑

12

(continues)

APPENDIX B   *(continued)*

Comments?

Is there anything else you would like to tell us about how you think the City of Eugene should attempt to solve its budget problem? If so, please use this space for that purpose.

Thank you very much for completing this questionnaire!

144

EUGENE DECISIONS   **Our City...**

...Our Future

November, 1991

This is a survey about city services and city taxes. The City of Eugene no longer has enough money to continue offering all current services. If nothing is done to close the gap between the cost of services and the money available to pay for them, the City of Eugene will face an $8 million shortfall by 1994.

Should services be cut? If so, what services? Should taxes be raised or new taxes introduced? If so, how much should they be raised and/or what new taxes should we adopt? Should more of the cost of offering a service be paid directly by the people who use them? If so, for what services should user fees be charged? This survey seeks your advice on these very difficult decisions. While these are tough decisions, you do not need to be an expert in city government to give us your opinions and suggestions.

With this survey we are sending along a copy of a newspaper tabloid that is also being sent to every household in Eugene. The tabloid will tell you more about the Eugene Decisions process and contains background information on city services, user fees, and taxes. You may find the tabloid helpful as you complete this questionnaire.

We deeply appreciate the time you are taking to complete this questionnaire. The questions may be about city services and city taxes, but in a larger sense, the survey is about the future of Eugene.

We have included a stamped, pre-addressed return envelope. If, however, that envelope becomes misplaced, please return this questionnaire to:

Eugene Decisions
P.O. Box 3318
Eugene, Oregon 97403

1

(continues)

APPENDIX C   *(continued)*

Where the Money Goes
Eugene General Fund Expenditures

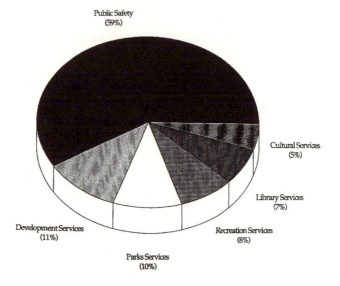

Public Safety
(59%)

Cultural Services
(5%)

Library Services
(7%)

Development Services
(11%)

Recreation Services
(8%)

Parks Services
(10%)

Source: Eugene Decisions

2

(continues)

146

 Part I.   How Much Do You Support Using <u>Taxes</u> For City Services

The City of Eugene has to reduce some services in order to balance its budget without raising taxes or fees, but opinions on which services to cut are mixed. The questions below describe the consequences of reducing or eliminating specific city services and ask how much you would support paying an additional tax to keep those services. (Fees for these services, for a variety of reasons, are not considered possible options. So, the services below must be paid for by taxes, or they cannot be provided by the city). The less you support the taxes, the more you would be willing to accept a service reduction or program elimination.

For each question, please indicate whether you strongly support, somewhat support, somewhat oppose, or strongly oppose paying the amount of taxes required to offer the existing level of service. Please check the box that best fits your opinion. If you don't know or are not sure, check "no opinion".

How much do you support paying the yearly tax to offer the current service level for....

1. **Police services** are those that respond to police calls, enforce laws, investigate criminal cases and support neighborhood block watch and block home programs. To avoid reducing these services, how much do you support an additional tax of $14 paid by every household in the City (including yours)?

Strongly Support	Somewhat Support	Somewhat Oppose	Strongly Oppose	No Opinion .
[]	[]	[]	[]	[]

2. **Fire and Emergency Medical Services** include fire protection, emergency medical, ambulance, and other rescue operations. To avoid reducing these services, how much do you support a tax of $10 paid by every household in the City (including yours)?

Strongly Support	Somewhat Support	Somewhat Oppose	Strongly Oppose	No Opinion
[]	[]	[]	[]	[]

3. The **Special Events** program promotes many events in the community, including the Eugene Celebration. Loss of funding would result in fewer and/or smaller events. To continue the program, how much do you support an additional tax of $4 paid by every household in the City (including yours)?

Strongly Support	Somewhat Support	Somewhat Oppose	Strongly Oppose	No Opinion
[]	[]	[]	[]	[]

3

(continues)

APPENDIX C   *(continued)*

Using Taxes For City Services

Continued...

4. The **Sister Cities** program provides for cultural exchanges with Eugene's sister cities in Korea, Nepal, Japan, and the Soviet Union. To continue the program, how much do you support an additional tax of $1 paid by every household in the City (including yours)?

Strongly Support	Somewhat Support	Somewhat Oppose	Strongly Oppose	No Opinion
[ ]	[ ]	[ ]	[ ]	[ ]

5. The **Business Assistance Team** helps new small businesses to start in the community, as well as helping existing local small businesses to survive. To continue the service, how much do you support an additional tax of $6 paid by every household in the City (including yours)?

Strongly Support	Somewhat Support	Somewhat Oppose	Strongly Oppose	No Opinion
[ ]	[ ]	[ ]	[ ]	[ ]

6. City support for the **Metro Partnership Contract** works to attract new businesses to locate in the Eugene area. To continue this service, how much do you support an additional tax of $2 paid by every household in the City (including yours)?

Strongly Support	Somewhat Support	Somewhat Oppose	Strongly Oppose	No Opinion
[ ]	[ ]	[ ]	[ ]	[ ]

7. The **Downtown Development** program promotes the private development of downtown Eugene and manages the mall. To continue the program, how much do you support an additional tax of $3 paid by every household in the City (including yours)?

Strongly Support	Somewhat Support	Somewhat Oppose	Strongly Oppose	No Opinion
[ ]	[ ]	[ ]	[ ]	[ ]

8. The **Affordable Housing and Neighborhood Development** program develops new low cost and low rent housing, and provides emergency shelter for homeless families. To continue the services, how much do you support an additional tax of $2 paid by every household in the City (including yours)?

Strongly Support	Somewhat Support	Somewhat Oppose	Strongly Oppose	No Opinion
[ ]	[ ]	[ ]	[ ]	[ ]

9. **Land Use Planning Services** manages the City's land use rules including the

4

(continues)

APPENDIX C   *(continued)*

Using Taxes For City Services

Continued...

historic preservation program. Loss of the program means that it is taken over by the County or State, perhaps resulting in service delays and some loss of local control. To continue the service, how much do you support an additional tax of $22 paid by every household in the City (including yours)?

Strongly Support	Somewhat Support	Somewhat Oppose	Strongly Oppose	No Opinion
[]	[]	[]	[]	[]

10. Eugene's 21 chartered **Neighborhood Groups** provide opportunities for citizens to participate in decision making with the City. Without City support, some of these groups may cease to exist. To continue City backing for the groups, how much do you support an additional tax of $2 paid by every household in the City (including yours)?

Strongly Support	Somewhat Support	Somewhat Oppose	Strongly Oppose	No Opinion
[]	[]	[]	[]	[]

11. **Human Services Contracts** assist homeless and low income people with food, shelter, medical attention and safety. To continue the program, how much do you support an additional tax of $9 paid by every household in the City (including yours)?

Strongly Support	Somewhat Support	Somewhat Oppose	Strongly Oppose	No Opinion
[]	[]	[]	[]	[]

12. The City's **Public Building and Facilities** program pays for renovation and major repair of City owned buildings and equipment. Reduced funding is likely to result in considerably raised future costs. To continue the service, how much do you support an additional tax of $65 paid by every household in the City (including yours)?

Strongly Support	Somewhat Support	Somewhat Oppose	Strongly Oppose	No Opinion
[]	[]	[]	[]	[]

(continues)

APPENDIX C *(continued)*

Part II. How Much Do You Support Using Taxes For Service Improvements?

The four City service areas listed below are under consideration by the City Council for increased service. We would like to know whether you support these service improvements and the taxes needed to provide them.

For each service, please indicate whether you strongly support, somewhat support, somewhat oppose, strongly oppose or have no opinion about raising taxes for each of these areas. Please check the box that best fits your opinion.

1. **Improved fire and emergency response** - The improvement in fire and emergency response time would improve the city's ability to respond to calls from 74% to 90% of the city within four minutes. To expand this program, would you support a tax of $17 paid by every household in the city?

Strongly Support	Somewhat Support	Somewhat Oppose	Strongly Oppose	No Opinion
[]	[]	[]	[]	[]

2. **Affordable Housing** - This improvement would expand the level of housing rehabilitation for low income residents and for rental properties, as well as assist non-profit housing development corporations with start-up money. To expand this program, would you support a tax of $4 paid by every household in the city?

Strongly Support	Somewhat Support	Somewhat Oppose	Strongly Oppose	No Opinion
[]	[]	[]	[]	[]

3. **Community Policing** - This improvement would add 63 public safety positions over 5 years (34 in the first year) emphasizing crime prevention, education, and joint problem solving between police and citizens, in order to address the root causes of crime. To establish this program, would you support an additional tax of $58 paid by every household in the city?

Strongly Support	Somewhat Support	Somewhat Oppose	Strongly Oppose	No Opinion
[]	[]	[]	[]	[]

4. **Community Arts** - This improvement would expand local support for the arts and improves existing facilities at the community center for the performing arts (WOW Hall) and the Maude Kerns Art Center. The expansion also includes a cultural tourism program to market Eugene's cultural arts. To expand this program, would you support an additional tax of $10 paid by every household in the city?

Strongly Support	Somewhat Support	Somewhat Oppose	Strongly Oppose	No Opinion
[]	[]	[]	[]	[]

6

(continues)

APPENDIX C   *(continued)*

▰▰▰ Part III. How Much Do You Support Paying <u>User Fees</u> for City Services

Some of the services that government provides can be funded through user fees paid directly for services received, such as a paying a fee every time someone uses a city swimming pool. Where user fees are possible, do you think fees should be charged? If so, how much? For the services listed below, do you feel that user fees should be used to pay the full cost of providing the service, part of the cost (say 25%, 50% or 75% of the cost) or no part of the cost?

> **An Example:**
> The chart for the Eugene public library (below) shows that if no user fees were charged, a typical household would pay $40 per year in taxes to operate the library.
>
> | Yearly Library Card Fee | $0 | $36 | $72 | $108 | $144 | Yearly Library Card Fee |
> |---|---|---|---|---|---|---|
> | Annual Tax | $40 | $30 ✔ | $20 | $10 | $0 | Annual Tax |
> | | [ ] | [✔] | [ ] | [ ] | [ ] | |
>
> If an annual membership fee of $36 were charged for use of the library, the annual tax needed to operate the library would decrease from $40 to $30. For the public library to be fully paid for by user fees (that is $0 from taxes), a yearly membership fee of $144 would need to be charged to each library user. Any of the combinations shown in the chart of yearly membership fees and taxes would fund the library at its current level of service.
>
> What combination of taxes and user fees would you recommend? If you recommend a user fee of $36 you would check the box (as shown) under the $36 user fee/ $30 annual tax combination.

For the following services, please check the box which most closely describes your preferred combination of fees and taxes.

1. The Eugene **public library** is paid mostly by taxes, now about $40 per household. Do you think a yearly fee should be charged the approximately 20,000 households currently using the library and, if so, how much should the yearly fee be? Please check the box that best describes your view of the right split between a library user fee and taxes.

Yearly Library Card Fee	$0	$36	$72	$108	$144	Yearly Library Card Fee
Annual Tax	$40	$30	$20	$10	$0	Annual Tax
	[ ]	[ ]	[ ]	[ ]	[ ]	

(continues)

APPENDIX C   *(continued)*

User Fees For City Services

Continued...

2. The **library bookmobile** is paid for totally by taxes, now about $1 per household. It provides service to individuals who have difficulty getting to the library on their own, such as senior citizens and disabled. Do you think a yearly fee should be charged the approximately 1,000 users of the library bookmobile and, if so, how much should the yearly fee be?

Yearly Book- mobile Fee	$0	$25	$50	$75	$100	Yearly Book- mobile Fee
Annual Tax	$1	$.75	$.50	$.25	$0	Annual Tax
	[ ]	[ ]	[ ]	[ ]	[ ]	

3. The **Hult Center** provides a place for local, national, and international artists to perform. The Hult Center operations are now paid for by a combination of user fees (tickets) and taxes. Ticket prices now average $13, and the average household contributes about $22 in taxes. What combination of ticket price and taxes would you prefer?

Ticket Price	$13	$14.50	$16	$17.50	$19	Ticket Price
Annual Tax	$22	$16.50	$11	$5.50	$0	Annual Tax
	[ ]	[ ]	[ ]	[ ]	[ ]	

4. City **swimming pools**, are primarily supported by a combination of swim class fees (now about $30 per class) and taxes (now $12 per household). What combination of swim class fees and taxes would you prefer?

Swim Class Fees	$30	$50	$70	$90	$110	Swim Class Fees
Annual Tax	$12	$9	$6	$3	$0	Annual Tax
	[ ]	[ ]	[ ]	[ ]	[ ]	

5. City **adult athletic** programs, such as softball and soccer are currently supported through a combination of fees paid by each team (now $300 per team) and taxes (now $5 per household). What combination of team fees and taxes would you prefer?

Team Fees	$300	$360	$420	$480	$540	Team Fees
Annual Tax	$5	$3.75	$2.50	$1.25	$0	Annual Tax
	[ ]	[ ]	[ ]	[ ]	[ ]	

8

(continues)

152

APPENDIX C   *(continued)*

6. The City's four **community centers** offer year-round recreational classes and provide a meeting place for a wide range of community groups. The community centers are currently paid for by a combination of activity fees (now about $30 per activity, such as aerobics) and taxes (now about $18 per household). What combination of activity fees and taxes would you prefer?

Activity Fee	$30	$42.50	$55	$67.50	$80	Activity Fees
Annual Tax	$18	$13.50	$9	$4.50	$0	Annual Tax
	[ ]	[ ]	[ ]	[ ]	[ ]	

7. The city outdoor and environmental program provides instruction in **outdoor activities**, such as rock climbing and skiing. These programs are supported by a combination of fees paid for outdoor activity instruction (currently about $30) and taxes (now about $2 per household). What combination of activity fees and taxes would you prefer?

Instruction Fees	$30	$42.50	$55	$67.50	$80	Instruction Fees
Annual Tax	$2	$1.50	$1.00	$.50	$0	Annual Tax
	[ ]	[ ]	[ ]	[ ]	[ ]	

8. The **specialized recreation program for the disabled** currently provides the only recreational programs for people who have disabilities (80% of whom are below the poverty level). This program is currently paid for mostly by taxes, now about $4 per household. Do you think a yearly membership fee should be charged for using the specialized recreation program and, if so, how much should the yearly membership fee be?

Yearly Membership Fee	$0	$75	$150	$225	$300	Yearly Membership Fee
Annual Tax	$4	$3	$2	$1	$0	Annual Tax
	[ ]	[ ]	[ ]	[ ]	[ ]	

9

(continues)

APPENDIX C   *(continued)*

User Fees For City Services

Continued...

9. The city provides **residential permits** that allow for building construction to begin. Permit services are currently supported by a combination of a fee paid every time a permit is processed (now an average of $1000 per permit) and taxes (now about $15 per household). What combination of permit fees and taxes would you prefer?

Permit Fee	$1000	$1175	$1350	$1525	$1700	Permit Fee
Annual Tax	$15	$11.25	$7.50	$3.75	$0	Annual Tax
	[ ]	[ ]	[ ]	[ ]	[ ]	

10. The city's **senior centers** provide and social and recreational opportunities for city residents over-55. This program is currently paid for mostly by taxes, now about $9 per household. Do you think a yearly membership fee should be charged for using the use of senior centers and, if so, how much should the yearly membership fee be?

Yearly Member-ship Fee	$0	$20	$40	$60	$80	Yearly Member-ship Fee
Annual Tax	$9	$6.75	$4.50	$2.25	$0	Annual Tax
	[ ]	[ ]	[ ]	[ ]	[ ]	

11. The city's **cultural arts** program sponsors the summer concerts in the parks. This program is currently paid for totally by taxes, now about $2 per household. Do you think a fee per concert should be charged and, if so, how much should the ticket price be?

Ticket Price	$0	$1	$2	$3	$4	Ticket Price
Annual Tax	$2	$1.50	$1.00	$.50	$0	Annual Tax
	[ ]	[ ]	[ ]	[ ]	[ ]	

12. How often do you or someone in your household use these city services — often, sometimes, or never?

	Often Use	Sometimes Use	Never Use
a) city library	[ ]	[ ]	[ ]
b) library bookmobile	[ ]	[ ]	[ ]
c) city swimming pools	[ ]	[ ]	[ ]
d) city athletic programs	[ ]	[ ]	[ ]
e) city community centers	[ ]	[ ]	[ ]
f) city outdoor activity instruction	[ ]	[ ]	[ ]
g) Hult Center	[ ]	[ ]	[ ]
h) specialized recreation program	[ ]	[ ]	[ ]
i) building permits	[ ]	[ ]	[ ]
j) senior centers	[ ]	[ ]	[ ]
k) concerts in the park	[ ]	[ ]	[ ]

10

(continues)

APPENDIX C   *(continued)*

User Fees For City Services

Continued...

13. Given the services you now use and the taxes you now pay, what is the most you think **you** should have to pay **in total** during any given month for all user fees, such as fees for using the swimming pools or enrolling in athletic programs?

$0	$10	$20	$30	$40	$50	$60	$70	$80	$90	over $90
[]	[]	[]	[]	[]	[]	[]	[]	[]	[]	[]

14. Earlier we asked you how much you prefer user fees compared with taxes as a way of paying for city services. We would now like to know how much you support paying a tax to **continue to offer the current level of service**. (Assume the amount to be raised through user fees will not change). Please indicate whether you strongly support, somewhat support, somewhat oppose, or strongly oppose using taxes to **maintain** the current level of service. The less you support the taxes, the more you would be willing to accept a service reduction. Please check the box that best fits your opinion. If you don't know or are not sure, check "no opinion".

How much do you support using **taxes** to maintain the current level of service for...

	Strongly Support	Somewhat Support	Somewhat Oppose	Strongly Oppose	No Opinion
a) city library (now a $40 tax per household)	[]	[]	[]	[]	[]
b) library bookmobile (now a $1 tax per household)	[]	[]	[]	[]	[]
c) city swimming pools (now a $12 tax per household)	[]	[]	[]	[]	[]
d) city athletic programs (now a $5 tax per household)	[]	[]	[]	[]	[]
e) city community centers now a $18 tax per household)	[]	[]	[]	[]	[]
f) city outdoor activity instruction (now a $2 tax per household)	[]	[]	[]	[]	[]
g) Hult Center (now a $22 tax per household)	[]	[]	[]	[]	[]
h) specialized recreation program (now a $4 tax per household)	[]	[]	[]	[]	[]
i) building permits (now a $15 tax per household)	[]	[]	[]	[]	[]
j) senior centers (now $9 tax per household)	[]	[]	[]	[]	[]
k) concerts in the park (now $2 tax per household)	[]	[]	[]	[]	[]

11

(continues)

APPENDIX C   *(continued)*

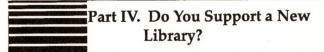

Part IV. Do You Support a New Library?

Below is an increase in a city service (the new library) under consideration by the city council. We would like to know whether you would support this service increase. If you do support the service increase, would you prefer to pay for it with a user fee, a tax, or some combination? Assume that the existing library services are maintained and funded through taxes.

1.   The **new library** in a reconstructed Sears building would provide over two times the space and an increased number of books and resource materials. Do you think a yearly fee should be charged to pay for the increased costs due to building and operating the new library and, if so, how much should the yearly fee be? Please check the box that best describes your view of the right split between a library user fee and increased taxes.

Yearly Library Fee	$0	$30	$60	$90	$120	Yearly Library Fee
Annual Tax Increase	$32	$24	$16	$8	$0	Annual Tax Increase
	[ ]	[ ]	[ ]	[ ]	[ ]	

[ ] I do not support the new library

12

(continues)

APPENDIX C   *(continued)*

Part V. Some Questions About Yourself

Finally, some questions about yourself so that we can better tabulate and interpret the results. All information, of course, is confidential.

1. Please tell us your age.

    _____ years old

2. Your sex:
    - ❑   male
    - ❑   female

3. How may persons are there in your household?

    _____ person(s)

4. How may persons under the age of 18 are there in your household?

    _____ persons(s)

5. How many persons over the age of 65 are there in your household?

    _____ persons(s)

6. Do you rent or own your home?

    - ❑   rent
    - ❑   own

7. If you own your home, please indicate the approximate amount of property tax you expect to pay this year?

    $_____   ❑   don't know

8. What is your highest level of education completed?

    - ❑   K-6 years (elementary school)
    - ❑   7-11 (some high school)
    - ❑   12 years (high school diploma)
    - ❑   13-15 (some college or post-high school training)
    - ❑   16 years (Bachelor's degree)
    - ❑   17 or more (graduate school)

13

(continues)

157

APPENDIX C   *(continued)*

More Questions.

Continued...

9. What is your approximate annual household income?

   ☐   under $20,000
   ☐ $20,000-$29,999
   ☐ $30,000-$39,999
   ☐ $40,000-$49,999
   ☐ $50,000-$74,999
   ☐ $75,000 and over

14

(continues)

APPENDIX C   *(continued)*

Comments?

Is there anything else you would like to tell us about how you think the City of
Eugene should attempt to solve its budget problem? If so, please use this space
for that purpose.

Thank you very much for completing this questionnaire!

15

(continues)

APPENDIX D OLS Regression Coefficients—Services

Independent Variables	Police	Fire-EMS	Park Maint.	Recreation	Hult	Planning	Human Services	Rec. for Disabled	Library	Book-mobile
Education										
BAORMORE	-0.4209	-0.2456	-0.6002***	-0.1955*	-0.2149***	-0.3367***	-0.0144	-0.0124	-0.0866	-0.0010
HSORLESS	0.0592	0.2322	-0.3083*	0.0827	0.0621	-0.2510	0.0399	-0.0210	0.1561	0.0201**
Income										
HIINC	0.3336	0.1159	-0.0111	0.0101	-0.1532*	0.1709	0.0252	-0.0071	0.0615	0.0006
LOWINC	-1.8601**	-0.8098	-0.4172	-0.2854	-0.2189	-0.3049	-0.0827	-0.0456	-0.2844	-0.0206
Household Char.										
HSHLD	-0.1137	-0.0451	0.0323	-0.0376	0.0076	-0.0321	-0.0206	-0.0034	-0.0146	-0.0006
RENT	0.3449	-0.0589	-0.0489	-0.2180*	-0.2106**	-0.1288	-0.0310	-0.0477**	-0.0357	-0.0101
USE	0.1303	0.0429	0.0289	0.0415	0.0402	-0.0103	0.0153	0.0001	-0.0275	0.0016
USE SERVICE	—	—	—	—	-0.1289	0.2301	—	-0.0198	-0.2074*	-0.0112
Respondent Char.										
FEMALE	0.0905	-0.0590	-0.0292	-0.1049	-0.0047	0.0096	0.0108	-0.0221	-0.0156	-0.0101*
AGE	0.0072	0.0108	0.0001	-0.0013	-0.0026	-0.0022	-0.0011	-0.0000[a]	0.0023	-0.0004*
Other										
GAPCLOSE	0.0449	0.0332	-0.0098	-0.0050	-0.0010	-0.0196	-0.0052	0.0022	-0.0002	-0.011
HSHL*LINC	1.3544***	0.6585***	0.2342*	0.2027**	0.1358*	0.1771	0.0586**	0.0348**	0.2173**	0.0110**
CONSTANT	-0.2027	-0.4776	0.9467**	0.7463***	0.7046***	1.5694***	0.1933**	0.0595	0.4381	0.0518***
R^2	.12	.09	.14	.08	.15	.05	.08	.09	.12	.12
Adj. R^2	.07	.04	.09	.02	.10	-.01	.02	.03	.07	.06

*** Significant at the .01 level, ** significant at the .05 level, * significant at the .10 level.

[a] $-1.8E-05$.

APPENDIX E   OLS Regression Coefficients—Taxes

Independent Variables	All Taxes	Corporate Income	Gross Receipts	Retail Sales	Payroll	Personal Income	Entertainment	Restaurant	Room	Utility
Education										
BAORMORE	0.8121	0.0362	0.2171	−0.0425	−0.2917	0.5496	0.0011	0.3843	−0.1379	0.0958
HSORLESS	1.9679	0.1108	0.4120	0.1333	0.3738	0.4341	0.2013*	0.1735	−0.0843	0.2133
Income										
HIINC	0.0419	−0.3535***	−0.3959	0.4038	0.0302	−0.2298	0.0068	0.4073	−0.0481	0.2209*
LOWINC	−1.0899	−0.3219	0.4405	0.3132	−0.8681	−0.8469	0.1189	0.3195	−0.2044	−0.0408
Household Char.										
HSHLD	0.0694	−0.0097	−0.1558	0.1924	−0.1004	−0.0076	0.0029	0.2036	−0.0443	−0.0118
RENT	2.0194*	0.0811	0.6630	−0.1970	0.7097**	0.4618	−0.1105	0.3831	−0.0646	0.0929
USE	−0.1709	0.0155	−0.0471	−0.2949*	0.1375	0.0238	0.0224	−0.0633	−0.0159	0.0510
Respondent Char.										
FEMALE	−0.1331	0.0170	−0.5482*	−0.1579	−0.0313	−0.2716	−0.0064	1.0726***	−0.0652	−0.1420
AGE	0.0222	0.0012	−0.0095	0.0040	0.0113	−0.0031	0.0064**	0.0125	−0.0026	0.0020
Other										
GAPCLOSE	0.9750***	0.0443***	0.1952***	0.2477***	0.0703*	0.1742***	0.0231**	0.1780***	0.0219	0.0210
HSHL*LINC	0.2847	0.1031	−0.3562	0.1382	0.3863	0.5000	0.0313	−0.6227	0.0413	0.0634
CONSTANT	−7.2317**	−0.2170	−0.1817	−1.6737	−1.0052	−1.5041	−0.5135**	−2.3383*	0.3273	−0.3207
R^2	.29	.09	.15	.13	.08	.11	.12	.14	.03	.06
Adj. R^2	.24	.04	.10	.08	.02	.06	.07	.09	−.02	.01

*** Significant at the .01 level, ** significant at the .05 level, * significant at the .10 level.

APPENDIX F Logistic Regression Coefficients—Services

Independent Variables	Police	Fire-EMS	Park Maint.	Recreation	Hult	Planning	Human Services	Rec. for Disabled	Library	Book-mobile
Education										
BAORMORE	-0.8570**	-0.8783**	-0.6506*	-0.7785**	-0.4823	-0.5485	-0.3252	-0.6889*	-0.5436	-0.5403
HSORLESS	-0.3309	-0.2581	-0.4868	-0.4001	0.3531	-0.3208	0.2986	-0.6754	-0.3062	1.0543**
Income										
HIINC	0.3004	-0.0751	-0.2703	0.2350	-0.6182	-0.0340	-0.2760	-0.2897	0.4511	0.0002
LOWINC	-0.6301	-0.7792	-0.9363	-0.4273	-1.3625	-0.9805	-1.1275	-1.3034	-0.1219	-1.7986*
Household Char.										
HSHLD	-0.0071	0.0893	0.1040	0.0404	-0.0098	-0.1019	-0.0423	-0.1704	-0.0563	-0.0898
RENT	0.1143	-0.0896	-0.3710	-0.5056	-0.6357	-0.4657	-0.4700	-0.9395*	-0.2714	-0.4094
USE	0.0723	0.0017	0.0068	0.1498	0.2240	0.2480	0.2075	0.0722	-0.0988	0.0405
USE SERVICE	-	-	-	-	-0.0770	-	-	-0.4277	-1.0250***	-0.4117
Respondent Char.										
FEMALE	-0.4827	-0.2686	-0.0044	-0.1385	0.0027	-0.1118	0.1716	-0.0594	-0.0543	-0.6410*
AGE	-0.0306**	-0.0048	-0.0335***	-0.0150	-0.0248**	-0.0268**	-0.0205	-0.0134	-0.0061	-0.0338**
Other										
GAPCLOSE	-0.0497	0.0057	-0.0689	0.0039	-0.0174	-0.0299	-0.0526	-0.0171	-0.0645	-0.1215**
HSHL*LINC	0.4240	0.3778	0.4425	0.2409	0.6569*	0.4402	0.6006*	0.4549	0.3229	0.7782*
CONSTANT	2.1572*	-0.6985	3.2709***	1.4123	1.9445*	3.0667	0.5445	1.0335	1.6225	2.5038*
% CORRECTLY CLASSFIED	61.93	78.68	69.04	67.01	66.50	76.14	68.02	72.59	72.59	74.11

*** Significant at the .01 level, ** significant at the .05 level, * significant at the .10 level.

APPENDIX G Logistic Regression Coefficients—Taxes

Independent Variables	Corporate Income	Gross Receipts	Retail Sales	Payroll	Personal Income	Entertainment	Restaurant	Room	Utility
Education									
BAORMORE	0.1025	-0.1363	-0.1290	-0.7754	0.7994	-0.5342	0.1207	-0.1658	0.0169
HSORLESS	0.3671	0.2315	0.6976	0.1310	0.7008	0.5141	0.3161	0.0874	1.0385
Income									
HIINC	-1.0926***	0.1147	0.4015	0.2838	-0.6021	0.2792	0.3711	0.3575	1.0629*
LOWINC	-0.7038	0.1918	0.0048	-1.6857	-1.0006	-1.1321	-1.2107	-0.7773	-0.6026
Household Char.									
HSHLD	-0.0475	-0.2631	0.0357	-0.3192	-0.1885	-0.1260	0.0100	-0.0093	-0.1760
RENT	0.3987	0.9647**	0.0469	1.5989***	0.9648	0.3036	0.8004*	0.9132**	0.8594
USE	0.0496	-0.0235	-0.1321	0.3792*	0.1392	0.1917	0.1642	-0.0628	0.2458
Respondent Char.									
FEMALE	0.0977	-0.5128	-0.1130	-0.4060	-0.8030	0.5442	0.8144**	0.9318***	-0.8551*
AGE	-0.0036	-0.0208	-0.0068	0.0225	-0.0102	0.0241*	0.0131	-0.0135	0.0010
Other									
GAPCLOSE	0.1324***	0.1585***	0.2124***	0.1614**	0.1489**	0.1406***	0.2152***	0.1441***	0.0856
HSHL*LINC	0.2105	-0.3189	0.0980	0.6965	0.5302	0.4923	-0.1497	0.1324	0.2252
CONSTANT	-1.8624*	-1.5227	-3.3984***	-5.5242	-3.8329**	-4.0839***	-4.9742***	-2.1882*	-3.5188**
% CORRECTLY CLASSIFIED	70.05	82.23	77.66	90.36	89.85	75.63	73.10	68.02	86.80

*** Significant at the .01 level, ** significant at the .05 level, * significant at the .10 level.

References

Aday, R. H.; and L. A. Miles. 1982. "Long-term Impacts of Rural Migration of the Elderly: Implications for Research." *Gerontologist.* Vol. 22. Pp. 331–336.

Advisory Commission on Intergovernmental Relations. 1992. *Changing Attitudes Towards Governments and Taxes.* Washington, DC: Author.

Ansolabehere, Stephen; Roy Behr; and Shanto Iyengar. 1993. *The Media Game: American Politics in the Television Age.* New York: Macmillan.

Appleby, P. H. 1949. *Policy and Administration.* Birmingham: University Of Alabama Press.

Arnstein, S. R. 1969. "A Ladder of Citizen Participation." *Journal of the American Institute of Planners.* Vol. 35. Pp. 216–224.

Arrington, Thomas S.; and David D. Jordan. 1982. "Willingness to Pay Per Capita Costs As a Measure of Support for Urban Services." *Public Administration Review.* Vol. 42. Pp. 168–171.

Atkinson, Rob; and Stephen Cope. 1995. "Community Participation and the Evaluation of Urban Regeneration Strategies." Paper presented at the interdisciplinary conference "Ideas Of Community," organized by the Centre for Social and Economic Research at the University of the West of England, Bristol, September 13–15.

Banfield, Edward C.; and James Q. Wilson. 1963. *City Politics.* Cambridge, MA: MIT Press.

Barber, Benjamin. 1984. *Strong Democracy: Participatory Politics for a New Age.* Berkeley: University Of California Press.

Beck, Paul Allen; and Thomas R. Dye. 1982. "Sources Of Public Opinion on Taxes: The Florida Case." *Journal Of Politics.* Vol. 44. Pp. 172–182.

Beck, Paul Allen; Hal Rainey; Keith Nichols; and Carol Traut. 1987. "Citizen Views of Taxes and Services: A Tale of Three Cities." *Social Science Quarterly.* Vol. 68. Pp. 223–243.

Beck, Paul Allen; Hal Rainey; and Carol Traut. 1990. "Disadvantage, Disaffection, and Race as Divergent Bases for Citizen Fiscal Policy Preferences." *Journal of Politics.* Vol. 52, No. 1. February. Pp. 71–93.

Berne, Robert; and Richard Schramm. 1986. *The Financial Analysis of Governments.* Englewood Cliffs, NJ: Prentice Hall.

Berry, Jeffrey M.; Kent E. Portney; and Ken Thomson. 1993. *The Rebirth of Urban Democracy.* Washington, DC: Brookings Institution.

Bessette, Joseph M. 1994. *The Mild Voice of Reason: Deliberative Democracy and the American National Government.* Chicago: University Of Chicago Press.

Bishoff, Don. 1993. "Did Tax Drive Get Fair Shake?" [Eugene, OR] *Register-Guard.* March 31. P. B1.

Bjornstad, David J.; and James R. Kahn 1996. *The Contingent Valuation of Environmental Resources: Methodological Issues and Research Needs.* Cheltenham, UK; and Brookfield, VT: Edward Elgar.

Borscheding, T. E.; and R. T. Deacon. 1972. "The Demand for Service of Non-Federal Governments." *American Economic Review.* Vol. 62, No. 5. Pp. 891–901.

Boycko, Maxim; Andrei Shleifer; and Robert W. Vishny. 1996. "A Theory of Privatization." *Economic Journal.* Vol. 106, No. 435. P. 309.

Bradford, David F.; R. A. Malt; and Wallace E. Oates. 1969. "The Rising Cost of Local Public Services: Some Evidence and Reflections." *National Tax Journal.* Vol. 22. June. Pp. 185–202.

Bradley, Ann. 1995. "Public Agenda Captures Voice of the People." *Education Week.* Vol. 15, No. 6. October 11. P.1.

Butler, Stuart. 1991. "Privatization for Public Purposes." In William T. Gormley Jr., ed., *Privatization and Its Alternatives.* Madison: University of Wisconsin Press. Pp. 17–24.

Center for Civic Networking. 1995. "Information Infrastructure: Public Spaces for the 21st Century." [Online] http://civic.net/ccn.html

Citrin, Jack. 1979. "Do People Want Something for Nothing?" *National Tax Journal.* Vol. 32, No. 2 (Supplement). Pp. 113–130.

City of Eugene [Oregon]. 1993. *Eugene's Government.* Eugene, OR: Author.

City of Sparks [Nevada]. 1986. "Budget Ballot." *Sparks City Hall Reporter.* Spring.

Clark, Terry Nichols. 1974. "Can You Cut a Budget Pie?" *Policy and Politics.* Vol. 3, No. 2. Pp. 3–31.

Clinton, Bill; and Al Gore. 1992. *Putting People First: How We Can All Change America.* New York: Times Books.

Cole, Richard L. 1973. *Citizen Participation and the Urban Policy Process.* Lexington, MA: Leighton Books.

Cole, Richard L.; and David Caputo. 1984. "The Public Hearing as an Effective Citizen Participation Mechanism." *American Political Science Review.* Vol. 78. Pp. 404–416.

Collier, Steve. 1987. "City to Mail Survey to 1500 Residents." *Springfield* [Oregon] *News.* August 15. P. 1.

Courant, Paul N.; Edward M. Gramlich; and Daniel L. Rubinfeld. 1980. "Why Voters Support Tax Limitation Amendments: The Michigan Case." *National Tax Journal.* Vol. 33, No. 1. Pp. 1–20.

Cronin, Thomas E. 1989. *Direct Democracy: The Politics of Initiative, Referendum, and Recall.* Cambridge, MA: Harvard University Press.

Crosby, Ned. 1991. "The Citizens Jury Process as a Basic Democratic Reform." Revised version of a paper presented at the Conference on Competing Theories of Post-Liberal Democracy, University Of Texas, Austin, February 8–10.

Crosby, Ned. 1993. *The Basics of the Citizens Jury Process.* Minneapolis, MN: Jefferson Center for New Democratic Processes.

Crosby, Ned; Janet M. Kelley; and Paul Schaefer. 1992. "Citizen Panels: A New Approach to Citizen Participation." *Public Administration Review.* Vol. 46, No. 2. Pp. 170–178.

de Tocqueville, Alexis. 1899. *Democracy in America. Part 1.* New York: D. Appleton. Original work published 1838.

deLeon, Peter. 1992. "The Democratization of the Policy Sciences." *Public Administration Review.* Vol. 52, No. 2. Pp. 125–129.

Dillman, Donald A. 1978. *Mail and Telephone Surveys: The Total Design Method.* New York: Wiley.

Downs, Anthony. 1957. *An Economic Theory of Democracy.* New York: Harper and Row.

Farnham, Paul G. 1990. "Impact of Citizen Influence on Local Government Expenditures." *Public Choice.* Vol. 64, No. 3. Pp. 201–212.

Ferejohn, John A.; and James H. Kuklinski. 1990. *Information* and *Democratic Processes.* Chicago: University Of Illinois Press.

Fisher, Glenn W. 1961. "Determinants of State and Local Government Expenditures: A Preliminary Analysis." *National Tax Journal.* Vol. 14. December. Pp. 349–355.

_____. 1964. "Interstate Variation in State and Local Expenditures." *National Tax Journal.* Vol. 17. March. Pp. 55–74.

Flannigan, William H.; and Nancy H. Zingale. 1991. *Political Behavior of the American Electorate.* Washington, DC: Congressional Quarterly Press.

Follett, Mary Parker. 1924. *The Creative Experience.* New York: Longmans, Green and Co.

Fowler, Floyd J., Jr. 1974. *Citizen Attitudes Toward Local Government, Services, and Taxes.* Cambridge, MA: Ballinger.

Gabler, L. R. 1971. "Population Size As a Determinant of City Expenditures and Employment—Some Further Evidence." *Land Economics.* Vol. 47, No. 2. May. Pp. 130–138.

Glaser, Mark A.; and W. Bartley Hildreth. 1996. "A Profile of Discontinuity Between Citizen Demand and Willingness to Pay Taxes: Comprehensive Planning for Park and Recreation Investment." *Public Budgeting and Finance.* Vol. 16, No. 4. Pp. 96–124.

Glass, David; Peveril Squire; and Raymond Wolfinger. 1983–1984. "Voter Turnout: An International Comparison." *Public Opinion.* December-January. Pp. 49–51.

Goodnow, Frank J. 1900. *Politics and Administration.* New York: Russell and Russell.

Gore, Al. 1992. *From Red Tape to Results: Creating A Government That Works Better & Costs Less: Report of the National Performance Review.* Washington, DC: Government Printing Office.

Gormley, William T., Jr., ed. 1991. *Privatization and Its Alternatives.* Madison: University of Wisconsin Press.

Gramlich, Edward M.; Daniel L. Rubinfeld; and Deborah Swift. 1980. "Why Voters Turn Out for Tax Limitation Votes." *National Tax Journal.* Vol. 34, No. 1. Pp. 115–122.

Greenstone, David J.; and Paul E. Peterson. 1973. *Race and Authority in Urban Politics.* New York: Russell Sage Foundation.

Greider, William. 1992. *Who Will Tell the People? The Betrayal of American Democracy.* New York: Simon and Schuster.

Hallman, Howard. W. 1992. "Citizen Roles in City Budget Making: Experience of Three Cities. *National Civic Review.* Vol. 81 (Supplement). Pp. 1–8.

Hamilton, Alexander; James Madison; and John Jay. 1982. *The Federalist Papers (1787–1788).* New York: Bantam Books.

Hatry, Harry P.; and Louis H. Blair. 1976. "Citizen Surveys for Local Govern-
ments: A Cop-Out, Manipulative Tool, or a Policy Guidance and Analysis
Aid?" In Terry Nichols Clark, ed., *Citizen Preferences and Urban Public Policy.*
Beverly Hills, CA: Sage. Pp. 129–142.

Herring, Pendelton. 1936. *Public Administration and the Public Interest.* New York:
McGraw-Hill.

Hinckley, Ronald H. 1992. *American Public Opinion* and *National Security.* New
York: Lexington Books.

Hirsch, Werner. 1970. *The Economics of State and Local Government.* New York:
McGraw-Hill.

_____. 1973. *Urban Economic Analysis.* New York: McGraw-Hill.

Holcombe, Randall G. 1985. *An Economic Analysis of Democracy.* Carbondale:
Southern Illinois University Press.

_____. 1996. *Public Finance: Government Revenues and Expenditures in the United
States Economy.* Minneapolis/St. Paul, MN: West.

Holmes, Thomas P. 1990. "Self-Interest, Altruism, and Health Risk Reduction:
An Economic Analysis Of Voting Behavior." *Land Economics.* Vol. 66, No. 2.
Pp. 140–149.

Hyman, David N. 1993. *Public Finance: A Contemporary Application of Theory to Policy.* Fort Worth, TX: Dryden Press.

Jackson, Andrew. 1837. *Messages of General Andrew Jackson: With a Short Sketch of
His Life.* Concord, NH: J. F. Brown and W. White.

Jefferson, Thomas. 1984. *Writings (1774–1826).* New York: Literary Classics.

Jefferson Center. 1993. *America's Tough Choices Citizens Jury: Report on Federal Budget Panel with Appendices.* Minneapolis, MN: Jefferson Center.

Kahneman, Daniel; and Amos Tversky. 1982. "The Psychology of Preferences."
Scientific American. No. 246. Pp. 160–173.

Kalt, Joseph P.; and Zupan, Mark A. 1984. "Capture and Ideology in the Economic
Theory of Politics." *The American Economic Review.* Vol. 74. June. Pp. 279–300.

Kathlene, Lyn; and John A. Martin. 1991. "Enhancing Citizen Participation: Panel
Designs, Perspectives, and Policy Formulation." *Journal Of Policy Analysis and
Management.* Vol. 10, No 1. Pp. 45–63.

Kay, Alan; Frederick T. Steeper; Hazel Henderson; Celinda Lake; and David J.
Hansen. 1992. *What the American People Want in the Federal Budget.* Washington,
DC: Americans Talk Issues Foundation.

Kelman, Steven. 1987. "Public Choice and Public Spirit." *The Public Interest.*
Spring. Pp. 80–94.

Kettl, Donald. 1993. *Sharing Power: Public Governance and Private Markets.* Washington, DC: Brookings Institution.

Kirkwood, Craig W.; and James L. Cormer. 1993. "The Effectiveness of Partial Information About Attribute Weights for Ranking Alternatives in Multivariate
Decision Making." *Organizational Behavior* and *Human Decision Processes.* Vol.
54, No. 3. P. 456.

King, Desmond S.; and Jon Pierre. 1990. "Introduction." In Desmond S. King and
Jon Pierre, eds., *Challenges to Local Government.* Sage Modern Politics Series,
Vol. 28. London: Sage Publications. Pp. 1–14.

Kopp, Raymond J.; Werner W. Pommerehne; and Norbert Schwarz, eds. 1997. *Determining the Value of Non-Marketed Goods: Economics, Psychological, and Policy Relevant Aspects of Contingent Valuation Methods*. Boston: Kluwer Academic Publishers.

Kweit, Mary Grisez; and Robert W. Kweit. 1981. *Implementing Citizen Participation in a Bureaucratic Society*. New York: Praeger.

Ladd, Helen F. 1990. *Effects of Population Growth on Local Spending and Taxes*. Cambridge, MA: Lincoln Institute of Land Policy.

Ladd, Helen F.; and Julie Boatwright Wilson. 1982. "Why Voters Support Tax Limitations: Evidence from Massachusetts Proposition 2½." *National Tax Journal*. Vol. 35, No. 2. Pp. 121–148.

Ladd, Helen F.; and John Yinger. 1989. *America's Ailing Cities*. Baltimore, MD: Johns Hopkins University Press.

Leblanc, Ron. 1988. "Direction '88: A Community Interaction Process." In *1988 ICMA Awards Program*. Washington, DC: International City and County Managers Association.

Lemov, Penelope. 1991. "The Axe and the Victims." *Governing*. August. Pp. 26–30.

Levine, Charles H. 1980. *Managing Fiscal Stress: The Crisis in the Public Sector*. Chatham, NJ: Chatham House.

Lewis, Alan. 1979. "An Empirical Assessment of Tax Mentality." *Public Finance*. Vol. 34, No. 2. Pp. 245–254.

Lilienthal, David E. 1944. *TVA: Democracy on the March*. New York: Harper and Brothers.

Long, Norton. 1949. "Politics and Administration." *Public Administration Review*. Vol. 9. Autumn. Pp. 257–264.

_____. 1952. "Bureaucracy and Constitutionalism." *American Political Science Review*. Vol. 46. September. Pp. 808–818.

Lowi, Theodore J. 1969. *The End of Liberalism*. New York: Norton.

Lyons, William. 1994. "City of Knoxville, Tennessee: 1994/1995 Budget Survey Results." [Professional report].

Martin, Michael W.; and Jane Sell. 1980. "The Marginal Utility of Information: Its Effects upon Decision Making." *The Sociological Quarterly*. Vol. 21. Pp. 233–242.

Martin, Roscoe C.; Frank Munger; Jesse Burkhead; Guthrie Birkhead; Harold Hemran; Herbert Kagi; Lewis Welch; and Clyde Wingfield. 1965. *Decisions in Syracuse: A Metropolitan Action Study*. Garden City, NY: Anchor Books.

Mazer, Stacy. 1996. "1996 State Tax Initiatives." *NASBO Information Brief*. Vol. 4, No. 2. Chicago: National Association of State Budget Officers.

McIver, John P.; and Elinor Ostrom. 1976. "Using Budget Pies to Reveal Preferences: Validation of a Survey Instrument." In Terry Nichols Clark, ed., *Citizen Preferences and Urban Public Policy*. Beverly Hills, CA: Sage. Pp. 87–110.

McKinney, Michael. 1996. "Helping Citizens Understand Budget Decisions: The City of Fort Worth's Budget Guide and Simulator Diskette." *Government Finance Review*. April. Pp. 17–20.

Melton, Wayne. 1986. "Sparks People Say Protection No. 1 Priority." *Reno Gazette-Journal*. April 16. P. C3.

Meltsner, Arnold J. 1971. *The Politics of City Revenue*. Berkeley: University of California Press.

Merrill, Bruce D. 1995. "Citizen Evaluation of the City of Tempe." Report prepared for the City of Tempe, Arizona. April 5.

Meshenberg, Michael J. 1989. "Influencing Chicago's Budget: Getting Citizens into the Act." [Pamphlet]. Chicago: Center for Economic Policy Analysis. December.

Mikesell, John L. 1991. *Fiscal Administration: Analysis and Applications for the Public Sector*. Pacific Grove, CA: Brooks/Cole.

Miller, Thomas I.; and Michelle A. Miller. 1991. "Standards of Excellence." *Public Administration Review*. Vol. 51, No. 6. Pp. 503–514.

Mitchell, Robert; and Richard Carson. 1989. "Using Surveys to Value Goods." *The Contingent Valuation Method*. Washington, DC: Resources for the Future.

More, Thomas. 1988. *Utopia*. Edited by George M. Logan and Robert M. Adams. Cambridge, UK: Cambridge University Press. Original work published c. 1555.

Morgan, David R.; and William Pammer Jr. 1988. "Coping with Fiscal Stress: Predicting the Use of Financial Management Practices Among U.S. Cities." *Urban Affairs Quarterly*. Vol. 24, No. 1. September. Pp. 69–86.

Morgan, Douglas; Kelly G. Bacon; Ron Bunch; Charles D. Cameron; and Robert Deis. 1996. "What Middle Managers Do in Local Government: Stewardship of the Public Trust and the Limits of Reinventing Government." *Public Administration Review*. Vol. 56, No. 4. Pp. 359–366.

Mosher, Frederick C. 1974. *Watergate: Implications for Responsible Government: A Special Report at the Request of the Senate Select Committee on Presidential Campaign Activities*. New York: Basic Books. Also in Jay M. Shafritz and Albert C. Hyde, eds. 1992. *Classics of Public Administration*. Belmont, CA: Wadsworth. Pp. 411–418.

_____. 1982. *Democracy and the Public Service*. New York: Oxford University Press.

Mueller, Dennis C. 1979. *Public Choice*. Cambridge, UK: Cambridge University Press.

Mullins, Daniel R.; and Mark S. Rosentraub. 1992. "Fiscal Pressure? The Impact of Elder Recruitment on Local Expenditures." *Urban Affairs Quarterly*. Vol. 28, No. 2. Pp. 337–354.

National Civic League. 1994a. "Chattanooga, Tennessee." [Online] http://www.csn.net/ncl/tn1.html

_____. 1994b. "Fort Collins, Colorado." [Online] http://www.csn.net/ncl/col.html

Neijens, Peter; Jan A. Deridder; and Willem E. Saris. 1992. "An Instrument for Collecting Informed Opinions." *Quality and Quantity*. Vol. 26, No. 3, Pp. 245–258.

Nelson, Michael. 1982. "A Short Ironic History of American National Bureaucracy." *Journal of Politics*. Vol. 44. Pp. 746–777.

Niemi, Richard G. 1984. *Controversies in Voting Behavior*. Washington, DC: Congressional Quarterly Press.

Oregon Department of Revenue. 1990. *The Basic Budget Book*. Salem: Finance and Taxation Unit, Local Government Section, Department of Revenue, State of Oregon.

Osborne, David; and Ted Gaebler. 1992. *Reinventing Government: How the Entrepreneurial Spirit Is Transforming the Public Sector*. Reading, MA: Addison-Wesley.

Ostrom, Vincent. 1989. *The Intellectual Crisis of Public Administration.* Tuscaloosa: University Of Alabama Press.

O'Sullivan, Arthur. 1996. *Urban Economics.* 3rd ed. Chicago: Irwin.

Pack, Janet Rothenberg. 1991. "The Opportunities and Constraints of Privatization." In William T. Gormley, Jr., ed., *Privatization and Its Alternatives.* Madison: University of Wisconsin Press. Pp. 281–306

Perkins, G. M. 1977. "The Demand for Local Public Goods: Elasticities of Demand for Own Prices, Cross Prices, and Income." *National Tax Journal.* Vol. 30. December. Pp. 411–419.

Peters, B. Guy; and Donald J. Savoie. 1996. "Managing Incoherence: The Coordination and Empowerment Conundrum." *Public Administration Review.* Vol. 56, No. 3. Pp. 281–289.

Pierre, Jon. 1995. "The Marketization of the State: Citizens, Consumers, and the Emergence of the Public Market." In B. G. Peters and D. J. Savoie, eds., *Governance in a Changing Environment.* Montreal: McGill-Queen's University Press. Pp. 55–81.

Piven, Frances Fox; and Richard A. Cloward. 1988. *Why Americans Don't Vote.* New York: Pantheon Books.

Plous, S. 1993. "The Effects of Question Wording and Framing." In *The Psychology of Judgement and Decision Making.* New York: McGraw-Hill. Pp. 64–76.

Portal, Ann. 1987. "Springfield Seeks Residents' Wishes." [Eugene, OR] *Register-Guard.* July 30. P. B1.

Preston, Samuel H. 1984. "Children and the Elderly: Divergent Paths for America's Dependents." *Demography.* Vol. 21. Pp. 435–457.

Public Agenda. 1995. "Public Agenda."[Brochure]. New York: Author.

Raimondo, Henry J. 1992. *Economics of State and Local Government.* New York: Praeger.

Redford, Emmette Shelburn. 1969. *Democracy in the Administrative State.* New York: Oxford University Press.

Reese, Thomas J. 1978. "The Thoughts of Chairman Long, Part 1: The Politics of Taxation." *Tax Notes.* Vol. 6. February 27. P. 199.

Register Guard [Eugene, OR]. 1993. "Did 'Decisions' Predict?" [Editorial]. April 3. P. A10.

Reich, Robert. 1992. *The Work of Nations: Preparing Ourselves for 21st Century Capitalism.* New York: Vintage Books.

Renn, Ortwin; Tomas Webler; Horst Rakel; Peter Dienel; and Branden Johnson. 1993. "Public Participation in Decision Making: A Three Step Procedure." *Policy Sciences.* Vol. 26. Pp. 189–214.

Ritzdorf, Marsha; and William Simonsen. 1994. "Socio-Demographic Characteristics and Preferences for User Fees Versus Taxes." Paper presented at the Urban Affairs Association Annual Conference, New Orleans, March 2–5.

Rohr, John A. 1986. *To Run a Constitution: The Legitimacy of the Administrative State.* Lawrence: University of Kansas Press.

Rose, Douglas D. 1988. "Citizen Participation in Public Decision Making." *American Political Science Review.* Vol. 82, No. 2. P. 630.

Rosen, Harvey. 1992. *Public Finance.* Boston, MA: Irwin.

Rousseau, Jean-Jacques. 1987. *Basic Political Writings*. Edited by Donald A. Cress. Indianapolis, IN: Hackett.

Rundquist, Barry; Sharon Fox; and Gerald Strom. 1995. "The Illinois Voter Project: An Experiment in Using Issue Information to Increase Citizen Participation in the 1994 Illinois Gubernatorial Election." Paper presented at the Annual Meeting of the American Political Science Association, Chicago, August 31–September 2.

Savas, E. S. 1987. *Privatization: The Key to Better Government*. Chatham, NJ: Chatham House.

Scavo, Carmine. 1993. "The Use of Participative Mechanisms by Large U.S. Cities." *Journal of Urban Affairs*. Vol. 15, No. 1. Pp.93–109.

Schacter, Hindy Lauer. 1995. "Reinventing Government or Reinventing Ourselves: Two Models for Improving Government Performance." *Public Administration Review*. Vol. 55, No. 6. Pp. 530–537.

Selznick, Philip. 1949. *TVA and the Grass Roots*. Berkeley: University of California Press.

Simonsen, William. 1994a. "Aging Population and City Spending." *Journal of Urban Affairs*. Vol. 16, No. 7. Pp. 125–140.

_____. 1994b. "Changes in Federal Aid and City Finances: A Case Study of Oregon Cities." *Publius: The Journal Of Federalism*. Vol. 24, No. 2. Pp. 37–51.

_____. 1994c. "Citizen Preferences and Budget Policy." Proceedings of the Joint Urban Affairs Association, University of Bristol and University of Wales Seminar, "Shaping the Urban Future: International Perspectives and Exchanges," Bristol, July 11–13.

Simonsen, William; Nancy Johnston; and Russell Barnett. 1996. "Attempting Non-Incremental Budget Change in Oregon: An Exercise in Policy Sharing." *American Review of Public Administration* Vol. 26, No. 2. June. Pp. 231–250.

Simonsen, William, and Mark D. Robbins. Forthcoming. "The Benefit Equity Principle and Willingness to Pay for City Services." *Public Budgeting and Finance*.

_____. Forthcoming. "The Influence of Fiscal Information on Preferences for City Services." *Social Science Journal*.

Smith, Vernon. 1980. "Experiments with a Decentralized Mechanism for Public Good Decisions." *American Economic Review*. Vol. 70. September. Pp. 584–599.

Sniderman, S.; M. Brody; and P. Tetlock. 1991. *Reasoning and Choice: Explorations in Political Psychology*. New York: Cambridge University Press.

Society of Friends. 1999. "Meetings for Business." [Online] ftp://ftp.clark.net/pub/quaker/business.txt

South, Scott J. 1991. "Age-Structure and Public Expenditures on Children." *Social Science Quarterly*. Vol. 72, No. 4. Pp. 661–675.

Starr, Paul. 1991. "The Case for Skepticism." In William T. Gormley Jr., ed., *Privatization and Its Alternatives*. Madison: University of Wisconsin Press. Pp. 25–38.

Statistical Abstract of the United States. various years. Washington, DC: U.S. Bureau of the Census.

Stiefel, Leanna. 1990. *Statistical Analysis for Public and Nonprofit Managers*. Westport, CT: Praeger.

Strange, John H. 1972. "The Impact of Citizen Participation on Public Administration." *Public Administration Review*. Vol. 32 (Special Edition). September.

Pp. 457–170 as reprinted. Also in Joseph A. Uveges Jr., ed. 1975. *The Dimensions of Public Administration*. Boston, MA: Holbrook Press. Pp. 554–579.

Swan, James H.; Carroll L. Estes; and Juanita B. Wood. 1983. "Fiscal Crisis: Economic and Fiscal Problems of State and Local Governments." In Carroll L. Estes, Robert Newcomer, and Associates, eds., *Fiscal Austerity and Aging*. Beverly Hills, CA: Sage. Pp. 113–132.

Thomas, John Clayton. 1995. *Public Participation in Public Decisions*. San Francisco: Jossey-Bass.

Topf, Richard. 1989. "Political Change and Political Culture in Britain." In John Gibbin, ed., *Contemporary Political Culture: Politics in a Postmodern Age*. Sage Modern Politics Series, vol. 23. London: Sage Publications. Pp. 52–80.

Tulloss, Janice K. 1995. "Citizen Participation in Boston's Development Policy: The Political Economy of Participation." *Urban Affairs Review*. Vol. 30. March. Pp. 514–553.

Tversky, Amos; and Daniel Kahneman 1974. "Judgement Under Uncertainty: Heuristics and Biases." *Science*. Vol. 185. Pp. 1124–1131.

U.S. Advisory Commission on Intergovernmental Relations. 1992. *Changing Public Attitudes on Government and Taxes*. Washington, DC: Author.

U.S. Bureau of the Census. 1990. *Social and Economic Characteristics: Oregon*. 1990 CP–2–39. Washington, DC: U.S. Government Printing Office.

U.S. Bureau of the Census. 1992. *Money Income of Households, Families, and Persons in The United States*. Washington, DC: U.S. Government Printing Office.

Van Valey, Thomas L.; and James C. Petersen. 1987. "Public Service Science Centers: The Michigan Experience." In Jack Desario and Stuart Langton, eds., *Citizen Participation in Public Decision Making*. Westport, CT: Greenwood Press. Pp. 39–64.

Vanhoose, Linda. 1993. "Speak Out Again." *Lexington* [Kentucky] *Herald-Leader*. February 3. P. 1.

Vernez, Georges. 1976. *Delivery of Urban Public Services: Production, Cost, and Demand Functions, and Determinants of Public Expenditure for Fire, Police, and Sanitation Services*. Santa Monica, CA: RAND Corporation.

Vroom, V. H.; and R. Yetton, 1993. *Leadership and Decision Making*. Pittsburgh: University of Pittsburgh Press.

Wallsten, Thomas S., ed. 1980. *Cognitive Processes in Choice and Decision Behavior*. Hillsdale, NJ: Lawrence Erlbaum Associates.

Walters, Laurel Shapers. 1993. "Factions Impede School Reform." *Christian Science Monitor*. July 26. P. 13.

Wamsley, Gary L.; Robert N. Bacher; Charles T. Goodsell; Philip S. Kronenberg; John A. Rohr; Camilla M. Stivers; Orion F. White; and James F. Wolf. 1990. *Refounding Public Administration*. Newbury Park, CA: Sage.

Watson, Douglas; Robert Juster; and Gerald Johnson. 1991. "Institutionalized Use of Citizen Surveys in Budgetary and Policy Making Processes: A Small City Case Study. *Public Administration Review*. Vol. 51. Pp. 232–239.

Weeks, Edward C. 1995. "Deliberative Democracy Project." [Online] http://utopia.uoregon.edu/www/research/ddp.html

Weeks, Edward C.; Kaye Robinette; and Shawn Boles. 1993. Citizens Smart Enough to Make Tough Choices." [Eugene, OR] *Register-Guard*. April 12. P. A9.

Weeks, Edward C.; and William Simonsen. 1992. *Eugene Decisions: Results of Citizen Input*. Eugene, OR: City of Eugene. January.

Weeks, Edward C.; and Susan Weeks. 1992. *Eugene Decisions: Results of Citizen Input*. Eugene, OR: City of Eugene. July.

Weicher, John C. 1970. "Determinants of Central City Expenditures: Some Overlooked Factors and Problems." *National Tax Journal*. Vol. 23, No. 4. Pp. 379–396.

Welch, Susan. 1985. "The 'More for Less' Paradox: Public Attitudes on Taxing and Spending." *Public Opinion Quarterly*. Vol. 49. Pp. 310–316.

White, Leonard D. 1948. *The Federalists*. New York. Macmillan.

_____. 1956. *The Jacksonians: A Study in Administrative History 1829–1861*. New York: Macmillan..

Wildavsky, Aaron. 1988. *The New Politics of the Budgetary Process*. Glenview, IL: Scott, Foresman.

Wilson, L. A. 1983. "Preference Revelation and Public Policy: Making Sense of Citizen Survey Data." *Public Administration Review*. Vol. 43, No. 4. Pp. 335–343.

Wilson, Woodrow. 1887. "The Study of Administration." *Political Science Quarterly*. Vol. 2. July. Pp. 197–222.

Winter, Soren; and Poul Erik Mouritzen. 1997. "Why People Want Something for Nothing: The Role of Asymmetrical Illusions." [Working paper].

Wolfinger, Raymond E.; and Steven J. Rosenstone. 1980. *Who Votes?* New Haven, CT: Yale University Press.

Wright, Jeff. 1993a. "City Manager Credits Eugene Decisions." [Eugene, OR] *Register-Guard*. October 12. P. B1.

_____. 1993b. "Did Flaws in Eugene Decisions Scuttle Tax?" [Eugene, OR] *Register-Guard*. March 28. P. B1.

_____. 1993c. "Eugene Leaders Ask: What Now?" [Eugene, OR] *Register-Guard*. March 25. P. A1.

Yankelovich, Daniel. 1992. *Coming to Public Judgment: Making Democracy Work in a Complex World*. Syracuse, NY: Syracuse University Press.

Yankelovich, Daniel; and Sidney Harman. 1983. *Starting with the People*. Boston: Houghton Mifflin.

Yantis, John. 1995. "Residents Give City High Marks." *Tempe* [Arizona] *Community News*. April 13. P. 1.

Yinger, John. 1990. "States to the Rescue? Aid to Central Cities Under the New Federalism." *Public Budgeting and Finance*. Summer. Pp. 27–44.

Zaller, John R. 1992. *The Nature and Origins of Mass Opinion*. New York: Cambridge University Press.

Zax, Jeffrey S. 1989. "Initiatives and Government Expenditures." *Public Choice*. Vol. 63, No. 3. Pp. 267–277.

Index

When we began conversations about this text, we decided we would stray from the stiff, formal, academic format that is so often used. We favored a style of writing—and approach—we believe is more friendly, down-to-earth, fun, conversational and informal. This is in an effort to enhance learning.

Part of our attempt to portray a relaxed communication style is by placing bylines at the beginning of every chapter, and including short biographies and photos of the authors at the end of this preface. We encourage you to spend a few minutes reviewing that information in an attempt to get a better sense of our backgrounds.

As you begin reading *Reporting That Matters: Public Affairs Coverage*, don't be afraid of the term *public affairs reporting*—or the generally advanced nature of texts on public affairs reporting.

In its simplest form, reporting of public affairs is nothing more than informing the public of information that people need, information that comes primarily from public agencies or entities. It is about issues that concern people.

Obtaining information, however, isn't always easy. While the public's business certainly should be conducted in public, too many officials are less than forthcoming with information people need and want to know—and have a right to know.

This text is not remedial in nature, so begin by remembering some of the basic and key building blocks to good reporting and writing:

- **Use simple sentences**, usually with only one thought.
- **In most cases**, don't switch tenses. Find the best one to tell the story and stay with it.
- **Active voice is** always better than passive voice.
- **Avoid the safe** but formatted writing style of transition . . . quote . . . transition . . . quote . . . transition . . . quote. This is not good writing. It is the only transcription of linked thoughts.
- **Tell a story**, but don't force it. Let the story tell itself. Don't overwrite.
- **Use precision in writing**; the correct word for the correct usage. Avoid jargon and complicated words.
- **Use a dictionary**, thesaurus and stylebook.
- **Keep yourself out** of the story (avoid the use of *I*, *we*, and *us* except in first person stories, which should be rare and reserved for columns and other commentary pieces).

Reporting of public affairs isn't easy. But those who do it well make a difference in the world. Remember the words of Peter Bhatia, executive editor of the *Oregonian* and a former president of the American Society of Newspaper Editors (ASNE), spoken to the South Asian Journalists Association (SAJA) in 1999:

I don't want to sound like an old man but I find that the current generation is not prepared to work hard. As baby boomers it was beaten into us that you can't expect things handed to you. You've got to have your own initiative and the willingness to go that extra mile.

It's important to be focused on becoming the best journalist and create your own opportunities. Combine that with hard work and this is an industry where you can succeed.

Do work hard but also make sure that you work harder than others. Seek out people who can teach you and help you achieve your goals; look for opportunities to increase your skills.

Acknowledgments

Journalism has been a major component of the lives of the authors of this textbook. We acknowledge the professionals who provided tips and samples of their work for this text. We are grateful to the many journalism organizations and groups for their existence and the availability of the material that has been collected and presented. We also acknowledge our students and professional and academic colleagues and bosses; Allyn & Bacon for this opportunity, specifically Molly Taylor, Michael Kish, Karen Mason and Suzanne Stradley for their patience and their low-key encouragement as this project moved forward; Pat McCutcheon of WestWords, Inc., for his detail and thoroughness during the production process; and Cheryl Adam, an exceptional copyeditor.

John Irby also acknowledges his wife, Lisa, and children for their support and love, and Dr. Alex Tan, director of the Edward R. Murrow School of Communication at Washington State University, for his continuing support and encouragement.

Kenton Bird thanks Ted Stanton, formerly of the Moscow *Idahonian*; Colorado State University Professor Emeritus Garrett W. Ray; Ken Olsen, a reporter for the Vancouver (Washington) *Columbian*; Vicki Rishling, lecturer in the University of Idaho School of Journalism and Mass Media; and his wife, Gerri Sayler, for her patience and understanding why the dining room table was always covered with clippings and notes.

Susan English acknowledges Karen Dorn Steele, a veteran journalist at the *Spokesman-Review*, for inspiring her through hard work and perseverance and for writing important stories and unknowingly inspiring many journalists to pay attention to public affairs.

We would like to acknowledge the valuable contributions that the reviewers to this text made. The reviewers were Glen L. Bleske, California State University, Chico; Steven E. Chappell, Truman State University; Bradley J. Hamm, Elon University; Robert D. Highton, University of Nevada; Ann L. Landini, Murray State University; Edward G. Weston, University of Florida; and Sheila M. Whitley, North Carolina A&T State University.

Experts Who Supplied Professional Tips

- Chapter 1: Mark Briggs, content and strategy manager for interactive media, *News Tribune*, Tacoma, WA
- Chapter 2: Patrick Webb, managing editor, *The Daily Astorian*, Astoria, OR
- Chapter 3: Brye Butler, reporter, *Abilene Reporter News*, Abilene, TX
- Chapter 4: Bill Bell, editor-publisher, *Whittier Daily News*, Whittier, CA
- Chapter 5: Ken Olsen, freelance magazine writer, Spokane, WA
- Chapter 6: Steve McClure, managing editor, the *Daily News*, Moscow, ID
- Chapter 7: Christopher Smith, Associated Press correspondent, Boise, ID

- Chapter 8: Bill Morlin, investigative reporter, the *Spokesman-Review*,
- Chapter 9: Bryan Gruley, Chicago Bureau chief, *Wall Street Journal*, C
- Chapter 10: Julie Sullivan, investigative reporter, the *Oregonian*, Portla
- Chapter 11: Hannelore Sudermann, assistant editor and senior writer *State Magazine*, Pullman, WA, and Colleen McBrinn, assistant features *tle Times*, Seattle, WA
- Chapter 12: Jim Borden, managing editor, the *Gazette*, Kalamazoo, MI
- Chapter 13: Vicki Rothrock, freelance correspondent, Hong Kong
- Chapter 14: Neil Modie, reporter, the *Seattle Post-Intelligencer*, Seattle,
- Chapter 15: Priscilla Salant, manager of rural policy and assessments, of Agriculture, Economics and Rural Sociology, University of Idaho, M and Dan Popkey, columnist, the *Idaho Statesman*, Boise, ID
- Chapter 16: Maxine Bernstein, reporter, the *Oregonian*, Portland, OR
- Chapter 17: Sheila R. McCann, co-editor of Social Justice Team, the *Sa bune*, Salt Lake City, UT
- Chapter 18: Hannelore Sudermann, assistant editor and senior writer, *State Magazine*, Pullman, WA
- Chapter 19: Dave Boling, sports columnist, *News Tribune*, Tacoma, WA Kershner, columnist and theater critic, the *Spokesman-Review*, Spokane, W
- Chapter 20: Anna King, reporter, *Tri-City Herald*, Kennewick, WA
- Chapter 21: Brent Champaco, reporter, *News Tribune*, Tacoma, WA
- Appendix A: Ralph Pomnichowski, freelance writer-photographer, Great
- Appendix B: James P. Medina, business editor, *Ventura County Star*, Ventu

ABOUT THE AUTHORS

John Irby

John is an associate professor and associate director of undergraduate studies in the Edward R. Murrow School of Communication at Washington State University in Pullman, Washington. For four years he also served as journalism degree program coordinator. The main courses he teaches are news writing and reporting, news editing and public affairs reporting.

He joined the WSU journalism faculty in the fall of 1999 after more than twenty-five years of experience in newspapers. John began his career in community journalism as a reporter and photographer at a 4,000-circulation weekly in southern California, and later worked as an editor at the 450,000-circulation *San Francisco Chronicle*. He has also held the publisher's job at small and medium-sized daily newspapers and was editor-in-chief of two newspaper groups with more than 100,000 circulation.

John and his wife, Lisa, development strategy manager for the College of Business and Economics at WSU, have four sons: Derren, 20; Dustin, 16; Noah, 9; and Hank Aaron, 7. Personal interests include writing, family, religion, the Internet, reading, films, art, music, sports and travel. He is a member by blood of the Choctaw Tribe and Nation of Oklahoma.

Kenton Bird

Kenton is an associate professor and director of the University of Idaho's School of Journalism and Mass Media.

He holds a bachelor's degree in journalism from UI, where he was editor of the student newspaper, the *Argonaut*. He attended University College, Cardiff, Wales, on a Rotary fellowship, earning a master's degree in journalism history; and Washington State University, earning a Ph.D. in American studies. During his 15-year career as a reporter and editor, he worked for newspapers in Moscow, Lewiston, Sandpoint and Kellogg, Idaho, and spent a summer at the *Washington Post*. In 1989, he was chosen as a congressional fellow of the American Political Science Association, working as a congressional staff member in Washington, D.C. While in graduate school, he taught part-time at WSU and UI.

In 2002, Kenton was one of three UI faculty members chosen to be a humanities fellow of the College of Letters, Arts & Social Sciences.

Kenton lives in Moscow, Idaho, with his wife, Gerri Sayler, an artist and former journalist.

Susan English

Susan is an assistant professor of journalism at Gonzaga University, where she teaches media ethics, journalism history, literary journalism and writing and reporting courses.

She has taught courses at the University of Idaho, Whitworth College and Eastern Washington University, including public affairs reporting, cultural diversity and the media, magazine writing and media law. She has also been on the faculty for ethics workshops at the Poynter Institute.

Susan earned her bachelor of arts degree in communications at Washington State University and her master's degree from Gonzaga. She did her graduate work in media ethics.

Prior to joining the faculty at Gonzaga, she was a writer and editor at daily newspapers for twenty-six years. In addition, she has written for a number of magazines; co-authored *Inside Out Northern Rockies: A Best Place Guide to the Outdoors,* published by Sasquatch Publishing; and contributed to a number of other guidebooks published by Random House and Sasquatch Publishing.

David Cuillier

David has worked for a dozen years as a public affairs reporter and city editor at daily newspapers in the Pacific Northwest, including Vancouver, Washington; Boise, Idaho; Kennewick, Washington; and Everett, Washington. He began teaching public affairs reporting and computer-assisted reporting at the University of Arizona in fall 2006 after completing his doctorate at Washington State University and teaching part-time at the University of Idaho.

Cuillier is a research assistant for AccessNorthwest at Washington State, where he studies citizen and press access to public records. Some of his research has included assessing public attitudes toward press access to public records, an examination of online access to court documents and an analysis of more than forty access audits conducted in the United States since 1995.

He received his bachelor's degree in journalism from Western Washington University in 1990, and his master's degree in communications from WSU 2003.

He lives in Tucson, Arizona, with his family.

1 The Changing World of Journalism

BY JOHN IRBY

From the beginning, a caterpillar is constantly changing until it becomes a butterfly. Journalism also is constantly changing with rapid technological advancements. Convergence is a common subject and consideration as the industry continues to change in ways hardly imagined.

Years ago, writer Stanley Walker wrote a tongue-in-cheek characterization of a stereotypical journalist for the 1930s, which was popularized by the movie *The Front Page.*

The movie plot finds a ruthless managing editor of a Chicago newspaper angry because his ace reporter plans to leave the paper to get married. While he trains a replacement, it gets a bit hectic as a convicted killer escapes from a bumbling sheriff.

Walker's characterization was published in a portfolio titled "Aids in Newspaper Writing," which was distributed in college journalism classes. Here's what he wrote:

What makes a good newspaperman? The answer is easy. He knows everything. He is aware not only of what goes on in the world today, but his brain is a repository of the accumulated wisdom of the ages.

Moreover, he is somewhat psychic, and is able to sense what the news will be tomorrow, and next month, and even next year. He writes prose that is crisp but graceful. He can perform any job in journalism. He is not only handsome, but he has physical stamina, which enables him to perform great feats of energy.

He can go for nights on end without sleep. He dresses well and talks with charm. Men admire him; women adore him; tycoons and statesmen are happy to share their secrets with him. He takes a drink, but never gets drunk. He is good to his family, if any.

He hates lies and meanness and shams, but keeps his temper. He is loyal to his paper and to what he looks upon as his profession; whether it is a profession, or merely a craft, he resents attempts to debase it. When he dies, a lot of people are sorry, and some remember him for several days.

He leaves little money, but he had a pretty good time.

It obviously was a different era. Journalists and newspaper reporters used to be well respected. Today, unfortunately, although most are very professional, reporters and editors are sometimes compared, in terms of credibility, to used-car salesmen.

That's partly their fault, and partly society's fault.

Nonetheless, newspaper daily circulation has been declining for years. In 1987, daily newspaper circulation reached an all-time high of 62.8 million, but it fell to 54.6 million at the beginning of 2005.

The number of newspapers has also shown a decline from 1940, when there were 1,878 daily newspapers in the United States, to 1,457 as 2005 began.

The U.S. population, however, has grown dramatically. In 1970 the population estimate was 203 million, and in July 2004 it was 293 million.

For years newspaper executives have debated the reasons for this decline, and one thing they have generally been able to agree on is that the strongest circulation support comes from older readers. For instance, 72 percent of those 65 or older read a daily newspaper, but only 24 percent of 18- to 24-year-olds read daily.

If that isn't scary enough, it is frightening to think that older readers are a finite market and that newspapers continue to see readership decline among the young. Much has been said, and some things have been done, to cultivate youthful readers. Still, the decline continues in a free-fall spiral.

With such trends, the future is clouded for a mature industry that has for many of those declining years been resistant to readership change, partly because of profit increases despite fewer readers.

Attracting a new generation of readers might be the only salvation for the once great and now last mass medium. One thing is clear. Change has jerked the industry along, sometimes kicking and screaming, for the past several years. Significant efforts have taken place in areas such as civic journalism, participant observation, interactivity and convergence.

Generation Y

Chris Rock, NSYNC, Kobe Bryant, Shaggy, P. Diddy and Jennifer Lopez all have at least one thing in common. They became Generation Y icons. Musicians, actors, athletes and celebrities are recognizable to a high percentage of society, but even more so to Generation Y, the 11- to 29-year-old sons and daughters of Baby Boomers or Gen X'ers.

Media focused on Generation Y treat content much differently than traditional newspaper companies. Areas of information concentration include a daily dose of irreverent reporting, access to things like a date channel, auctions, classifieds, music and videos, sports, concert schedules, quizzes, horoscopes and celebrity and artist spotlights.

Many boys, girls and young adults claim that newspapers don't know much about them—and that newspapers might not understand the importance of Generation Y to the future of print media.

"The next generation of Americans is wired, worldly and wondering if the news their parents read isn't a bit like an Oldsmobile, a vehicle for an earlier generation," said Chris Peck, editor of the *Memphis Commercial Appeal.* "Their music is different, their cultural icons are different, their values are different from the Generation X and Baby Boomers before them."

Generation Y's attractiveness is linked not only to their high number of members but also to their interest in news and fondness of reading. This is a generation that makes marketers salivate, and reporters and editors must learn to be sensitive to the role it will play in the changing world of journalism.

Generation Y, also known as Echo Boomers and Millennial Kids, is a huge target audience. Classified as those born between 1977 and 1995, nearly 79 million of them will be targeted as newspaper readers when they are between the ages of 25 and 43 in the year 2020 (32 percent of the population).

Some quick facts:

- **They have significant** buying power; they spend about $245 billion a year.
- **They are a** visual generation, aren't afraid of work, but would prefer to play.
- **They seek quick** gratification, and see technology as a tool.
- **They live for** today. Before September 11 and the resulting terrorist and war actions, they never lived through periods of risk, failure or economic depression.
- **Their attitude is** to "spend now and pay later." The prevailing belief is that the good times will never end.
- **They enjoy video** games—and their choice of medium is the World Wide Web.
- **They value individuality** and self-expression.
- **They are the** most ethnically diverse generation ever in the United States.
- **They are environmentally** conscious, and family and community are important to them.
- **They are not** as brand conscious or loyal to brands as past generations.

Gen Y likes humor, irony and the truth. They believe education is cool and integrity is admirable, and their parents are their role models. They're blunt, savvy and contradictory.

Gen Y likes to have fun. They are unpretentious and they exude attitude. But what often makes sense to them is Greek to older, and by traditional standards wiser, newspaper editors.

Marketers have suggested that businesses should capitalize on Gen Y's unique characteristics by accepting and emphasizing their strengths and by facing their weaknesses by poking good-humored fun at them.

That might be a mantra that reporters, editors and newspapers should adopt in certain areas of coverage.

J. Walker Smith, a managing partner at Yankelovich Partners, which specializes in generational marketing, said: "'Most marketers perceive them as kids. When you do that, you fail to take in what they are telling you about the consumers they're becoming. This is not about teenage marketing. It's about the coming of age of a generation."

A study of Gen Y students and their media habits and content interests took place at Washington State University in 2001–2002. Student responses were interesting, but not always surprising.

"Whatever affects me" was the number 1 response to the question of what the generation considers news and information. Readers have for years said they wanted news and information of interest. The difficulty comes in determining what that is. Local news, sports and entertainment news were mentioned most often as news of interest.

Television, as expected, was the leading outlet for news, with newspapers a close second. The Internet finished third.

When asked what it would take in content and/or delivery modes for Gen Y to be connected to and reliant upon a newspaper for news and information, the number 1 response was credibility.

"Make it more credible/truthful/factual, less biased, have different points of view, different voices, uplifting and positive news."

Time and convenience were also cited, as were readership aids such as a better index, organization, reduced jumps, shorter stories, cleaner ink and larger print.

There were a few surprises in the study, including Gen Y caring deeply about international and world news. Other highly ranked areas of news and information interest included politics and government, economy/business/finance and weather.

The fourth highest choice for obtaining daily news and information was "word-of-mouth," more often than not from "Mom."

When asked about personal values, family and friends were mentioned most often. Education and religion were also mentioned often as values.

Reducing cost was listed as an avenue to help Gen Y be more connected with a newspaper. In other words, the generation can fork over $3 for a double mocha latte, but has a hard time justifying 50 cents for a newspaper.

Gen Y also seems somewhat angry or edgy—or at least painfully honest. When asked what else they'd like the media to know about Generation Y, students responded: "We are not happy with the way things are set up for us in the world, inheriting past generation problems and a culture of violence. . . . We hate surveys. . . . We are told we are losers by the media and we are not. . . . We are easily distracted by booze and sex."

The question still remains, however, how reporters, editors and newspapers can engage the generation and retain those who already have the newspaper habit.

Peck, who took part in the study while at the *Spokesman-Review* in Spokane, Washington, said: "I observed that forces more powerful and pervasive than terrorism are altering the media landscape in places where a free press exists. Demographics and technology are the two most powerful of these. And, unless traditional media respond quickly to changing demographics and new technology, their future is dim."

Peck said Gen Y considers newspapers relics that are too distant, too preachy and not interactive enough. He fears a worst-case scenario in which traditional news outlets die a slow death, smothered by talk show hosts, reality TV and Web blogs.

"The challenge for media with Gen Y," Peck said, "will be to more actively engage this emerging generation in the process of gathering and telling the news. . . . People who are looking for news also have a voice in how the news is covered and how it connects to their lives.

"This concept requires significant changes in the way the media do their work. The most significant, and humbling, of these changes is being willing to open up the newsroom and encourage journalists to involve the public more in the gathering of news."

Should newspapers concentrate all of their efforts on a new generation of readers?

"Not so fast," says Doug Floyd, editorial page editor of the *Spokesman-Review* in Spokane, Washington. "Would we in the newspaper business be wise to identify all of Gen Y's interests and non-interests and make our publications fit that mold? Is that the way to guarantee the next generation's newspaper-reading habits will be properly formed? Not so fast.

"Indeed there are some features that Generation Y members share, and not just their born-to-the-mouse comfort with computers. . . . They are alike in how unalike they are. For all the attention that has been focused on them as a cohort, they may be a generation that defies stereotyping more than any other to date."

Interactive Journalism

It has been suggested that to capture Gen Y's attention, the message has to be brought to where they congregate, whether it's the Internet, a snowboarding tournament, cable TV, a coffee shop or wherever. Content of interest, researchers claim, can be funny or disarmingly direct, or somewhere in the middle. It can be in various formats, including print, or presented in various manners—as long as it is engaging and, oftentimes, interactive.

Civic journalism, which will be discussed in the next section of this chapter, was the beginning of significant interaction between the media and the public. It is being practiced more and more across the country—but it seems to be morphing into a new form of interactive journalism.

Jan Schaffer, director of the Pew Center for Civic Journalism until it closed in 2003, is now director of J-Lab, the University of Maryland's Institute for Interactive Journalism (www.j-lab.com). Its mission reads: "J-Lab is an incubator for innovative news experiments that use new technologies to help people actively engage in critical public issues. Its core mission is to improve public life by transforming journalism for today and re-inventing it for tomorrow."

Schaffer made a futuristic statement about change at a media convergence session in 2002 at the University of South Carolina: "You could think of it this way: Future news might well be less about story telling—the stories we journalists want to write, produce or tell—and more about story making—the stories that our consumers are assembling for themselves via their own process of gathering information, sifting through the onslaught of daily info-bits and participating in learning about things."

The Pew Center for Civic Journalism and J-Lab have been involved across the nation in groundbreaking and interesting work in projects they not only encouraged but also in many cases partnered. Go to www.j-lab.org/ and www.pewcenter.org for more information about the project examples listed below or others that are also described on those Web sites.

In the state of Washington, the *Everett Herald* let residents vote on the town's waterfront development by creating a clickable map with icons that could be dragged to make development decisions at four waterfront sites. Game players submitted their final versions of the map over the Internet, and their votes were tallied for news stories.

Also in Everett, the *Herald* analyzed more than thirty-five thousand crime reports between 2001 and 2002 and presented findings in an interactive map. Users click buttons to get color-coded breakdowns of crime categories, or click on a specific neighborhood to get detailed statistics.

At the *Seattle Times* and on its online site, Seattletimes.com, an online game was created to allow readers to "build" solutions to area transportation problems. It used a calculator format similar to one used a year earlier in an online budget game, to let participants map the future, suggesting what transportation projects are most important and how much they would be willing to pay for them. More than two thousand people filled out the form, suggesting that the public was willing to fund government-proposed projects through gas and car taxes rather than sales tax. The results were considered, and the regional transportation board changed its plans.

In Kansas, the *Topeka Capital-Journal* faced coverage of an unruly city council with an online version of TV's *Survivor.* Those interested could go online and "vote off" council members based on their bad behavior.

In Alaska, journalism students at the University of Alaska–Fairbanks put together a multimedia presentation about how residents feel about the USA PATRIOT Act and the war on terror.

In North Carolina, the *Winston-Salem Journal* used 360-degree photography, clickable maps, videos, quizzes, interactive graphics, timelines and video clips in a multiple-part series that "helped define Winston-Salem's race relations."

Kyle M. Orland wrote the following article for J-Lab: The Institute for Interactive Journalism, after the first Batten Awards for Innovations in Journalism in 2003 in Washington, D.C.

Future News Is Foreshadowed at Batten Awards

WASHINGTON, Sept. 15, 2003—Dan Gillmor sees a day when reporters use suitcase-sized, satellite uplinks to report on leads culled from customized, syndicated feeds. He sees readers using cell phones to take pictures and upload them in public Web logs. He also sees emerging technology creating a new, far more participatory journalism.

(continued)

(continued)

"Journalism . . . has been a lecture. We say here's the news . . . and you buy it or you don't. I'm pretty sure we're turning into something between a conversation and a seminar," said the *San Jose Mercury News* columnist, blogger and news futurist in keynoting the first Batten Awards for Innovations in Journalism.

In a modern newsroom, he said, the conversation should work this way: "We tell you what we know . . . you tell us if you think we're right. We talk about it, and then we move on to keep the thing going and to learn more and tell more and help each other."

Gillmor's remarks capped a morning symposium and awards ceremony, held Sept. 15 at the National Press Club in Washington, D.C., in which finalists showcased various ways they were connecting with news audiences.

"The public has a wealth of information that informs our opinion in the newsroom," said Michael Skoler, director of news at Minnesota Public Radio, a Batten Award runner-up for its "Budget Balancer" exercise. "We then use our editorial judgment to determine what goes back out."

Gillmor agreed: "The readers, by definition, have more facts and nuance at their command collectively than we do individually. That's not threatening, that's a huge opportunity for us."

Gillmor said that opportunity has been built into the Web since its inception: "When Tim Berners-Lee created HTML and the Web, he meant that to be a read-write medium, not just a read-only medium. It became kind of read-only before the tools were there to write on the Web as easily as you could read from it."

The rapid emergence of Weblogs (or "blogs," as they're often called) is helping to make it "the writable Web, not just the readable Web," Gillmor said.

MSNBC.com, the $10,000 winner of this year's Batten Awards, exemplified the Web's writable side. MSNBC.com's "Big Picture" series of interactive, multimedia features allowed visitors to learn about and then voice their opinion on topics ranging from the war in Iraq to the 2002 congressional elections and the Oscars.

Ashley Wells, MSNBC.com's senior interactive producer, said the initiative attracted more than one million unique broadband users.

Interestingly, he told the symposium, the Iraq War package held the audience longer than the others—more than one-third of the users spent more than 10 minutes per visit, some longer.

MSNBC.com's use of slide shows, videos, interactive sidebars, votes and feedback "may be paving the way for when TV is merged with the Web," Wells said. "Then, maybe we'll know enough about it to transform television news to make it more interactive, more engaging, more in-depth and really help evolve journalism. That's what I'm really excited about."

VillageSoup.com President Richard Anderson discussed the community Web sites built for Belfast, Camden and Rockland, Maine, which won a Batten Award honorable mention. "Their community is online, it's not just their newspaper online," he told the group.

The *San Francisco Chronicle*'s "Two Cents" initiative was also cited as an honorable mention for giving a corps of more than 1,400 local correspondents the opportunity to weigh in and write for the paper. "I consider this more a leap in philosophy than a leap in technology," said creator and community editor Heidi Swillinger.

Leaps in technology, though, prompted the *Chicago Tribune,* a Batten Award runner-up, to produce what Senior Editor Tony Majeri called a "multi-sensory" time capsule of the

(continued)

(continued)

9/11 attacks on the World Trade Center. Struck by how people still hoard the "Nixon Resigns" front pages, Majeri said, he sought to harvest from the *Tribune*'s sister TV stations and newspapers various 9/11 multimedia reports and turn them into an historical keepsake, one that would build on the "notion of how people both emotionally as well as intellectually" learn about things. The resulting CD-ROM helped sell an extra 100,000 newspapers and was shared with schools.

Keynoter Gillmor saw the techniques showcased in the Batten Award winners as forerunners of other emerging trends that promise to impact future journalism.

Civic Journalism

Civic journalism is not new. It has been around for years in one form or another, under one name or another. It did, however, draw much attention over the past ten to fifteen years, having been largely marketed, publicized and parented by the Pew Center for Civic Journalism and several key editors and educators across the nation.

Civic journalism is explained on the Pew Web site (www.pewcenter.org) as follows: "Civic journalism is both a philosophy and a set of values supported by some evolving techniques to reflect both of those in your journalism. At its heart is a belief that journalism has an obligation to public life—an obligation that goes beyond just telling the news or unloading lots of facts. The way we do our journalism affects the way public life goes. Journalism can help empower a community or it can help disable it."

Some of the elements or tenets of civic, or public, journalism are strongly debated by reporters and editors at large, medium and small newspapers. But many are just good quality journalism—period. And more and more journalists have supported the idea that civic journalism is, indeed, a key to resolving some of what ails the industry.

Jay Rosen of New York University, one of the true believers of civic journalism, made the following statement, sort of a framework for civic journalism: "If journalism can be described as a purposeful activity, then its ultimate purpose is to enhance democracy. Thus, democracy not only protects a free press, it demands a public-minded press. What democracy also demands is an active, engaged citizenry, willing to join in public debate and participate in civic affairs. Part of journalism's purpose, then, is to encourage civic participation, improve public debate, and enhance public life, without, of course, sacrificing the independence that a free press demands and deserves."

Journalism is a purposeful activity. It is not meaningless, and it has a specific goal to inform. But newspapers also have a goal as businesses to make money.

Democracy, including the First Amendment, protects a free press. But it can be argued that democracy does not demand a public-minded press. Democracy is government in which people have the power, and there is a principle of equality and opportunity in democracy, but there is nothing that demands a public-minded press. Still, much of the press understands the value in being public minded, but there is not a direct link to be drawn from democracy.

PROFESSIONAL TIPS

Mark Briggs

Mark Briggs is content and strategy manager for interactive media at the *News Tribune* in Tacoma, Washington, and editor of thenewstribune.com. He is the former new media director at the *Herald* in Everett, Washington, and has won several national awards for innovation in online journalism. He also serves as an adjunct professor at Seattle University teaching communications courses.

Question: What are the best things and worst things about civic journalism?

Civic journalism, done well, increases the relevancy for a news organization within a community. This is especially important now with the increasing fragmentation of all news media. If a news outlet loses relevancy, it will quickly lose audience and viability in the marketplace of ideas and information, as well as the marketplace for business.

Unfortunately, the concept of civic journalism has a regrettable connotation within the journalism profession. The primary complaints against it remain grant-funding for journalism projects that might compromise a news organization's objectivity, and the perception that some civic journalism creates news to report on (by hosting town hall meetings, for example). Still other complaints center on the effort to help communities solve problems instead of just reporting on them.

At the *Herald,* we recognized that most communities want to solve their problems; they just don't know how. So by reporting the story of "How would you solve this problem?" we are forced to be more interactive and engaging with our readers because we need information from them. Then, by reporting our findings with comments and evaluations from public officials, we are connecting the two essential components of our democracy—the taxpayers with notions of how their money should be spent, and those responsible for doing the spending.

By any measure, this is good journalism and consistent with the idea that we are part of the public trust and a community watchdog while retaining our role as messenger instead of active participant.

Question: What changes are ahead for the world of journalism?

The battle to remain relevant lures news organizations increasingly toward the cesspool of "infotainment." Celebrities and sensationalism continue to deteriorate the quality of journalism today, hastened by increased profit pressure from Wall Street. Infotainment is easy, but good journalism is hard. Ultimately, like politics, all news is local. Advances in technology will allow news organizations to drill down deep into communities in ways not previously possible.

Technology will also require news organizations to keep pace with the splintered ways in which readers will demand to receive—and interact with—their news.

The readers will play a role in tomorrow's journalism that they do not today. This is good news for the profession, since it will increase the relevancy of any news organization that adapts and innovates as quickly as readers' needs and expectations.

(continued)

PROFESSIONAL TIPS Continued

Question: Why is interactivity important?

People don't trust the news media. Newspaper readership and television news viewers are in steady decline. Voting in public elections is down. Yet there's never been more access to information. So how do journalists connect the dots? Innovation and interactivity hold the key.

Digital communication tools like e-mail, the Web and cell phones with built-in cameras make increased interactivity relatively easy for news organizations. Good journalism means knowing the communities you serve, and these technologies mean every newspaper and TV station has multiplied the eyeballs it potentially has "in the field." Using these tools will make journalists more knowledgeable about their subjects and open up the process of journalism to more people, increasing relevancy to the stories published and peoples' trust in the people reporting them.

Question: Do you have any additional comments?

The business of news is a concept that students and young journalists need to understand. Resources and pay are issues in most newsrooms today, and journalists must come to grips with their role in the businesses that employ them. Quality, relevant engaging content will attract and maintain the audience needed to improve resources and increase pay. Owners, boards of directors and shareholders run newspapers to make money, and every journalist should accept that. But journalism is important work, and reporters, editors and photographers should recognize the better the product they create, the better the chance of growing the business.

Exception can also be taken with Rosen's statement about democracy demanding an active, engaged citizenry, and public debate and participation in civic affairs. That might have been the case in years gone by, but for the most part we do not have an active or engaged citizenry or large-scale participation in civic affairs. The press can—and does—generate a significant amount of public debate, but we do not live in a democracy that demands those things.

Many opponents to civic journalism claim that journalism's purpose should not be to encourage civic participation but rather to only inform the public; if participation results, it is a welcome by-product. They also suggest that an enhancement of public life is another welcome by-product of journalism, but is not a primary motivation.

Is civic journalism the savior of newspapers in the twenty-first century? That's a question Chris Peck addressed at the Pew Center for Civic Journalism's luncheon for the Association for Education in Journalism and Mass Communication (AEJMC) on August 6, 1999 (www.pewcenter.org/doingcj/pubs/chrispeck.html).

Peck, a former president of the Associated Press Managing Editors group (one of two major editor organizations in the nation), has played a very public role in civic journalism.

As editor of the *Spokesman-Review,* Peck popularized "pizza parties," where his newspaper gave free pizza to small focus groups to discuss topics and report back to the paper.

Peck and other civic journalists, as well as many traditional journalists, routinely reference tenets used at the *Spokesman-Review* that include the following:

- **Reporting should accurately** reflect the people it serves.

- **Reporters and editors** possess a unique power to help solve problems.

- **Editorial pages should** shift from insider politics and run nontraditional columns.

- **Facts should not** be intermingled with opinion.

- **Editors and reporters** should listen to what readers are saying about their newspapers' shortcomings.

None of those "civic journalism" principles are revolutionary or new. Yet controversy and caution have raged.

Jeffrey Mohl, former editor of *Quill* magazine, said in the August 2000 edition: "This sometimes-critical approach to journalism is a diversion from the century-old ideal of objectivity, and many professionals predict it will kill the critical edge and search for truth that the news media is supposed to provide."

In the same edition, Steve Sidlo, managing editor of the Dayton, Ohio, *Daily News,* said if civic journalism is going to be taught in a university environment, it should be taught without overemphasizing the name.

"I would avoid making a big deal out of phrases like 'civic' or 'public' journalism," Sidlo said. "I'd teach the value of listening. I teach how to subtly get at what people really think. When we are too noisy on 'civic journalism' techniques, we take the eye off the ball. We get caught up in the debate of techniques and lose the goal—getting citizens more involved in decision-making and understanding complex issues."

Civic journalism has pushed the thought processes at many American newspapers.

The Journalism Values Institute has suggested that the highest calling of newspapers is to truly consider the needs and concerns of readers. In that regard, it developed and/or altered six traditional journalistic core values, hoping to help newspapers reconnect with readers. Here are JVI's core values:

- **Balance was modified** to include fairness and wholeness: not just getting both sides of a news event, but also trying to look beyond the conflict and include the underlying tensions.

- **Accuracy now includes** authenticity: not just getting the facts right, but also getting the right facts, including context, background and perspective.

- **Leadership is now** more than being a community watchdog and bringing community issues to light. It includes focus and framing of issues, challenging people to confront difficult issues, stimulating discussion and showing people potential answers or solutions.

- **Public access means** helping citizens connect with one another through the newspaper.

- **Credibility is not** just being accurate and reliable, but also assuming responsibility for how a community views itself.

■ **And finally, editorial** judgment has changed from simply telling readers the news to helping them understand how the news affects them.

The *Spokesman-Review* seriously began its civic journalism push in 1993 on its editorial pages, which had previously been written and edited by and for "white guys in ties," according to former managing editor Scott Sines.

Two focus groups told the *Spokesman-Review*: "Get out of your ivory tower and into the community. Put more women on the editorial board. Write shorter editorials and sign them. Publish less opinion by the experts and more by ordinary folks. More diversity, please."

Peck has made many public and provocative statements about civic journalism, including some of those in his AEJMC speech, in which he called for journalism schools to train:

> a new journalist, a person who can run a focus group. This new journalist would also know how to do civic mapping and how to frame stories so that they connect the dots on key issues so that fragmented elements of the public can see where others are coming from.
>
> Public editors, or civic editors, or interactive editors will also have to be developed so that everyone from the rich to the poor to Christian conservatives to non-believers is represented.
>
> Newspapers can't have brick-and-mortar headquarters but should have powerful greenhouses for cultivating civic life.
>
> When an interactive or civic editor detects a cause that resonates across social, class and racial lines, the paper would build a bridge, one story at a time, between the separated publics. Story by story the newspaper would knit together a fractured community and repair the idea of the common good.

Steve Smith, who succeeded Peck as editor of the *Spokesman-Review,* has been a civic journalist for many years. When he was editor of the Colorado Springs *Gazette,* he says he challenged journalists to invent a better kind of journalism through public listening, alternative framing and tapping new voices. He said he believed civic journalism required "new tools, new reflexes, new routines and a new language."

At its basic level of understanding, civic journalists believe government and public life aren't working as well as they should, and that content coverage and techniques must be changed because newspapers and journalists have a responsibility to do something about the problems.

James K. Batten, namesake of the previously mentioned Batten Awards, rose from reporter to chairman of Knight-Ridder Newspapers. He died June 25, 1995, after a long battle with brain cancer. Batten's comments and commitment to finding a way to combat readership decline—and financial concerns—helped open the door to civic journalism. He gave a speech in 1990 about newspapers and communities. In the speech he quoted John Gardner, an advocate for a wide range of nonprofit groups, including churches, schools, hospitals and neighborhood organizations: "Communities have been disintegrating for a long time, and the sense of community is increasingly rare. A steadily increasing proportion of our people do not belong to any community; they float around like unconnected atoms; they have no sense of any common venture. So why vote? Why read the newspaper?" Batten and others reasoned that civic journalism could help repair fracturing communities and bridge a gap between them and newspapers.

Davis "Buzz" Merritt, former editor of the *Wichita (Kansas) Eagle,* is another of the founders of the movement. Over the years he has formed the following definition: "Public journalism is a set of values about the craft that recognizes and acts upon the interdependence between journalism and democracy. It values the concerns of citizens over the needs of the media and political actors, and conceives of citizens as stakeholders in the democratic process rather than as merely victims, spectators or inevitable adversaries. As inherent participants in the process, we should do our work in ways that aid in the resolution of public problems by fostering broad citizen engagement."

Civic journalism continues to evolve as a work in progress, having grown over the years in many respects out of widespread professional and consumer dissatisfactions.

Daniel Yankelovich wrote a book titled *Coming to Public Judgment: Making Democracy Work in a Complex World.* His theories included three areas of possible change for journalists.

- **Consciousness raising.** He said journalists could reduce the chances of people giving up on issues if they, journalists, help set agendas that would help citizens focus public attention.

- **Working through.** Journalists can aid this process, he said, by reducing issues to choices, finding the core values, spelling out the costs and consequences of each choice, bridging the expert–public gap, facilitating deliberation and promoting civility (putting things in everyday language and facilitating discussion in a civil and open-minded way).

- **Resolution.** The final step, he said, is journalists helping the public make a stable, responsible choice, with the media championing those decisions.

Arthur Charity, in his book *Doing Public Journalism,* said: "Public journalism is nothing more than the conviction that journalism's business is about making citizenship work."

He also suggested that newspapers have a larger role in society than just helping along decisions; public journalists must find ways to strengthen their community's goodwill and develop cooperative habits; journalists need to become activists; and those who buy newspapers should be called *citizens,* not *readers.*

Mapping the Beat

While individual beat coverage will be discussed later in this book, one of the most successful processes claimed as a component of civic journalism is beat mapping.

Beat mapping is recording significant and relevant information about a beat. There are many traditional public affairs beats (and sources), such as law enforcement (police chief), courts (attorneys, judges), government (elected and appointed officials) and business (presidents, chief financial officers).

But mapping a beat has much more depth and many more layers than just the obvious. The better public affairs reporters will map a beat that will include workers; people of color; diversity in gender, sexual orientations and other areas; those underrepresented; areas of civil liberty and even human health.

In other words, while straight news beats would likely focus on political and economical organizations, public affairs beats explore social issues that envelop people where they live, work, hope and fear. Beat maps can aid dramatically in this process.

The beat system has been used for years by most newspapers and has been modified somewhat by teams over the past several years, but when you think about it, teams are also organized by beats.

Beats for newspaper reporters are nothing more than specific areas of coverage—organized by location or subject—where a regular set of sources has been used. Traditionally they have been built around the established power structure and social order, which pretty much limited reporters to using the same sets of sources.

Beat mapping includes trying to find nontraditional sources, people who can provide different perspectives. Civic (or beat) mapping is about engaging knowledgeable experts, officials and ordinary people.

Maps will often include "third places" (nontraditional places where people gather) and identify "connectors" (people who can connect you with other people), "catalysts" and "go-to-people"—those who are proactive and get things going.

Maps can take on various formats (paper or electronic) but should be clear and to the point. They should include story ideas, topics, subtopics, source areas, place areas, incidental and private places, a brief history of the beat and additional appropriate information, facilities and services. Maps should also include a description of the beat or community, a list of beat/community concerns and interests, locations of hangouts or places where people gather and names and phone numbers of active, involved beat/community citizens.

While reporters put together maps to help them in coverage, they are extremely valuable when a new reporter steps into a beat or is substituting on a beat.

The Pew Center for Civic Journalism listed "Seven Knowledge Keys" for mapping a community:

- **Civic places:** The places where people get together to talk, and what you can learn in each place.

- **Sources:** Authentic, credible, trusted and beyond the official layer and "man on the street" mentality.

- **Sense of place:** A brief history of the people and issues; the feel of the topic.

- **People:** The norms and practices that shape interactions.

- **Issues:** What is really important? What is the buzz? What is the language people use (how are they describing things and sharing information)?

- **Aspirations:** What hopes do people have for now and for the future?

- **Stereotypes:** Preconceived notions, biases (the ones you have as well as others).

Media Convergence

One of the key components of civic journalism has been the partnering with other media, first newspapers with television and/or radio, and then next with the Internet. It has been proven that multimedia coverage will increase familiarity and interest with issues.

But this isn't completely new, as media groups have shared information for years, often driven more by economic considerations rather than interactive and civic concerns.

Today it is called *media convergence,* when ownership groups diversify and merge. It is more and more common for a company to own not only newspapers but also TV or radio stations, and to have a major Web operation—even in the same market as cross-ownership laws allow.

Groups also "cluster" newspaper properties to not only share information but also reduce costs.

Critics abound, raising questions about corporate boardroom and shareholder involvement, and arguing that commercialism damages journalism and adds to the already eroding trust and belief in the integrity of news by readers, listeners and viewers. They also believe there are ethical concerns.

Some old-school newspaper journalists probably never imagined that trash-can-kicking editors and hardcore cop reporters would be doing television stand-ups. Nor would many industry old-timers have guessed that today's reporters would be providing shorter, alternative stories for online Internet consumption—even before the daily was published.

The evolution of American newspapers is constant, and change accelerated rapidly in the 1990s and early 2000s. Media convergence is one of the constant themes of discussion. What will the journalist of the future look like? What competencies will he or she have?

Some newspaper companies and individual properties are leading the convergence way, at least publicly—the Tribune Company in Orlando, Media General in Tampa and the New York Times Co. in Sarasota. The American Press Institute and the Poynter Institute are leading professional education/academic efforts.

Universities across the country have taken a cue by changing curriculums to include teaching traditional print journalism students to capture sound bites with digital handheld cameras—and stream video on the Web.

Traditional broadcast students are also being assigned to write weather columns and opinion pieces for a lab newspaper or in-class exercise.

Multimedia desks are being set up in professional and collegiate newsrooms, with print and broadcast editors sitting side by side, sharing resources, ideas and news.

It's a curious media world, indeed.

Blogging and Citizen Journalists

Never pick a fight with someone who buys ink by the barrel. That somewhat familiar old saw isn't nearly as valid as it once was. Nor does the saying "the power of the press" elicit the same caution it once did.

There are many reasons, but one that is foremost today is the fact that almost anyone can be a journalist because of technological advancements, specifically computers and the World Wide Web.

Ted Koppel, former anchor and managing editor of the ABC News program *Nightline,* said the following at the Red Smith Lecture in Journalism at the University of Notre Dame in 2000: "I don't know how many of you have ever paused to think about this, but journalism is one of the very few professions that requires no training whatsoever. Clearly you cannot become a doctor or a lawyer without training. You need training to become a carpenter or plumber. But to be a journalist in America requires nothing more than your assertion that you are one. You don't need a license. You don't have to belong to a union. No permit is necessary."

Koppel's statement is close to the truth, yet a great deal of training does take place at universities and newspapers across the United States. Koppel went on to say: "The technologies of delivering information have changed but the fundamentals of honest reporting haven't. . . . Establish a set of guiding principles for yourselves . . . emphasize honesty, fairness, decency. . . . The central purpose of journalism is the communication of ideas."

The communication of ideas is what drives citizen journalists today, as they seem to have cropped up everywhere on Web sites with blogs. What is a blog (short for Web log)? It is an online diary, a personal chronological log of thoughts published on a Web page. It is typically updated daily, and the blog usually reflects the personality and opinion of the author.

As an example, the *Spokesman-Review* newspaper Web site (www.spokane.net) has links to almost twenty-five newspaper-sponsored blogs and eighty local blogs.

The newspaper blogs range in topic from Washington State University Cougars athletics to movies to the conflict in Iraq.

The links to local blogs are much more diverse, including:

- **A Family Runs Through It:** This blog is written by Phil Corless, a twenty-year resident of Idaho and a stay-at-home dad for five years. He says his world revolves around his kids, and he started his blog after finding a dearth of Web sites and information about family news and activities. His log on August 2, 2005, read: "My kids are fascinated by my feet. The two toes next to each of my big toes are webbed. No, I'm not a good swimmer. I'm proud to be the only one of my Grandma's 20+ grandchildren who inherited her webbed toes." The blog includes a photo of his feet.

- **Kick Shoe Kooy:** Author Cathy Kooy says she and her alter ego Thelma live in a two-story farmhouse with a wrap-around porch in an arid, Wild West region of Washington state (also known as Ephrata). A victim of both the lure of the Angel of Woo and the Red Stapler, she is considering therapy, but is afraid they will tattoo the word *NUTTER* on her forehead.

■ **The Unbearable Bobness of Being—Triangulate the Madness and Obfuscate the Sadness:** Bob Salsbury says he grew up in the Spokane Valley and still lives there with his three kids. He enjoys canoeing, camping, hiking, mountain biking, going to the lake, rockhounding, lapidary, skiing and carving evil little trolls out of bars of soap. Bob started blogging after people begged him to. Here is an excerpt from his August 2, 2005, entry:

Arm Wrestling Mithra for One More Day
More Vacation Thoughts
If my children were grown and sufficiently immune (or adequately resistant) to embarass-ment by their father's behavior and lifestyle choices, I would quit my career, sell my house, yank my retirement, and purchase a VW Synchro Westfalia and live on Pacific Ocean beaches. I'm serious about this. Life is too short for suburbia. Life is perfect for tides and storms.

On the beaches I would read books and beachcomb for hours and surfcast and learn to love seafood grilled over driftwood fires and I would go back to my camper each evening and write novels and poems and journals of every little thing. . . .

At night I would roll over and hold my love tightly and tell her "tomorrow I'll make you pancakes and bacon but right now let's challenge the moon for supremacy over the pull on our hearts."

Blogger Rory O'Connor wrote in July 2005: "The advent of the 'blogosphere' (there are now more than 30 million Web logs) offers even more choices and voices, as dissatis-fied media citizens increasingly take matters into their own hands to create 'citizens' media.'"

He went on to write about OhmyNews, a citizen media project in South Korea that has a simple slogan: "Every citizen is a reporter."

OhmyNews, he said, "posts 150–200 stories a day, attracts millions of daily readers and has tens of thousands of registered citizen journalists. A staff of less than 50 editors and reporters assist in fact-checking and editing, but ordinary citizens—including house-wives and elementary students—do most of the reporting and writing."

Blogger Jeff Jarvis claims on his blog, Buzzmachine: "No one owns journalism. It is not an official act, a certified act, an expert act, a proprietary act. Anyone can do journal-ism. Everyone does. Some do it better than others, of course. But everyone does it."

Personal interest drives blogs, including politics for many bloggers.

Barb Palser, *American Journalism Review's (AJR)* new media columnist and the director of content for Internet Broadcasting Systems, wrote in the August–September 2005 issues of *AJR* magazine: "The state of the blogosphere is also fluid and fast-develop-ing. The first line of blog swarms pounded the national press, but bloggers are already growing more enmeshed in political causes and becoming more active at the local level. How bloggers are moderated in these activities—by an implicit and self-imposed code of conduct, government regulation or nothing at all—will influence their role in tomorrow's mass communication landscape. How the mainstream media react to bloggers and other challenging voices—by ignoring them, engaging them or attempting to co-opt them—will do the same."

While blogging communication is still evolving, one consideration in the evolution will be the bottom line. Advertising has long driven the media, taking on more and more importance over content and information throughout history. Such might be the case with blogs.

CHAPTER EXERCISES

1. Write a two-page original essay about civic journalism, with a conclusion (at least two paragraphs long) of your personal beliefs on the topic.

2. Select one of the civic journalism "names" in this chapter, and do an Internet search and a ten-minute classroom presentation (or written report) about them.

3. Civic mapping is about engaging not only experts and officials, but also the ordinary people who are knowledgeable about the community or beat you are covering. Turn in an electronic-based map of the beat you have been assigned in this course. Your instructor will provide details.

4. Approach five Generation Y students who you do not know, and interview them about their media habits. Ask them the following six questions, and write a three-page essay/analysis of their responses:

   ■ **What do you** consider news and information, and, as a member of Generation Y, what do you personally want and need to know?
   ■ **Tell us how** and when, on a daily basis, you typically get your news and information.
   ■ **What are the** media stereotypes of Gen Y?
   ■ **What are the** personal values that define your generation and are important in your life?
   ■ **What would it** take in content and/or delivery-design modes for you to be connected to and reliant upon a newspaper for your news and information?
   ■ **What else do** you want to add about Generation Y and the media?

5. Keep a forty-eight-hour media diary/log of how you obtain news and information. Write a two-page essay summarizing how you get news and information.

6. Keep a blog or written journal for the rest of this semester.

Generating Story Ideas

BY JOHN IRBY

Did you ever wonder how many revolutions an amusement park ride like this makes in a day? Or how many people ride it in a day? Or how much electricity it takes to run it? There are limitless story ideas if one isn't afraid to wonder.

Every other year the kids, my wife and I buckle up our seatbelts, load far too many necessities into the family van and drive out of Pullman, Washington. We drive seventeen hundred–plus miles to Escanaba, Michigan, passing through communities like Kellogg, Idaho; Havre, Montana; Minot or Fargo, North Dakota (depending on the route); Duluth, Minnesota; and Ashland, Wisconsin.

We spend about three and a half days on the road, eating fast food for sustenance and sleeping on rock-hard mattresses in clean but moderately priced hotels.

Diet drinks and water are kept cold by melting 99-cent convenience-store bags of ice in a blue cooler wedged between two front bucket seats.

Snacks can be found in a bag on the floor near the feet of screaming and fighting back-seat kids ("Are we there yet?"). The kids are somewhat amused, but never completely satisfied, by watching cartoon and children's videos on a thirteen-inch television-VCR resting on top of the cooler.

Once we arrive at my mother-in-law's two-bedroom "doll house," we do next to nothing for two or three weeks. Oh sure, we play cards a few evenings with the relatives, wagering nickels and dimes on low-stakes games of chance.

We even go to a Friday-night fish fry, attend the 4th of July parade in neighboring Gladstone, let the kids splash in the community wading pool, rent movies from Block-buster and entertain ourselves by window shopping at Wal-Mart, K-Mart and ShopKo.

Like I said—we do next to nothing.

That's our idea of a vacation, taking time to rest and relax, to unwind and rewind.

Begin at the Beginning

Students, however, might not understand. Escanaba—or Kellogg, or Havre, or Minot, or Fargo, or Duluth, or Ashland—aren't in the fast lane (U.S. Highway 2 is only two lanes much of the way). Those cities are miles away from Atlanta, Boston, Chicago, Dallas, Denver, Houston, Kansas City, Los Angeles, Miami, New York, Portland, San Francisco, Seattle or Washington, D.C., the type of cities where many students usually want to live and work; places where there is action and excitement.

That, in fact, is my background. I grew up in Los Angeles (Compton and Bell Gardens) and spent much of my professional newspaper career in southern California. The pace was, as the cliché goes, fast and furious.

Today I hear students routinely say that after graduation they will move to a large city and get a job. They have reporting and writing dreams of covering education for the *Seattle Times,* or government for the *Washington Post,* or immigration for the *Los Angeles Times,* or entertainment for the *Miami Herald,* or foreign affairs for the *New York Times.*

Most, however, will start as reporters or copy editors for newspapers like the Escanaba *Daily Press,* circulation 13,659; Havre *Daily News,* circulation 10,201; Shoshone *News-Press* in Kellogg, circulation 2,591; or, if they are lucky, the larger *Daily News* in Minot, circulation 34,544, where a marketing campaign was once built around the slogan "Why Not Minot?"

Some will even end up at weekly community newspapers, which, by the way, are often the best places to start. Dreams can easily be placed on hold for these experiences that go a long way toward achieving those dreams.

Fresh-out-of-college journalists will begin by covering the pros and cons of a traffic-light controversy on Main Street U.S.A., or a new recycling project in which small-town residents must separate their own cans, bottles and newspapers into blue, yellow and white bins.

Admittedly, there generally isn't as much going on, or as much excitement, in smaller communities as there is in major metropolitan areas and cities. But that doesn't mean there isn't a plethora of story ideas—and excitement—waiting to be found in places like Kellogg, Havre, Escanaba or Minot.

For instance, on August 20, 2003, *Escanaba Daily Press* Reporter Eric Bradley wrote about John Gannon, a local native and Iraq war veteran.

Bradley wrote about Gannon's experiences in war:

> [T]he work was so intense and so demanding that Gannon didn't realize he had turned 22 until well after noon on his birthday, March 28. He was sitting in a fox hole, dirty and on guard.

Not only is there power in those words, but there is also interest on two fronts; first, news about the war in Iraq and, second, familiar but vastly different experiences. Gannon was having a birthday, something we all have, yet he couldn't initially realize it. For most of us, it is a special day, one saturated with well-wishes, presents and cake. Gannon, unfortunately, couldn't afford to think much about his birthday. He was concerned with staying alive.

Jerome Tharaud of the Havre (Montana) *Daily News,* provided another example the same day, writing about health care for American Indians:

> "The health disparities in Indian Country are overwhelming," Chippewa Cree Tribal Chair Alvin Windy Boy Sr. said. ". . . the federal government spends about $1,530 per person for health care for Indians, compared with an average of about $3,500 for all Americans. It's no different than Third World conditions. How could a country claim to be so strong to other countries when their backyard is riddled with health disparities?"

And finally, in Minot, North Dakota, Andrea Domaskin of the *Daily News* told the story of the Babe Ruth World Series in nearby Williston that drew seventeen thousand spectators in the first two days and utilized four hundred volunteers. While the event took three years to plan, according to Domaskin's story, Williston may see a $1.5 million impact.

Walking the Dog

Every morning while in Escanaba, I take my mother-in-law's dog for a half-hour walk as the rest of the family sleeps. I have an internal alarm clock. I can never sleep past 6:30 A.M., another thing many college students probably can't understand.

Toby, a 9-year-old Dalmatian, loves his morning walk. One morning we walked to the Upper Peninsula State Fair Grounds, and he ran free on the infield of a racetrack that hasn't had a racing hoof print or tire track for several years.

One morning, off in the distance, a thick plume of dark smoke rose wide and high over an area that appeared to be downtown.

Was there a story in that smoke? Of course!

Story ideas most often come naturally if a reporter possesses or develops three simple skills, the last being the most difficult:

1. **Observation**
2. **Curiosity**
3. **Follow-up action**

A huge cloud of smoke in the sky is something most people will notice. Most would also be curious. But not many would follow up and act—gather information and write a story—about what is burning. The majority of people wait until they hear about it on the radio, watch it on television, read about it in the newspaper or listen to a description from a friend or relative.

Observation, curiosity and follow-up actions are the basics of story generation.

As a former reporter, I couldn't resist walking toward the smoke until I found the fire. Thankfully, I had not witnessed a tornado or I might be with Dorothy in Kansas.

Following is part of the *Daily Press* story that afternoon (Thursday, July 24, 2003). Not necessarily the best writing, but functional deadline writing that included the basic facts.

Downtown Blaze: Ness Glass Gutted in Morning Fire

By Lynn Johnson

ESCANABA—Fire guttered a Ludington Street business this morning.

A large fire broke out around 6 a.m. at Ness Glass, 1509 Ludington St., flooding a six-block area with heavy, gray smoke. No one was injured in the blaze, according to Escanaba Public Safety. The building is completely gutted.

Escanaba Public Safety and the Ford River Volunteer Fire Department responded to the blaze. When they arrived, flames had already taken over most of the rear of the two-story building.

The fire was contained by 9 a.m., but firefighters continued to battle hot spots. Exact cause of the blaze was unknown. . . . The second floor of Ness Glass contained five apartments. According to owner Barry Ness, four of the units were occupied by a total of seven tenants and at least one overnight guest. . . . Ness wasn't positive the building was insured.

Generation Y and News

It is important for students who are preparing for professional news writing or editing careers to understand that people get information in a variety of ways, and how they get information can have a bearing on how stories are generated.

In a 2002 study and survey about Generation Y (in this survey, those roughly between the ages of 6 and 25), Washington State University college students were asked where they get their daily news and information.

The first three responses were television, newspapers and the Internet. The next response was somewhat surprising—"word of mouth."

Peggy Kuhr, former managing editor of the *Spokesman Review* in Spokane, Washington, and now the Knight Chair in Community Journalism at the William Allen White School of Journalism and Mass Communications at the University of Kansas, took part in the study and survey. She wrote the following in a publication titled *Reaching Generation*

Y, Back to the Future (Again), providing insight into story-idea generation: "What I hadn't fully realized," Kuhr wrote, ". . . was the intersection between the importance of family and Generation Y and news. These young people get a lot of news from their family and other people close to them. . . . One survey said: 'Mom tells me. She listens to news in the car.' Another said: 'Mom sends me articles to read.'"

Newspapers are written for a mass audience. But more attention should be paid to Generation Y, which is currently more than 20 percent (about 60 million) of the population, and will one day swamp Baby Boomers.

What Generation Y sees or defines as news, what interests the target audience, whatever it is, should be strongly considered in story generation.

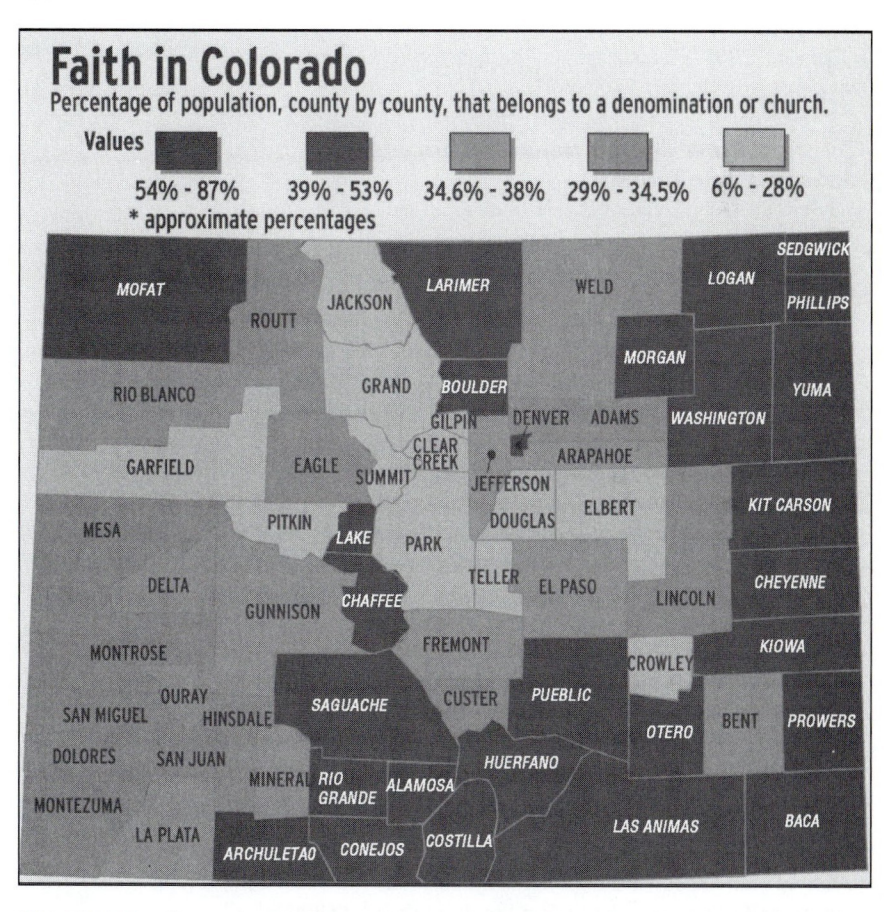

FIGURE 2.1 Generation Y claims to have strong values when it comes to faith, even though its members might not display those feelings in a traditional manner, such as regularly attending church services. Why do they often avoid church services? That question could be the genesis of a story appealing to a nontraditional reader market (college students). This graphic could provide a wealth of story ideas.

The Gazette

PROFESSIONAL TIPS

Patrick Webb

Patrick Webb is managing editor at the *Daily Astorian,* a 10,000-circulation, five-day, afternoon family-owned newspaper on the northern Oregon Coast. Webb is a native of England who immigrated to the Northwest in 1980. He has worked at Astoria since 1997 and became managing editor in January 2001. He manages a thirteen-person newsroom that includes five reporters.

Question: How do you generate story ideas in a small town?

They are all around you. But you must look and listen. I encourage reporters to bring in their own story ideas, to add to ones I assign to them. The easiest and most pleasant job for an editor is setting priorities with a bright, observant reporter when there are plenty of options.

One of the most difficult things to do, if there are no ideas on the table, is to sit down and think, "What are we going to write about today?" That taxes the brain, and we all want to avoid that!

Often an idea is good, but the timing is wrong. If that is the case, I will let a reporter or intern know that—and urge them to keep the idea on their future to-do list. If it is something we have covered already, then my challenge is to say to them, "What is the new angle on that?"

Readers like stories that answer the question "Whatever happened to . . .?" But there must be something different, some progress. These strategies are designed to avoid deflating the reporter's ego by suggesting that their idea is bad or that "we've done that!"

Other ways are to drive about town with your eyes really open. What do you see, and what is missing? Or to ask sources when you have finished an interview, "What else is going on that you haven't seen in the paper?" When you tackle budget cuts, go to the person on the end that was cut. For instance, ask a teacher: "What is missing from your classroom this year?" They will tell you.

Question: What makes stories interesting?

People . . . people . . . people. Just like a real-estate salesman who can almost become boring saying, "Location . . . location . . . location," over and over again, I am guilty of saying, "People . . . people . . . people," to my reporters. And I don't intend to change that approach.

In the 1980s there was a big move in American journalism to encourage reporters to write about how the city council decisions affected Joe Public. It was a welcome move, and our best reporters have embraced it. Save the "inside baseball" minutiae of the city council debate for the weekly gossip column—if there is any humor there. Instead, focus on "Why should I care?" and "How will it affect me?"

It needs, however, to go beyond tokenism. Having a story that begins with Joe Taxpayer, which then flows into the city council report, is a good starting point. But then you must follow up. Is Joe Taxpayer representative of middle ground or extremes?

One story in Camas, Washington, where I worked in the early 1980s, was about a recycling fanatic who complained to the city that garbage service was a mandatory charge on his combined

(continued)

PROFESSIONAL TIPS   Continued

water–sewer bill. He didn't think it fair for him to pay the collection charges because he recycled and burned rubbish and thus created no refuse for city crews to collect. It made a fun story, of the little guy against city hall, but no one else came forward saying they did the same.

Question: What problems do beginning reporters have in developing story ideas?

Because we start reporters at $11 an hour, and are a long way from "big-city" attractions, we tend to attract beginning journalists straight out of college who are mostly young. This is not necessarily bad. They bring enthusiasm and new ideas, and they look at things with a fresh eye—including things we longtimers take for granted.

But there is a flip side. They live in rented apartments and are often single. Cynics might suggest that is good for an editor, because they have no life outside work. But it means they have little

perspective on paying taxes or raising children. And it means their social life often is with other journalists, which is dangerous because it can make them prematurely cynical and out-of-touch with readers.

One reporter who appeared in local drama productions often appeared bleary-eyed at staff meetings during dress rehearsal week. But he had the advantage of regularly mingling with ordinary but articulate people who were not journalists and could offer input on what the paper did and did not cover.

The biggest issue for beginning journalists, however, isn't that they are green or too starry-eyed. It is they don't always know what we have or have not reported. . . . On Day 1 of their orientation we make sure they know how to research our archives. My admonition is: "If you have an idea, great, but check what we have done before. If it is something new, go for it. If it has been done before, let's look for a new angle."

Generation Y, for instance, listed the following as primary areas of news and interest in *Reaching Generation Y, Back to the Future (Again)*: "Whatever affects me, international and world news, sports, current or major events, local information and entertainment, politics and government, people-focused news, lifestyle news, relationships and family."

Those areas are not much different from what newspaper readers have said they have wanted for years, even though there might be differences in the context, definition and substance.

Searching for Story Ideas

Story ideas can come from anywhere, from anyone and at anytime. The best reporters realize this, because they know if they don't come up with their own ideas, a cranky editor will make story assignments, some of which might be a bit of a stretch.

Searching for story ideas resulted in Washington State University student Renée Mizar visiting the campus multicultural center. She had became aware of the center after attending a nearby theater performance, but she wondered how many other students didn't know about the center, which occupied a less-than-visible location on the edge of campus.

Mizar found out that in generating story ideas, it is important to put aside preconceived notions and to keep an open mind about expectations.

She felt somewhat intimidated and awkward as she entered the Native American Student Center. But she was greeted with friendliness, and her apprehension eased.

She learned there were numerous Native American student groups on campus, yet there was a tight-knit, family-like feeling among the Native American student population.

Next she went to the African American Student Center. She was welcomed into a casual and friendly atmosphere. She was given a tour and learned the center was open to everyone, not just students of color.

After her visit, she said she felt "somewhat silly" for being nervous about going to the multicultural center. She was impressed by the hospitality and friendliness, and was encouraged to come back any time.

She came away with excellent story ideas, based on her one-hour visit when observation turned into curiosity. Here are three:

- **Focus on the** ways students remain connected to their culture after going to college. Explore the ease or difficulty of students' ability to transition to college life while remaining faithful to their ethnic heritage and cultural traditions and practices. Look at what effect the campus and environment have. The article could take the form of a personal profile, looking at the life of one person in particular or a group of people from the same ethnic or cultural background. The article could explore in-depth what challenges the student faces and if they feel comfortable in displaying aspects of their culture (i.e., through such areas as their clothing, language or jargon) and practicing unique cultural traditions.

- **Focus on the** multicultural center and the specific minority student organizations that are a part of it, including the African American, Native American, Latina/o and Asian American/Pacific Islander student centers. Present the services, events and programs the centers provide, such as a student mentoring program. Also, chronicle the history of the center, such as when it was established and how that came about. Address the university's reputation in terms of diversity and how it compares to other universities. Delve into history, chronicle the scope of ethnic and cultural diversity at the university and how it has changed and grown over the years and discuss the direction in which it is currently headed.

- **Focus on a** member of a minority group and their ability to identify with people of their own culture or ethnic background at the university. Has their personal experience of being a minority influenced their attitudes toward people of other backgrounds and cultures? Do they think they are more aware and understanding of people of other backgrounds, and has this changed since coming to the university? Focus on if the student has ever encountered discrimination or had to overcome stereotypes based on their cultural, racial or ethnic backgrounds. More specifically, have they ever encountered this at the university? If so, how was the situation handled, and did it change their outlook about the university?

Curiosity Is King

Have you ever wondered about anything? Do you wonder about everything? For instance, who wrote the book of love?

The Backstreet Boys sang the song "You Wrote the Book on Love." Spring Hermann wrote a young adult adventure romance novel titled *Who Wrote the Book of Love,* but the Monotones sang the original hit song "Who Wrote the Book of Love."

Wonder is a wonderful thing, but it shouldn't be confused with the type of wonder involved in the Seven Wonders of the Ancient World, where any number of story ideas can be generated.

SEVEN WONDERS OF THE ANCIENT WORLD

1. The Great Pyramid of Giza
2. The Hanging Gardens of Babylon
3. The Statue of Zeus at Olympia
4. The Temple of Artemis at Ephesus
5. The Mausoleum at Halicarnassus
6. The Colossus of Rhodes
7. The Lighthouse of Alexandria

Take, for instance, the Lighthouse of Alexandria. It was once shown on Roman coins. What structures, landmarks or buildings are shown on American coins? A story about the images, how they got there and what they represent could be an interesting and educational story or series.

What do you know about the statue of Zeus at Olympia? He was the spiritual leader of gods and men. His main attribute is the thunderbolt, and he controlled thunder, lightning and rain, or so the legend goes. Weather is clearly an area for limitless story ideas. What causes thunder, lightening or rain? Did you know the Olympics were held in Olympia to honor Zeus?

Wonder, when it comes to public affairs reporting and generating story ideas, is having your feelings or thoughts aroused by something strange or surprising. It means wanting to learn more about something. It means being a bit amazed, astonished or surprised at something. It means to be filled with curiosity or doubt.

For instance, have you ever wondered?

- **Why does one** intersection have a four-way stop sign when there is very little traffic traveling north-south?

- **How can the** mayor afford a Ferrari sports car when his annual salary is only $15,000?

- **Why does Wal-Mart** build a superstore in one city while it would seem to make more sense for the retailer to open in a neighboring community?

- **Why are there** so many potholes in the streets?

- **Why does tuition** continue to increase?

- **Why do gasoline** prices seem to always go up, but never down?

There is wonder in everything. It just takes a little thought, maybe even some imagination, and story ideas are abundant (for additional story ideas, see the Human and Nonhuman Sources section in Chapter 3, Finding and Cultivating Diverse Sources).

CHAPTER EXERCISES

1. Go to http://ce.eng.usf.edu/pharos/wonders/, pick one of the "Seven Wonders" and click on the photo. Read the location, history and description information, and write a detailed story idea for your student or community newspaper. Make sure it has a local angle or connection, possibly a public affairs–type story.

2. Go to http://ce.eng.usf.edu/pharos/wonders/other.html, pick one of the "Modern Wonders" and write a detailed story idea for your student or community newspaper. Make sure it has a local angle or connection, possibly a public affairs–type story.

3. Go to www.scopesys.com/anyday/, and highlight your birthday. Write a three hundred-word story about the significant public affairs events in history that occurred on your birthday.

4. Spend one hour walking around your campus or city, and compile a detailed list of five story ideas for your student or community newspaper. Identify the public affairs "connection" or "beat" on each idea. Ask your professor if he or she will provide extra credit if you submit the ideas to the student/community newspaper and a story is reported, written and published.

Finding and Cultivating Diverse Sources

BY JOHN IRBY

Reporters are taking the easy road when they get both sides of a story. To serve readers, reporters must recognize that there are many voices in between polarized points of view and it is important to find, cultivate and use a diversity of sources.

It shouldn't have to be said, but it is worth repeating time and again—proper sources are important in reporting. The best writers aren't always the best journalists, because they don't always understand the importance of gathering good information. Writing good stories isn't possible without finding and cultivating diverse sources.

How a reporter finds sources, how a reporter cultivates sources, how he or she gets them to talk and how a journalist keeps those sources comprise the theme of this chapter.

The Sources among Us

Anyone can be a source. Some might be more valuable or worth developing more than others, and sources aren't always "officials." In fact, some of the best sources are not officials, but are as diverse as neighbors, clerks, disgruntled employees, stay-at-home moms and undercovered or ignored voices.

Sources can even be found and cultivated in an elevator.

Two weeks after the terrorist attacks of September 11, I walked up the hill from the parking lot, then entered a brick building and an elevator down the hall.

Two men stepped on with me, and the door slowly closed. I didn't know either well, but I had seen them in the building in the past. We had exchanged pleasantries, talking briefly in the halls and in the elevator about the weather, Saturday football games or the lack of salary increases.

As we were riding from the ground floor to the second level, in what has to be one of the world's slowest elevators, one of the men said: "I guess Arabs are leaving the university in droves. I was talking to someone in multicultural services and he said thirty-five students have withdrawn. They (foreign students) are scared to death."

Was that a story? Yes.

OK, maybe it was a story tip. But those men were "sources" of information I had cultivated over a period of time with hallway and elevator small talk. They had become comfortable enough in my presence to say what was on their mind.

These are the kinds of tips that come when journalists cultivate sources; tips that lead to high-interest stories.

In this case, as a journalism professor rather than a reporter, I passed the information on to the student daily newspaper. But if I had been a community newspaper reporter covering a major university and the education beat, I would have asked follow-up questions of the man talking.

"Who in multicultural services told you that?"

"Have you heard anything else?"

"What do you make of the student response?"

"Do you know any students?"

Ultimately, university officials would need to be contacted as a source, but oftentimes the best strategy is to gain as much information as possible before going to official sources.

It's analogous to an attorney asking probing questions of a key witness. The best attorneys will not ask tough questions unless they already have a good idea of the answer. The best reporters are the same: they don't like to ask questions of key sources unless they have a good idea of the answer.

So, before contacting university officials, I would have called the adviser to the campus Middle Eastern Students' Association (MESA).

Just for fun, I did. She had also been a source I had cultivated (in theory), as we previously met for lunch and had helped each other on a couple of university-wide projects. She was comfortable telling me information off the record, which gave me the answers to the questions I would ask of official sources.

She told me the university was offering full tuition and book refunds to Middle Eastern students who returned home. Some, about fifteen at the time, had decided to leave, and the university had counseled the students so they could leave in good standing and easily return when they felt safe.

The adviser also said about fifty-five students attended the MESA meeting two nights earlier, about forty more than usual, and many told stories about having rocks, as well as verbal and other physical threats, thrown at them.

She asked if I wanted the names of students to call and interview. As I was about to say yes, I remembered I was no longer a reporter and declined, somewhat sadly. But if I had still been a reporter pursuing the story, I would have had several sources, obtained through cultivation.

It would have been a great story.

Source Cultivation and Ethics

John Sherman is the city supervisor (city manager) in Pullman, Washington, and is the major decision maker in a city of 138 employees. He has direct or indirect supervision of most of the city's departments.

Pullman is a community that in many ways would be similar to other cities where young journalism graduates might begin their professional newspaper careers.

Education and farming are the main economic drivers. The city area is 8.93 miles, with 59 miles of streets (excluding the university). There are nearly as many parks (12) as traffic signals (17), and there are 1,273 street lights.

Pullman is a college town with a population of about 25,000; more than half of the 19,000 students at Washington State University are counted in that number.

Even with a major university, it is a small community. It isn't uncommon to see acquaintances and friends at the grocery store, cinema, or tiny airport; walking downtown; or sharing faith at church.

I attend church with Sherman.

From time to time, we have conversations about city government and/or policies at the university. He is comfortable talking with me. In a way, you could say I have cultivated him as a source of information.

"The new hospital was full and sending patients to Moscow [Idaho]," Sherman said one Sunday morning. "There were a lot of surgeries and a number of students checking in with the flu."

Story tips? Yes.

In early September 2002, police officers were called to a fight at the Attic, a night-club above the Top of China, a downtown restaurant.

Law enforcement's use of force and pepper spray was questioned. More than one hundred innocent people suffered secondary exposure to pepper spray, most of whom were unaware of a fight and the actions taken by police to intervene.

One day at church, Sherman volunteered in a discussion that the university had agreed to pay for half of an investigator's costs of an independent and neutral assessment of the police actions at the Attic.

Was Sherman a source? Had I cultivated him? Yes, and yes. But there's a larger question to consider: is it ethical to use such information as "source information" when it is supplied by a friend? As a reporter, could I—should I—use that information? Is this using a friend?

Maybe.

Reporters in small communities will have a greater probability of sources becoming friends, or friends becoming sources. People who reporters associate with, people they spend time with away from work, oftentimes end up being sources.

Reporters are never "off the clock." It's the nature of the profession. It is important that reporters understand potential conflicts, making their positions clear in advance by cautioning friends that they might want to consider or be careful of what information is shared. Reporters don't use their friends if they are honest with them about who they are and what they do for a living.

In the Attic situation, I passed the tip on to the campus cable television station.

Searching for Sources

Reporters can often find sources by working the phones, but they can usually be more effective by working the fields—meeting people out of the office, face to face, to generate richer responses.

In gathering information for the proper framing of a story, reporters need to search out different perspectives or points of view, not just "both sides of an argument." Those voices are usually found in traditional places.

In "Finding Third Places: Other Voices, Different Stories," part 3 of a four-video series by the Pew Center for Civic Journalism, Dan Chapman, city hall reporter for the *Charlotte (North Carolina) Observer,* said: "I just go and plop down in a barbershop for a couple of hours, and once you get on good terms with the barber, he'll introduce you to everybody else and you just sit there largely as a sponge, a fly on the wall and you take it all in."

By plopping down at the barbershop, Chapman is searching for sources, but not the "usual suspects." Some of the best sources can be found in what is termed *third places,* locations that traditionally weren't utilized by journalists but are becoming routine stops on beats.

But although third places are wonderful for finding sources, all sources aren't created equal. Some experts or public officials are needed for stories, and they might not be found at a "third place."

For instance, a reporter could select a university professor to provide information about the stress that students face during finals week. A professor might be a logical, traditional and easy source, but maybe not the best source. Professors might believe they know all about the stress of finals week, especially because they were once students. But a better source would be those experiencing stress right now—students. And the source variety should include considerations of gender, age, class, ethnicity and other diverse concerns. That will make a more complete story.

The best stories include a variety of sources—and a mix of the type of sources used. A reporter writing a story about police should include as sources women and people of color, not just white male officers.

Unfortunately, women and minorities are dramatically underrepresented in newspapers. One reason that seems obvious is that a high percentage of newspaper managers are white and male.

In selecting sources, seek people who have lived the story you are trying to tell. I once moderated a debate that focused on the legalization of drugs. The county sheriff was a panelist and a good "official" source on the topic. But he would have been a terrible source for a story about what it is like to be "high" after smoking marijuana. Why? Because he admitted he had never smoked the drug. He had not lived the story and would have had nothing to contribute on that specific aspect.

Stories need not only sources that can provide facts—knowledgeable, impartial assessments—but also sources that can provide specific, human examples, which allow for richness and context.

Selecting appropriate sources is a demanding process. Far too many reporters take the easy way out and settle for the usual suspects.

Cultivating sources means taking people to lunch. It means listening to your neighbor over the backyard fence. It means setting aside at least two hours a week—or, better yet, an hour a day—getting out of the office and simply meeting people, going to places you've never been, riding a bus route, walking a neighborhood, volunteering at nonprofit or multicultural organizations or visiting a homeless shelter or soup kitchen.

The Psychology of Sources

How do reporters get sources to talk, and why do sources talk?

One year, a Diversity Celebration was held on campus. A source called a reporter for the student newspaper and said several multicultural organizations would picket the event and that several individuals would walk out during the celebration.

The source also said several people were unhappy about how the event was planned by the university, claiming there wasn't enough inclusiveness with individuals and organizations. And, there was a charge that the university was not serious about diversity efforts, that the celebration and other high-profile activities had been geared at image enhancement and not reality.

Why would a source come forward with such information? There could be many reasons.

Some sources have no motive other than wanting the truth to be told. Others, however, might have a motive, agenda, or vendetta. Still others may be ambitious or egocentric—thinking that being quoted might make them look important. Some might simply be interested in the topic and speaking their mind.

Sometimes sources don't want to talk because they are afraid of reprisals, or they might be afraid of how they might be incorrectly portrayed in the media.

Whatever the reasons to talk or be quiet, sources are more apt to talk if they believe your interest is genuine rather than manipulative, and if they believe they can trust you as a reporter.

Because of the public nature of some jobs, some sources are required to speak and provide information to the media. But many sources don't have to talk, and there is generally a reason they do or don't. Understanding that is key to obtaining correct information.

Usage Ground Rules

In all source–reporter relationships, there must be some understanding and basic ground rules. Caution—and traditional editors and professors—suggest that source attribution

PROFESSIONAL TIPS

Brye Butler

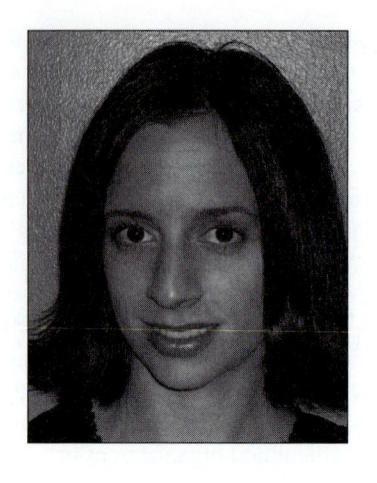

Brye Butler is the nonprofits reporter at the *Abilene (Texas) Reporter-News,* circulation 34,528, and former city reporter at the *Wichita Falls (Texas) Times Record News,* circulation 34,076. Butler is a graduate of Washington State University, where she was selected the top journalism graduate in 2001. She also was named Journalist of the Year in 2003 by the *Times Record News* and won the Scripps President's Choice Award by the Scripps Company in 2004.

Question: How do you find nontraditional sources, the ones that aren't the usual suspects, and how do you cultivate your sources?

1. Secretaries. It's almost a cliché at this point, but it's true. I cover city hall and am over there all the time, but not like they are. They see everyone who comes in and out and hear all the "water cooler talk." I'm most friendly with the city manager's secretary. It's easy. I remember her husband and kids' names, things she likes, what she does on the weekends. I work in a few personal things about my life, and I call before holidays to wish her a nice day off. In passing she mentions things she has heard, an upcoming meeting that has a hot issue, or she will tell me to ask so-and-so what they know about (fill-in-the-blank) pertinent issues.

2. Go knocking door-to-door. This isn't so easy. I end up apologetically explaining I'm not selling anything and that I am a person of high integrity with a degree, but yes, I'm soliciting—their opinion. People like to read about people. Issues are easier to understand with a face attached. A government story, city council action or potential action or a policy change is more interesting and real when the story has someone affected that is featured in it. For all these reasons, I'm not

afraid to go to someone's home and ask them what they think. It's nice when the photographer is willing to spend a little extra time and tag along as there are some strange people out there.

Here's an example of knocking on doors: city staff wanted to spend millions on construction for homes in a flood plain. Meanwhile, the city had been in a drought since November 2003, and there was also a drought from 1999 to 2001. Does this add up? I wondered, so I went to the neighborhoods—where the grass was brown and the trees were dying—and asked residents about flooding. It turns out despite the lack of water now, they have been flooded, and are worried. It seems once you lose your stuff one time, you definitely want some new channels to redirect water, whenever that rain may come.

3. Go to the meetings that seem insignificant, like city council–appointed "work sessions" and other planning or focus groups. I usually don't cover these live; I don't write up a meeting story for the next day's paper. But after a boring hour, I walk away with a few story ideas, met a few more people, shown my face and I've given out my business card with my contact info on it. In the daily grind, it's tough to make it to these, but worth it every now and again.

(continued)

PROFESSIONAL TIPS   Continued

Cultivating sources is one of my favorite aspects of working a beat. It's challenging and fun. I think it's a combination of proving yourself and humanizing yourself. First, I prove I'm capable and can do the job. I know my stuff and I'm a good journalist. Working with older, prominent men as part of covering the government beat is tough. It took time, but they know I'm not a silly little girl, but I'm fair and accurate. I often call or e-mail back after a story is written to double check and ensure accuracy. They know I'm thorough.

Also, I know sources will be more willing to talk to me if it's enjoyable. They're more willing to answer questions and take time out of their busy work day if it's not painful to talk to me. So, I get all my background/basics first. Instead of wasting the first few minutes of our time going over the background, I use that time to chit-chat. What are you and your wife doing this weekend? How was your daughter's first choir performance last week? Did your brother and his family enjoy their trip to the city last month? Then, I relate. Yeah, I don't

have kids to take trick-or-treating, but my husband and I had fun passing out candy last night. We ask each other questions, and then I transition into how work has been going lately and what I'm working on today. Then, bam, I interview. At the end, a little well wishing and a "Do you mind if I call you back after I've finished the article to double check a detail or two?" Of course, they don't mind, they say, and they tell me to be sure and say hi next time I'm at city hall.

The key for me is to make it easy to talk to me. This leads to people calling you with story ideas or information, or asking the editor specifically for you to write up the article/cover the event. This is the payoff. There's nothing better than when a source asks another reporter, "Where's Brye?" or, "We were hoping Brye would be here." They know you, trust you and want you to cover it, especially when the topic is touchy or unfavorable for them. They know you're not a friend, but they can trust that you'll be fair and correct.

---

should be used at all times. Reporters who follow that rule might never have to say they are sorry, except for cluttered writing.

Identity of sources is absolutely necessary when the source is critical to the value and perception of the news. But when something is a simple statement, something that is widely accepted, it doesn't always need to be attributed. All attribution does in some cases is clutter the writing.

Clarity should be a reporter's guide.

How and when to attribute, however, are only the beginning of what can sometimes become complicated understandings.

Far too many sources don't want their names attached to information they provide. Sometimes there are legitimate reasons, including possible retaliatory action or concerns of individual privacy or sensitivity.

But in most cases, reporters should not allow source anonymity. There are several legitimate reasons why it should be avoided, even though the two chief ones are sometimes ignored by reporters working for major newspapers and wire services.

First, it isn't uncommon for a source requesting anonymity to have an ax to grind or a trial balloon to float. The source might be trying to personally attack someone or something—or gauge public interest or lack of support—and not be held accountable or responsible.

Second, and even more importantly, anonymity erodes credibility. Readers often wonder why they should believe sources they can't identify. Readers often question the credibility of such stories and the claims they include.

Reporters should generally assume that everything a source says is on the record and can be used without restriction. It is best, especially with those who might not have much media knowledge or contact, to make this perfectly clear.

From time to time, sources will make a comment and then add, "Of course, that's off the record."

Is it?

If the reporter has set the ground rules in advance, then it is only off the record if the reporter now agrees. But if the reporter does not accept the "off-the-record" stipulation, he or she has an obligation to immediately let the source know that the comment was, indeed, on the record. A source will assume by a reporter's silence that the reporter is not going to use the information.

Human and Nonhuman Sources

Sources can provide off-the-record background information, which can be considered for publication if it is confirmed by other sources; there is no substitute for knowledge when a reporter is working on a story.

Reporters, however, need to excel at not only cultivating human sources but also learning their beats and communities, which contain nonhuman source background and story information.

Often the best place to start is a reporter's individual newspaper's library, generally today an electronic story archive.

But there are many other document or data sources. The most basic are the Internet, a dictionary, an encyclopedia, a thesaurus, a dictionary of quotations, a style book, a phone book and a reverse directory.

Following are some random but wonderful thoughts from students who visited various organizations to listen for and seek a diversity of sources and story ideas. These topics would likely be valid story ideas in virtually any market, or at least serve as teasers for brainstorming:

- **Service clubs:** Who are the people who belong, and what kinds of things do they do for the community? Who are the oldest and youngest members? What sacrifices do members make to take part in these groups?

- **Dangerous highways:** What roads are the most dangerous? How many accidents have occurred? How many people have been injured? What have officials done, or what are they doing, to find safety solutions?

- **Tuition increases:** Tuition has increased by 16 percent and will continue to increase unless parents, students and community members contact the legislature and put a stop to it. Most people aren't aware of the dramatic, skyrocketing increases.

- **Campus safety:** Students are always talking about this. How many students are injured by cars at improperly painted crosswalks or at intersections without stoplights? Are the campus crime reports accurate? Are all rapes and assaults being reported? Can anything be done to increase dorm security or walking on campus after dark?

- **Students with children:** Having a child is a twenty-four-hour job. Students generally don't have a lot of money, so the obvious question is whether sending a child to child care creates financial turmoil. Are students able to use financial aid for child care? There also has been a long-term debate about sending children to child care and how that affects their development. It would be interesting to do a day-in-the-life story of a student with children and see how they manage their day.

- **Veterans:** Many Vietnam veterans are at the age of retirement. One story idea would be to profile an individual who is in this situation. The concerns and special problems faced by a veteran could raise awareness. How does a person, specifically a veteran, face retirement? How well are veterans taken care of as far as retirement benefits are concerned? How many veterans were able to find steady employment after their service to allow them to retire adequately? Are disabled veterans able to receive low-cost comprehensive health care as they grow older?

- **Homeless missions:** It would be interesting to compare the lives lived by these men to their lives before their addictions and problems. Many are trying to rebuild their lives. They are working to rebuild their monetary situation, their employment and most importantly their families. Some have not seen their kids, parents and siblings in many years, having been shut out of the family because of their problems. Homeless missions house these men and help them get in contact with their loved ones and begin to rebuild those relationships.

- **Alcohol and the family structure:** How many families are torn apart because of the abuse of alcohol by one or both parents? What effect does alcohol abuse have on the children? What is the likelihood of a child of an alcoholic becoming an alcoholic?

- **Being gay on campus:** Because there is not a large gay population on campus, a story could be done on how it feels to be gay in a predominately non–gay/lesbian environment. The story could focus on the struggles of coming out of the closet and how hard it is in a conservative community. How does sexuality affect one's social and academic life? What kind of discrimination do gays and lesbians face? How can others be educated? The story could be told through the eyes of a gay or lesbian student, emphasizing realities and giving voice to underrepresented students.

- **Religious conversion:** It would make an interesting story to find an American-born woman who converted to the Islamic faith. What were her reasons for the conversion? Is she happy with her decision? Does she have regrets? The story would explore Muslim life from her experiences.

CHAPTER EXERCISES

1. Select one of the story ideas listed above, envisioning it as a local story. Put together a list of diverse sources who could be interviewed.

2. If you were covering crime, where would you go to get information? The police station! The police station is a traditional listening post where sources and story ideas can be found. But journalists who are interested in telling more about a community need to also establish listening posts in the places that fall outside the routine.

   Here is your assignment: determine a nontraditional listening post. It must be a place where you have never been and that are not likely to visit. It should include a group of people who are poorly understood and/or poorly covered (or undercovered) by the media. Spend at least one hour at your new listening post. Listen with all of your senses. Read bulletin boards, pamphlets and leaflets. Resist the temptation to interview people. Sit down and have a conversation. Listen carefully to the language people use to describe themselves and what they do.

   Write a two-page essay on your experience, explaining what you learned and how you felt. Answer the following questions: who comes here? What can I learn about this group of people from this place? How might the people I encounter here fit into everyday coverage?

   Compile a list of five sources and five detailed story ideas (at least two paragraphs on each story) spurred by your listening post visit.

3. This exercise will help you expand the number of places you go and the variety of people with whom you talk. Begin this assignment by drawing a map of your daily world. Place your desk in this course in the center of the map. Draw your routes to and from the desk to other parts of the building. Include where you enter the building and if you tend to talk with anyone along the way. Draw the route you take to school. Include landmarks, buildings, stores, cafes and so on. Provide as much detail as possible. Notice how you are probably a creature of habit in your routines. Notice the places you do not frequent in your community. Design an alternate route to and from class, then make a list of the new places you would experience.

4. Go to www.businessnamehere.com (you select the business). Review the site. Compile a list of basic background information. Compile a list of possible traditional and nontraditional sources for a story on this business.

5. A celebrity (you pick one, but make it a widely known person) is coming to town. Research him or her online, and draft five questions based on what you find. List the online sites and links to those sites that generated your questions.

4 Interviews

BY JOHN IRBY

If you were assigned to write about a celebration of Kamehameha the Great, you might interview many people, including descendants and event organizers. The quality of your interview, however, would depend upon learning basic facts such as the meaning of his name: the one set apart.

Although there are many elements to interviewing, a reporter can go a long way toward mastering the art by becoming accomplished in two basic areas. The first is learning what questions to ask—and how to ask them. The second is learning how to record the answers—and then asking follow-up questions. Mastering those areas, however, takes work and practice, and interviewing is much more complex that just asking questions and recording answers.

In this chapter you will learn how to prepare for an interview, how to phrase your questions, how to establish rapport with a source and how to ensure accuracy. You will also come to understand that in the interview process a reporter will gather information not only from what he or she is told in response to questions, but also from what is observed.

Where to Start

Success as a reporter—or success in any profession in which information is gathered—will hinge in part on the ability a reporter or person has in making a source comfortable. That's because sources oftentimes have information they don't particularly want to share, information that can be critical to a story or the public's right or need to know but also damaging to the individual or the group, business or organization they represent.

If a source perceives a hostile environment or one that is contentious—or even uncomfortable—the source isn't as likely to answer questions as honestly or openly as he or she might otherwise.

The best place to start establishing an interviewing style that affords source comfort is with preparation. It's analogous to what a student would do to prepare for a test—study. Before any interview, a reporter should research the subject and the source.

If a source believes a reporter is knowledgeable about the subject of the interview, he or she is more likely to speak openly and completely. But if sources doubt a reporter's ability to comprehend the subject, most will become guarded as to what they say.

The best reporters will gather as many facts as possible before the interview so that the face-to-face session will allow for reactions and interpretations to questions of substance, rather than spending valuable time on basic information that could have been found in advance.

Interviews are the best way to get opinions, but not the best way to gather purely factual information. You can generally obtain factual information—names, dates or figures—more quickly and reliably from written records or available data.

A second key to establishing an environment conducive to effective interview sessions is for a reporter to learn and develop how to use a conversational, personal tone with the source. When reporters interview by having a conversational discussion with a source, the results are generally much richer.

A Success Story

Charley Pride was born to poor sharecroppers in Sledge, Mississippi. He's also a member of the Country Music Hall of Fame and has a star on the Hollywood Walk of Fame.

As a young sportswriter at the *Nevada State Journal* in Reno, Nevada, I was assigned to attend one of his performances as a headliner at the celebrity room of a large Lake Tahoe casino, and then interview him. At the time, I didn't know the first thing about country music and had never heard of Charley Pride.

I had to question why a sportswriter would be assigned to write about a country singer. Rather than ask, which would have been the correct approach, I did some research, which was also the correct way to prepare for an interview.

I found out that Pride was one of the few blacks in country music. More specific to my sports-association question, I found out he had a baseball career before his success as a singer.

Pride had begun his music career while playing baseball as a member of the Memphis Red Sox in the Negro American League, singing and playing the guitar on the bus between ballparks.

I learned that after a failed tryout with the New York Mets, Pride played baseball in Montana—an interview preparation fact that helped secure one of the best interviews of my career.

When we sat down for the interview, I started with some small talk, such as pleasantries about enjoying his show, in an effort to provide a comfortable environment and put him at ease.

I suggested I wanted to find out about his singing success, but wanted to first share something we had in common. He asked what.

I told him about my baseball successes, and that I had once lived and worked in Montana and covered baseball games at some of the stadiums where he had played.

He became somewhat excited. He wasn't being interviewed by yet another reporter. He didn't approach our time together as an obligation required by his manager.

We were simply talking, enjoying our conversation, which was wide-ranging and included topics such as common restaurants, racial stereotypes and attitudes and cold Montana winters. It was a two-hour talk with Charley Pride.

Although I became a much better writer over the years, the story from that interview was a good read. Here is an abbreviated version:

Charley Pride knows what it's like to pick cotton and walk a dirt road. "Mississippi Cotton Picking Delta Town" is the title of the entertainment superstar's new single record. But Charley hasn't always turned out country music singles.

From Sledge, Miss., Pride used to hit singles, but he gave up his baseball cleats and uniform in 1964 for Tony Lama boots, silk shirts and stylish outfits.

Still, baseball is Pride's first love. It got him out of the Mississippi cotton fields and launched his country-music career.

During a break after his opening-night performances at Harrah's Tahoe Tuesday night, Pride lounged in his backstage suite and talked about his unusual entrance into the entertainment world.

Pride worked in the cotton fields as a boy, but it wasn't his idea of how he would spend the rest of his life.

"I was always sort of a skinny kid, and when I was about 12 I started getting interested in baseball," Pride said. "People used to say to me 'You'll never make it in baseball, you're too skinny.' You know, when you're growing up and people keep telling you these things, you start believing them.

"But you come to a point in your life when you stop for a minute and really think: is this true or is it not? I decided it wasn't true for me. I was skinny, but I had two arms, two legs, two eyes. Maybe I wasn't the best, but I wasn't the worst."

Pride told himself he was going to give baseball a whirl and see if he could make it. He fell in love with the game, put on some weight, honed his skills and abilities and saw his chance to get out of Mississippi.

At the age of 17, Pride had developed his talent to a level where he was playing for the Negro American League Memphis Red Sox. He later played for the Birmingham Black Barons.

"Back at that time, the Negro American League was sort of a training ground for the majors," Pride said. "I was a pitcher and an outfielder."

Pride also played in several exhibition games against teams comprised of the best black players from the major leagues.

"After the major-league season, the black stars would get a team together to barnstorm around the country playing the

(continued)

(continued)

best players from the Negro American League," Pride said, adding he played against Henry Aaron, Willie Mays and Ernie Banks.

"I don't remember if I struck out Aaron or not," Pride said. "But I do know he didn't get a hit off me."

Pride's success in the country-music field is due to a different set of circumstances.

"After I was dropped by the Los Angeles Angels, I joined the Pioneer League in Montana, playing baseball and working in a tin smelter in Helena," Pride said. "One night someone brought a guitar to the game and I sang over the public address system."

That experience launched Pride's singing career, leading to a night club job at the Main Tavern in Helena where he was later discovered, ending up in Nashville.

In the country-music field, Pride doesn't think he is a black pioneer.

"From society's standpoint I might be a pioneer as a black country singer, but from my standpoint I don't feel like a pioneer. I've been singing country music since I was young and I'm just a little more tan than most country-music singers."

Pride didn't make it to the big leagues in baseball, but through the game he made it to the country-music big leagues.

A Failure

Preparation and research do not always guarantee a good interview.

Kareem Abdul Jabbar was a 7-foot–2, 267-pound giant of a man on the basketball court. The New York native came west to play college ball at the University of California, Los Angeles (UCLA), where he led the Bruins to an 88–2 record.

Jabbar played in eighteen National Basketball Association (NBA) All-Star Games in a twenty-year career, and he holds NBA career records for most minutes (57,446), most points (38,387), most field goals made (15,837) and most field goals attempted (28,307).

He is one of the best basketball players of all time.

When I interviewed him, I knew a great deal about him, professional athletes and sports in general. I was well prepared for the interview, but I couldn't get him to open up.

It was a phone interview (not the best option), and every question I asked him, open- or closed-ended, was met with one of three one-word responses—yes, no, maybe—or the following seven-word response: "I don't have anything to say about that."

The problem wasn't a lack of knowledge or research, but rather timing. I called Jabbar at his hotel room and woke him up from a nap.

There was no story to write.

Conscious Decisions

Interview preparation involves more than just researching the subject and source. It also involves trying to determine the type of story that is most likely to be written and then making conscious decisions about how to prepare.

PROFESSIONAL TIPS

Bill Bell

Bill Bell has been editor for more than twenty years of the *Whittier Daily News* (and also publisher for more than the past ten). The *Daily News* is an 18,000 daily-circulation newspaper in Whittier, California, a community of about 85,000 people in Los Angeles County. The newspaper is owned by MediaNews Group, headquartered at the *Denver Post,* and is part of a three-newspaper cluster called San Gabriel Valley Newspapers, which includes the *San Gabriel Valley Tribune* and *Pasadena Star-News.* Bell has been a journalist in southern California for forty-seven years.

Question: What are some of the main problems a new reporter has with interviewing sources?

Problems new reporters have with interviewing sources surface during the editing process. It can become obvious that a reporter is actually putting quotes around what should have been paraphrased, probably because his/her note taking did not keep up with the source. This leads to all interviewees sounding a lot like the reporter or, worse yet, being misquoted. Editors must work with reporters to assure accurate quoting/paraphrasing of sources.

New reporters find themselves interviewing sources who are awesome in stature, who intimidate them, who they feel sorry for, who they instantly don't like, etc. Those factors are enemies of every journalist and every news report. They should be recognized and dealt with.

Question: What are three things that young reporters need to learn about interviewing?

1. They should be sure not to leave the interview without the following information: the correct name and spelling of the source, title if appropriate, age, address, where and how the source can be reached later if needed.
2. They should know why they have selected a source and what questions need to be asked.
3. They should leave their own personal feelings out of it and ask questions the readers want asked and answered. They must take care not to be overly impressed by some highly placed sources' status or unimpressed because another source has a lowly station in life.

Question: What are the advantages and disadvantages to telephone and e-mail interviews?

The advantages to both forms of electronic interviews are purely matters of time and convenience. They're easier and less time-consuming than in-person interviewing.

The disadvantages are significant. First, it is difficult to be sure you are interviewing who you think you are interviewing. Nor do you have any idea for sure how private or how public your interview is. Electronic interviewing deprives you of visual advantages of the source, such as physical presence, body language, facial expressions and, if you go to the source, his/her environment.

- **News:** When a news-story format is anticipated, reporters should base most of their interview preparation on the subject of the news or topic of interest.

- **Feature:** Interview preparation for a feature story will generally focus on the person and their personality. Interests, family, friends, hobbies, travels, habits, quirks and so on should also be researched.

- **Investigative:** Preparation for an investigative interview usually centers on the subject matter and the person(s) involved. Preparation for these interviews needs to be most comprehensive, again because of the legal comparison of an attorney not wanting to ask a question without knowing the likely answer. Reporters in investigative interviews can't afford to be surprised, and reporters must anticipate interviewing in an adversarial environment. Reporters will sometimes also go on "fishing expeditions" by obtaining facts from "people on the fringe" before interviewing the central source or sources.

Before any interview, a journalist should thoroughly consider four things: what is the purpose of the interview? What do I need to know about the person and subject before the interview? Have I planned properly? How am I going to execute the plan?

Other Considerations

There are many factors and considerations in interviewing. One is appearance, and reporters need to dress appropriately. For instance, it wouldn't be appropriate for a reporter to wear a halter top, shorts and sandals to interview a university president. Nor would it be wise to wear a suit and tie to interview a farmer in the middle of a field in 100-degree heat. The key to appearance preparation is to dress professionally, fitting in with the environment.

It's also advantageous to seek interviews on neutral turf. Sources will sometimes find power in their official surroundings, such as an office, and are not always comfortable in a newsroom.

Reporters should always prepare a list of questions in advance, even though there is no mandate that all questions must always be—or should always be—asked. Interviews can sometimes go in different directions than planned, nullifying the need to ask some of the prepared questions.

As an example, a reporter could be cruising through a list of ten prepared questions about a recycling plant when the mayor references a proposed $550 million electrical and ignition design and manufacturing plant that will employee 250 higher-than-average salaried workers. A good reporter will immediately switch the focus away from why tin and aluminum cans have to be sorted, and will concentrate on the major news development. The recycling story can wait for another day.

Still, having prepared questions, in most cases, will allow a reporter to concentrate on source answers rather than mentally search for the next question as a source talks, aiding the reporter to better understand what is being said—or not said.

Preparing for an interview also entails thinking in advance about how to ask questions. The phrasing of questions, or how they are structured, can have a significant bearing on the answers and framing of the story.

Reporters should not ask questions using certain words, inflection or inference that sends a signal about the response the reporter wants or expects. Reporters need to be aware of their biases and keep away from prejudiced questions.

Television newsmagazine shows are notorious for asking leading questions. The "Don't you think . . .?" lead-in is one of the chief offenders. It carries an implication that the reporter supports a specific point of view. A better lead-in is "What do you think?"

Reporters sometimes make statements, seeking to confirm their position from the source. For example, Mike Price was a successful college football coach at Washington State University who was hired at Alabama for his dream job of coaching the Crimson Tide. But he was fired seven months later, before ever coaching a game, after a night of partying at a strip club.

Would it be appropriate for a student reporter to ask in an interview: "The Mike Price situation is tragic. He made some very foolish mistakes. Do you have any comments?" No. It is questionable, leading terminology.

The reporter's statement is likely true. It was a tragic situation, and Price made some foolish mistakes. But reporters shouldn't put words in the mouths of those they are interviewing. Sources should not be told or led into what to say.

A better question would be: "What do you make of the Mike Price situation?"

Kimberly Kimby, a reporter at the *Orange County Register,* says on "Interviewing: New Questions, Better Stories," the first of a four-video series by the Pew Center for Civic Journalism: "I'm finding very often that when I say, 'Tell me more about that' or 'What do you mean by that?' that they don't mean what I thought at all."

Understanding the two basic question formats, and when to use each, is wise in preparing for an interview. KISS—"Keep it simple, stupid"—is also a good rule to follow, and aptly defines the two basic concepts of questions, open-ended and closed-ended.

Open-ended questions, which should be used most often, allow the person being interviewed some flexibility in answering. They are less direct, less threatening, and more exploratory. As an example, a reporter covering a fatal car accident could ask the same question in different ways.

"Officer, it kind of looks to me, and don't you agree, that the guy in the blue car was at fault?"

Or: "Officer, what happened here?"

The second version is clearly best. It isn't leading to some conclusion that the reporter has drawn, and it is simple. Reporters should use their training to do some detective work, resulting in some ideas and/or conclusions. But don't force them upon the source; use that information as background, if you need it.

This open-ended version of the question also gives the officer the flexibility to explain what happened, not just to say if he or she agrees or disagrees with the reporter's speculation.

There is a time, however, for closed-ended questions, usually when detail or specificity is being sought, including "yes" or "no" answers.

Michael Trihey, a very good newspaper reporter when he worked at the *Bakersfield Californian,* once conducted a jailhouse interview with a police officer waiting for trial on charges of killing two prostitutes.

Trihey's first question wasn't a closed-ended "Did you kill those women?" Nor did he ask a biased question such as "Do you think anyone will believe you didn't kill those women?"

Those types of questions could have been interview breakers.

Trihey, now assignment manager at KGET-TV (NBC), Bakersfield, California, started the interview with this question: "Tell me about your job as a policeman at the time the prostitutes were killed." He followed with "Did you have any relationship with the women who were murdered?"

His questions didn't accuse the officer of the murders. Trihey did, however, at the end of the interview, ask the closed-ended question: "Did you kill the two prostitutes?"

Establishing rapport in an interview is a concern that can be aided by advance planning and a proper attitude. Although there are occasions that dictate a more aggressive interviewer posture, the best interviews involve a respect for the source and a professional approach in attitude and actions.

If a source believes in an interview that the reporter is a real person, rapport has a real chance of being established. If the reporter demonstrates humility and searches for areas of common interest, rapport has a real chance of being established. But if a reporter comes across as arrogant or condescending, rapport will die a sudden death.

Those being interviewed will sometimes try to manage the news, or protect themselves, by placing stipulations on what they say in the following ways:

- **Off the record:** This means that nothing said can be used. The information might, however, help a reporter obtain that information or other information. Most reporters claim they have to accept "off-the-record" information to do their jobs properly. Editors generally acknowledge that there is some worth in off-the-record comments, but there are many cautions. If a source makes a statement and then claims the information is off the record, the reporter can accept or deny it is off the record. Whatever the decision, the reporter should inform sources at that time so they do not assume that he or she has accepted the information as off the record.

- **Deep background:** This term came into vogue during Bob Woodward and Carl Bernstein's Watergate coverage. It pertained directly to Deep Throat, identified in 2005 as Mark Felt, a former FBI agent, with the understanding that he or his position would never be revealed and that he would never be quoted. "Deep background" discussions were to only confirm or add perspective to information that had previously been obtained.

- **Not for attribution:** This refers to information that can be used but not attributed— basically the same as using an anonymous source. Information from anonymous sources is used in stories far too often by reporters. Interviews with anonymous sources might reveal a critical story or public information, but every effort should always be taken to obtain the information on the record.

From time to time—ever so sparingly—using anonymous source information in a story might be justified if the following considerations become reality.

- **All efforts must** be exhausted to obtain the information on the record.
- **The information is** critical information that the public needs to know.
- **Release of the** information will provide significantly more good than the bad caused by a lack of publication.

- **Readers must be** told in the story specifically why the source's identity can't be revealed, and the fullest possible identification without revealing identity must be included.

Many editors have additional rules before allowing publication of anonymous source material, including:

- **Reporters need to** distinguish between "leaked" facts and opinion.
- **Editors must approve,** in advance, a reporter's offer of anonymity.
- **If asked, the** reporter must share the name of the anonymous source with the editor.
- **Anonymous sources are** not allowed to make personal attacks on others.

"He said, she said" is a common debate. The best way to achieve accuracy in an interview is by taping the conversation. Transcription, however, can be a very time-consuming process, so many reporters become exceptional note takers. Taping is also something uncomfortable for some sources.

Paraphrasing can serve a journalist well, as quoting a source from an interview isn't always a simple process.

Should a reporter "clean up" a quote or use it verbatim? Follow *The Associated Press Stylebook and Briefing on Media Law,* which reads: "Never alter quotations even to correct minor grammatical errors or word usage. Casual minor tongue slips may be removed by using ellipses but even that should be done with extreme caution. If there is a question about a quote, either don't use it or ask the speaker to clarify. . . . In general, avoid fragmentary quotes. If a speaker's words are clear and concise, favor the full quote. If cumbersome language can be paraphrased fairly, use an indirect construction, reserving quotation marks for sensitive or controversial passages that must be identified specifically as coming from the speaker. . . . Remember that you can misquote someone by giving a startling remark without its modifying passage or qualifiers. The manner of delivery sometimes is part of the context. Reporting a smile or a deprecatory gesture may be as important as conveying the words themselves."

The Subtleties of Interviewing

The little things sometimes make a difference. When they are not addressed, they sometimes become big things. Here are several subtleties of interviewing, and although some might seem trivial, they are all important.

When possible, don't sit directly in front of a source as it can make him or her nervous or uncomfortable.

Permit sources to make eye contact—if, and when, they wish, but don't force the issue.

If taping an interview, ask for permission (after the tape is rolling so the answer is recorded); some sources are uncomfortable being taped. Never secretly tape anyone. When taping, place the recorder in an inconspicuous spot.

Take accurate notes.

Be a good observer. Some reporters see everything but don't observe anything. Sources aren't always honest. As an example, a source might say he or she was in the military in 2003 and a decorated Iraq War veteran, yet you observe a degree hanging on the wall from Stanford University with a 2003 date. It could be a simple mistake, but it should raise a reporter's skepticism and warrant a follow-up question.

A classic example of sources not always being honest, or using the media, occurred in a January 2005 edition of the student newspaper at Washington State University.

The story was about the students' elected vice president resigning. He was quoted as saying, "This was a hard decision," and that his resignation was based on not having enough time to spend with his friends, on his studies, and at his internship.

His fellow officers were quoted as saying, "I was a little overwhelmed at first and sad because I didn't want him to leave" and "We're really going to miss his spirit in the office. We have so much to do, we need to mourn and move at the same time."

The truth? He was asked to resign by the executive staff, which included the person who suggested that mourning was appropriate. The lesson: reporters need to dig deeper, go below the surface, ask appropriate questions and not accept as gospel everything they are told.

What you observe can have significant meaning. Researchers have studied nonverbal communication and suggest that a person might be unapproachable if they have folded arms, or that they might be under tension if they cross their ankles.

Ask follow-up questions. If a mayor explains the criteria used to fire a city manager and these criteria include age, don't accept that as something readers will understand, especially if you don't understand. Ask what the mayor means. Was the city manager too old or too young? Is it legal to hire or fire someone based on age?

Hear what isn't being said. Suppose that same mayor kept referring, almost as an afterthought, to the city manager's relationship with another department head. That might not have been listed as a reason for the dismissal, but could it actually have been the reason? That is real understanding—hearing sometimes what isn't being said but is being referenced.

Some Final Tips

Concentrate on using "how" and "why" questions. "Why did you do that? How did that happen?"

Ask those being interviewed to define terms you don't understand. "Can you define what you mean?"

Try to reason why a source is telling you something. Do they have suspect motives?

Ask questions that sources should be able to answer. For instance, it probably wouldn't be appropriate to ask a city transit manager why the police department is over budget. If a source can't answer a question, ask if he or she knows who would have the information.

Be detached. Rather than asking questions beginning with something like "I understand that you . . .," use the following nonpersonal position: "People say you have . . . "

Remember, if you don't ask, it isn't likely that certain information will be volunteered.

Ask people to define answers. If someone says they change "a lot" of tires during the winter, ask, "How many?" If something is unclear, ask for clarification by inquiring: "Are you saying . . .?" Ask for examples.

Translate jargon.

Verify statistics. If someone told you they were in New York on September 11, 2000, when terrorists attacked, what should you do? Check the date—it was 2001.

End every interview by asking, "Do you have anything to add, or is there anything I forgot to ask?"

Reporters should interview in person whenever possible, even though the phone can be an effective tool in gathering basic information and for routine interviews.

Be persistent and polite.

Always make it clear that you are a reporter and everything in the interview is on the record, unless otherwise agreed upon.

Ask only one question at a time.

Don't stay longer than you are welcome.

CHAPTER EXERCISES

1. Divide into teams of two; one student will play the role of a reporter, and the other will be interviewed. As the reporter, pretend you are working on a story about campus (alcohol use, racism or religion). You are planning to have plenty of official comment, but you also want comment from students. Spend a couple of minutes preparing five questions (beyond the basics of name, classification in school, etc.). You will want to ask the interviewee's personal views on alcohol use (or whatever topic). Ask specific questions. Don't accept only generalities. Push for examples. Get a few good quotes. When done, select a new topic and reverse roles. When both students have played the roles of reporter and interviewee, type your questions and answers, then turn them in.

2. Good stories can't be written without good information. Select one of the following three interview options:

   - **Interview a foreign-born student** on campus about cultural differences between his or her country and the United States.
   - **Interview someone who** works the graveyard shift. What is it like when the rest of the world works days?
   - **Interview anyone on** campus (other than a student) about the five greatest challenges facing your university or community.

   Do not interview someone you know. Prepare a list of ten questions (minimum) in advance (this does not include: "What's your name?" "How old are you?" etc.). After the interview, type the questions and the verbatim responses immediately underneath each question. Ask open-ended questions. Work as individuals, and do not conduct duplicate interviews (when you set up your interview, ask if anyone else has interviewed him or her; if so, find another person to interview). On your assignment, remember to translate notes (abbreviations, etc.) and write in complete sentences using correct language, grammar, syntax, spelling and AP style.

3. Interview your neighbor in this course. Find out something different, funny or interesting about him or her, and write a one-page *brite,* a short feature-like story.

5 Meetings, Speeches and Press Conferences

BY KENTON BIRD AND DAVID CUILLIER

"I call this meeting to order." Kids often seem to get right to the point, whereas it is typical for officials to "dance all around" questions. If this happens to you, politely find another way to ask the question, not letting the person avoid the question by double-talking.

From wood-framed city halls to brick courthouses to marble state capitols, meetings are how governments do much of their work. They are one of the main windows through which the public learns about the formation of public policy and how it affects their daily lives.

Meetings can be long, tedious and deadly dull; they can also be the sources of some of the most interesting, revealing and provocative stories about government at all levels. Meetings often give residents of a community the first warning of changes that will affect their daily lives: new schools, street repairs, tax increases and business openings and closures.

The reporter's challenge is to focus on substance, not process; avoid getting bogged down in minutiae; and use meetings as a springboard to stories that explain the workings of the council, commission or agency and why it matters to readers.

Similarly, bringing a speech to the printed page is not an easy task, particularly when radio or TV has already reported the highlights. A follow-up story can provide added depth and texture to a speaker's remarks, as well as audience reaction. An accurate and detailed story of a speech can give the public an insight into a significant public event.

Press conferences are a hybrid of meetings, speeches and interviews. Politicians and government officials use these pseudo-events to spin stories and shape public opinion. Reporters who refuse to accept statements at face value will ask probing questions and verify information from other sources, avoiding being manipulated. Finally, other events that involve talking heads require a blend of skills.

Meeting Advances

A reporter's work typically begins days before the opening gavel. The release of the agenda often is an opportunity to preview major issues and recap unfinished business. Many newspapers run advance stories intended to give citizens an opportunity to contact officials in advance or attend the meeting in person. Sometimes these are stand-alone stories; often, they are part of a weekly preview of government meetings.

Who sets the agenda is important. In small towns, the mayor might compile the agenda; in larger cities, the city manager or clerk would have this task. If an item on which a decision had been delayed from a previous meeting is missing from the agenda, that might be a story—an agreement could have been worked out behind the scenes, or the mayor might be trying to work out a compromise.

Whoever decides the agenda, he or she usually has a secretary or administrative assistant who actually assembles it. Check with this person often.

Release of the agenda—usually two or three days before the meeting—provides an opportunity for a reporter to reacquaint him- or herself with ongoing issues, review supporting documents from previous meetings and read the accounts of those meetings in the paper's archives.

Many agendas are accompanied by a packet of supplementary material: budgets, bids, staff reports. Knowing who is responsible for which agenda item enables interviews with key players in advance of the meeting.

At a minimum, an advance story contains the meeting's starting time and location; it's often helpful to provide logistical information such as where to park, how to get a copy of the agenda and whether the meeting will be televised on a public access channel.

An enterprising reporter can turn a routine advance story into a scoop by contacting board or council members in advance and asking them how they intend to vote on a controversial issue on the agenda. Not all elected officials will disclose their positions beforehand, but if they do, you've got a story that no one else does.

Here's an example from the *Coloradoan* in Fort Collins. Reporter Kevin Duggan turned a routine meeting advance into a background piece on a controversial human rights ordinance. An accompanying box, "What's Next?" gave a capsule preview:

City Braces for Renewed Rights Debate

Plan to Expand Protection to Homosexuals Draws Fire

By Kevin Duggan

Ring the bell.

The next round in the long fight over Fort Collins' Human Rights Ordinance and whether anti-discrimination protection should be extended to homosexuals is about to begin.

Tuesday, the City Council is scheduled to begin a formal consideration of proposed revisions to the ordinance, which has been the subject of public debate and study by a city-appointed task force for months.

Council members will be considering two ordinances. The first makes several changes to the city's anti-discrimination law, which was passed in 1972.

City law now prohibits discrimination in employment, housing and public accommodations on the basis of race, color, religion, disability, sex, national origin, marital status or—in the case of employment—age.

The proposed ordinance also would ban discrimination in the areas of housing and public accommodations on the basis of whether a person receives public assistance. It also refines several definitions in the law to closer reflect state and federal anti-discrimination laws, and alters the city's process for handling complaints.

The second proposed ordinance would add sexual orientation—defined as actual or perceived heterosexuality, homosexuality, bisexuality or asexuality—as a basis of discrimination in all three areas covered by the law.

That thorny issue has dominated the discussion of the ordinance in three public forums held by the city's Human Rights Ordinance Task Force and in letters and phone calls to council members.

Supporters of including sexual orientation in the law say homosexuals face rampant discrimination but have no legal recourse to battle it.

"People's private behavior is something that should not be used to judge their competence for a job or whether they should live in a particular place," said Barbara Gonzales.

Gay people need legal protection, Gonzales said, just as seniors and racial minorities do.

But opponents, many of whom say this is a moral issue, contend that homosexuals should not be singled out for "special" protection.

The gay lifestyle is a matter of choice, they say, while one's race is not.

Jon Patterson, a Fort Collins attorney, said the city should not use its authority to force landlords to rent to those with different "values and attitudes."

The same goes for telling employers whom they must hire, he said.

"I think it is wrong to put the power of the government on one side of this issue," Patterson said. "To do that has some serious potential for limiting freedom of speech, association, religion and use of private property."

Arguments on the issue are expected to be aired during a special hearing scheduled from 7:30 to 10:30 P.M. Tuesday at the Lincoln Center. The hearing will be held away from council chambers at City Hall in order to accommodate the expected large crowd.

The council will not take formal action on the ordinances Tuesday. That is expected to come Feb. 17, when the council is scheduled to have first readings of both proposals.

Final consideration of the ordinances is scheduled for March 3.

(continued)

(continued)

The council could choose to put either ordinance up for a public vote. Opponents of adding sexual orientation have been campaigning for an election, while supporters say an election would put the city in the position of letting the majority decide the issue.

A similar proposal was put on the city ballot in 1988. The issue was defeated at the polls after a bitter and divisive political campaign.

WHAT'S NEXT?

The first of three Fort Collins City Council hearings on proposed revisions to the city's Human Rights Ordinance is set for 7:30 to 10:30 P.M. Tuesday in the Canyon West Room of the Lincoln Center, 417 W. Magnolia St.

Speakers will be limited to two minutes to express their opinions on the two ordinances that the council will be considering.

The first council vote on the ordinances is scheduled for Feb. 17 at City Hall, 300 W. LaPorte Ave. Public hearings on the ordinance are expected to be limited to one hour each.

Final consideration of the ordinances is scheduled for the council's March 3 meeting. Again, public hearings on the ordinances are expected to be limited to one hour each. The meetings at City Hall are set to begin at 6 P.M.

Comments on the ordinances may be made by calling 493–2489, ext. 184, or by writing to the City Manager, P.O. Box 580, Fort Collins, CO 80522.

Another key way to advance a story in meaningful fashion is to find citizens affected by the proposed sewer rate increase, by new rules restricting home-based day care or by mandates for keeping sidewalks clean. In any case, put a human face on the story as often as possible.

Covering the Meeting

The mayor, board chair or presiding officer sets the tone for a meeting through his or her choice of apparel and degree of formality. If the men on the council wear jackets and ties and the women wear suits, the reporter should follow suit. Similarly, if the mayor favors plaid shirts and blue jeans, the reporter has license to dress more casually.

Go to the council chamber or meeting room early, arriving at least fifteen or twenty minutes before the scheduled starting time. This will give you time to find an appropriate seat.

Some bodies have designated press seats or even a media table; however, sitting there might make it difficult to pursue comments from citizens during the meeting. Some reporters are uncomfortable at being set apart from the rest of the public, wanting to avoid the appearance of having special privileges.

Steve Smith, editor of the *Spokesman-Review* in Spokane, Washington, and a proponent of civic journalism, argues that viewing the deliberations from citizens' perspectives is important. Regardless of where one sits, the most important thing is being able to see and hear the participants.

Another advantage of arriving early is the ability to talk to staff members and, if covering this body for the first time, to introduce yourself. Be sure that nothing has been added to the agenda since it was first released, and ask for copies of any supplementary material.

If you're new to the beat, be sure you know the names of all members of the board, commission or council, as well as the support staff such as the city clerk and attorney. Many agencies have placards or nameplates in front of each member's seat, but don't assume the person sitting behind the name is that member. (Sometimes a substitute will fill in for a legislator; sometimes the nameplates are simply out of place.) Double check to be sure you are spelling each name correctly.

Once the meeting is underway, watch the clock. Being able to say how long a hearing or debate lasted is a valuable detail. Pay attention to departures from the agenda. What issues have been moved ahead? What decision has been delayed until the end of the meeting—perhaps to when most of the audience has gone home? What informal conversations go on during recesses or breaks in the meeting?

Many boards or commissions use something called a *consent calendar* or *consent agenda* to deal with routine items—or those on which the presiding officer hopes to avoid debate. Typically, this agenda includes decisions such as authorizing payment of bills, accepting reports and referring matters to committee. The collected items may be adopted with a single vote—unless a member objects and asks for a proposal to be considered separately.

Occasionally, something that divided the council at a previous meeting shows up on the consent agenda. That's usually a sign that a deal has been worked out behind the scenes and dissenting members have been persuaded to drop their objections. If there's been an attempt to gloss over differences of opinion, find out why.

Observe public involvement in the decision-making process. The degree of interest from parents, residents of affected neighborhoods or organized factions is often an indicator of public interest. Be sure to get the names of everyone who speaks. At some public hearings, speakers are asked to sign up in advance, which provides a great tool for checking the spelling of names and finding an address or telephone number.

The mayor or presiding officer usually asks speakers to identify themselves by name and address, but this step may be overlooked at informal meetings or in small jurisdictions. Consider asking the mayor after the meeting to build this into the protocol for meetings—both to assist in reporting accurately who speaks at the meeting and for the benefit of citizens who attend.

If necessary, be prepared to follow a speaker into the lobby during a break in the meeting to confirm the spelling of a name or get a phone number for follow-up questions. When people step to the microphone and read from prepared remarks, make a note to ask for a copy.

Any time a crowd of citizens shows up at a council or board meeting, try to determine whether it's a spontaneous expression of public sentiment or an organized attempt to pack the meeting and influence policy.

Sometimes a church, parent–teacher organization or neighborhood group will use a telephone tree or e-mail list to generate a large turnout for a meeting. Find out who the group's president or spokesperson is, and follow up after the meeting. Be careful not to portray a carefully choreographed demonstration as a groundswell of public opinion.

Occasionally, a citizen will deliver an articulate observation about the future of the city or a caustic denunciation of the council's recent action—and then turn to the audience (or you in particular) and say, "That's off the record."

After the meeting, if convenient, or before the story runs, politely but firmly inform the speaker that everything said at a public meeting is on the record, and that if the speaker didn't want to be quoted, he or she should have chosen another forum to express his or her opinion.

Of course, if you're covering a meeting of a business organization or nonprofit group, open meeting laws don't apply. Even so, a statement before a group won't stay secret long. In that situation, the reporter might negotiate with the speaker over reporting the substance of the comment. Use common sense. In general, if it's said in public, it's fair game—whether the setting is the corner cafe where the chamber of commerce meets, the high school gymnasium or the hardware store.

Don't leave a meeting too early—even if you think the major items have been discussed. If your deadline prevents you from staying to the end, ask another reporter to alert you if anything major happens. Be prepared to call the mayor or clerk the next day with follow-up questions.

I've seen a city council reverse an annexation decision after lobbying by the mayor during intermission. And I've seen a school board go into a closed "executive session" at the end of its regular agenda, then reconvene in public session to make an unpopular decision after the affected and interested citizens have gone home. Be especially careful when a closed session is scheduled as the last item on a long agenda.

Writing the Meeting Story

While the meeting is underway, be thinking about your lead. Just as a sports writer tries to begin writing at halftime of a basketball or football game, so, too, a government reporter needs to be thinking before the meeting is over about what to include in his or her story.

Your lead might not be the most consequential decision, such as annexing property or the adoption of a budget. It could be the most interesting, unusual or provocative action—the one that sparked the sharpest debate among council members or the liveliest public reaction.

Remember that you're not giving the minutes of the meeting; that's the job of the board's clerk or recorder. Forget about the formalities: the call to order, the pledge of allegiance, the proclamations and presentations.

Beginning reporters often take a chronological approach, forgetting that the most important or interesting news can come far down the agenda. A reporter new to a beat might wish to run several possible leads past his or her assignment editor to see which has the greatest interest or timeliness.

Test your lead by asking yourself whether the decision's impact goes beyond people who work at city hall or the courthouse.

Richard Hendrickson, who teaches at John Carroll University in Cleveland, tells his students to pose this question: "Would I read this if I didn't have to write it? If the answer is no, you might want to ask yourself . . . if it is significant or interesting enough to anyone else to merit publication."

A reporter in a competitive situation should look one or two news cycles in advance and have several leads in his or her pocket. If the TV station and the morning paper lead with the zoning decision, you might wish to start your story with an increase in water and sewer rates.

One way to make your story distinct is to localize it: look for the impact on people or neighborhoods. If the decision will be felt in different ways in different parts of the city, find two or three examples.

A state or regional commission's decision can be broken down by city or district. Here is an example of showing the impact on a neighborhood. In an advance story, Kyle Henley of the *Coloradoan* focuses on the west-central neighborhood of Fort Collins and includes descriptions of the areas involved (a map would make it even easier for citizens to know which neighborhoods will be affected):

City Council to Plot Neighborhood Plans

Mountain Vista and West Central Areas Target of Long-Term Planning

By Kyle Henley

The city has plans. In fact, it has plans within plans.

On Tuesday night, City Council is poised to add to the list of plans, considering the Mountain Vista Subarea Plan and the West Central Neighborhoods Plan.

The West Central Neighborhoods Plan is the strategy the city is going to employ to guide the development and redevelopment of the 3-square-mile, L-shaped area southwest of Colorado State University.

The plan deals with such items as parks, land use, neighborhood appearance and design, housing, transportation, historic preservation and sense of community.

Because the planning area is next to Colorado State University, one of the key elements of the West Central Neighborhoods Plan is the interaction between students and residents.

It "attempts to deal with encouraging a mix of housing types so units are available for families of all incomes and to balance the needs for CSU student/rental housing, while mitigating the negative impacts within neighborhoods," City Planner Ken Waido said.

Due to the high number of students living in some of the city's most dense neighborhoods, traffic and parking are big issues in the West Central Neighborhoods.

The plan calls for better use of Center Avenue to alleviate congestion at the intersection of Prospect Road and Shields Street.

"Other policies and plans deal with adding bicycle routes and recommendations for pedestrian improvements," Waido said.

Unlike the West Central Neighborhoods Plan, which deals with an already

(continued)

(continued)

developed area, the Mountain Vista Subarea Plan creates a vision for an area that is largely rural.

Through City Plan, the city's 20-year plan for growth that was passed in 1997, officials decided Fort Collins would grow to the northeast, specifically into the 5.5-square-mile area bounded by Interstate 25, Vine Drive, Douglas Road and Leman Avenue.

City officials estimate the area will develop over the next 10 to 20 years and eventually be home to more than 5,000 homes.

But significant infrastructure investments—roads, sewers, utilities, police stations, fire stations, parks, libraries, etc.— need to be made before any of it can happen, said city planner Pete Wray. That cost could be as high as $200 million.

That means the city, and taxpayers, may need to look for ways to finance the plan.

"While developers will be expected to finance the infrastructure improvements necessitated by their projects, and some of those improvements, such as roads, will be very costly, it appears that traditional funding mechanisms . . . will not be adequate to pay for all the street improvements and community amenities the plan envisions," Wray said.

"This situation suggests that the city should consider the full range of infrastructure financing mechanisms."

If the council or board is divided over an important question, tell who voted on which side and why (some papers might do this in a sidebar or information graphic). Even if there is no decision, recap the arguments in favor and against a proposition. But remember that the outcome has more public interest than the parliamentary maneuvering that led to the final vote.

As with all types of public affairs reporting, try to place the news in context. Show how the latest decision connects with past actions. Is a large annexation consistent with a council's goals of managing growth? Does a zone change to allow a big-box retailer on the edge of town run contrary to a policy to encourage commercial development in the city's core?

The reporter needs to give enough background on a topic for casual or first-time readers without bogging down the story in history (some newspapers refer readers to the paper's Web site for previous stories about an issue).

A reporter can also give an indication of what happens next. If the decision is not final, when will it come back to the council? Many newspapers run box score–like summaries to give readers an indication of the next steps in the deliberative process.

Finally, don't feel obligated to include everything that happens at the meeting in your first story. As a city hall reporter in Moscow, Idaho, I found I could often generate a week's worth of follow-up stories from one council meeting. By conducting follow-up interviews with affected citizens and getting details of a project or plan from city staff, I could provide perspective, depth and explanation—something not possible when a decision is relegated to a bulleted paragraph after a one-sentence introduction: "In other action, the council . . . "

Some items discussed won't be worthy of a story in the days after the meeting, but deserve to be filed for future reference—particularly if they are part of a running story or ongoing local controversy.

In drafting a lead, look for the 3 C's—contrasts, costs and complaints. Those are great ways to tell readers or viewers "What does it mean for you?"

Speeches

Like meetings, speeches are public events that give reporters an opportunity to exceed the obvious ("The governor outlined his budget for the next fiscal year . . . ") and provide readers with information that augments what the audience heard in person.

Politicians, scientists, entertainers, business leaders and others use speeches as a way to educate, uplift and inspire. From campaign rallies to high school graduations, speakers offer policy goals, advice, wisdom and humor.

A reporter's ability to reach beyond the routine recap of the talk sets an insightful speech story apart from an ordinary one.

An advance story can provide useful background on the speaker, as well as give readers a chance to decide whether the speaker is worth hearing. The sponsoring organization might provide biographical information, but if not, a good public or college library will have reference works such as *Current Biography.*

An Internet search could provide additional details, but be careful that you use material that can be verified and identified.

In an advance story, be sure to provide the essentials: time, location, sponsor and whether tickets are required.

Arrive early at the lecture hall or auditorium. This provides an opportunity to count the number of seats—a task that's easier before the room fills with people. Knowing the room's capacity makes it easier to estimate the attendance. It's better to say, "The 600-seat auditorium was two-thirds full," than to report, "Several hundred people heard the speech."

At some formal speeches—a governor's state-of-the-state address or a university commencement—a prepared text might be available. The ability to follow the text makes note taking immeasurably easier, though it requires close attention to any deviations from the advance draft. Be sure to ask the sponsoring organization whether a prepared text is available.

Sometimes, a sponsor makes a speaker available for a press conference before or after the speech. This gives reporters a chance to ask clarifying questions or delve into topics not covered in the speech.

If possible, stick around after the speech to ask audience members for their reaction. The ability to discern how well a speaker connected with his or her audience is a key element of a successful speech story.

Here are tips for writing a speech story.

Identify the main themes. Remember, you're telling a story, not giving a transcript. Don't write down everything the speaker says. Try to capture the essence, not the entire speech.

Avoid vague leads that don't tell what the speaker said.

Don't write: "Director Michael Moore spoke Tuesday to a capacity crowd at Beasley Coliseum."

Instead, write: "Director Michael Moore urged Americans to become better informed about the political process and to vote for a new president in November."

Or, to get the action up front: "America must become better informed about the political process and vote for a new president in November, director Michael Moore told students at Washington State University."

Listen for quotations that support the main point. But use quotes selectively.

Pay attention to the audience: the numbers, the demographics, the reactions (laughter, sighs and nods of agreement). If questions follow the speech, get the names and identification for the questions.

Include biographical information about the speaker, perhaps details from the introduction that aren't well known. When former Attorney General Janet Reno visited the University of Idaho in 2001, *Spokesman-Review* reporter Hannelore Sudermann described Reno as an avid kayaker, the daughter of two newspaper reporters and the owner of a red pickup.

Tell how much the speaker was paid, if applicable, and the source of the money.

Note any protests inside or outside the auditorium. Sometimes their message is as interesting as the speech itself.

Observe how the speaker arrived and left the event. When media giant and environmental activist Ted Turner spoke at the University of Idaho, *Lewiston Morning Tribune* reporter David Johnson ended his story as follows: "Turner encouraged people to car pool, use mass transit and refuse to buy gas-guzzling automobiles. After his talk, Turner was escorted to a waiting UI forestry college Chevrolet Suburban and driven away to make his speech at Washington State University."

Press Conferences

Daniel Boorstin, in his book *The Image,* defined *pseudo-event* as an event that would not happen were it not for the presence of the news media. Boorstin used the staged press conference as an example of the media's reliance on official sources of news.

Yet unlike other pseudo-events—grand openings, ribbon cuttings, new product releases—press conferences can have some news value. At best, they are an opportunity to observe how well a public official or political candidate thinks on his or her feet; at worst, they are self-serving vehicles for the politician or officeholder to get a sound bite on a local TV news report.

Press conferences range from the spirited exchanges between the president and the White House press corps (an infrequent occurrence under President George W. Bush) to an informal, across-the-desk session with a mayor or university president and a handful of reporters. They're part speech, part group interview, and, when TV cameras are present, part theatrical presentation.

For government agencies and public officials, press conferences serve several purposes, including allowing news to be released to all local agencies simultaneously, avoiding the impression of playing favorites, bringing together several experts in one place, saving time for reporters and making efficient use of the principals' time (avoiding the need to give multiple answers to the same questions).

PROFESSIONAL TIPS

Ken Olsen

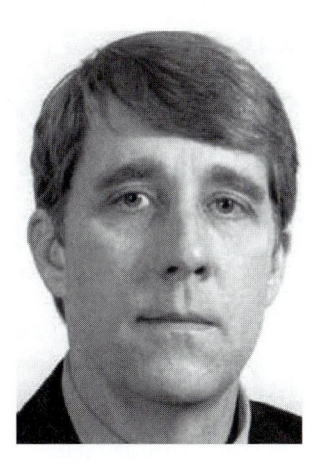

Veteran journalist Ken Olsen has covered nearly every kind of public agency during his twenty years of working for newspapers. He is now a freelance magazine writer based in Spokane, Washington.

Question: Given shrinking news holes and smaller newsroom staffs at many newspapers, how important is it to cover meetings of city councils and other agencies?

Once a reporter is familiar with a beat, the routine meetings of a government agency move way down the priority list. I suggest a three-part test:

1. What am I going to get by attending the meeting that I can't get elsewhere? (Possibilities are interviews with audience members, local color, etc.)
2. Can I better spend that time working on another story that puts me ahead of the competition?
3. Why can't I advance the story in more meaningful fashion than spending all of that time watching the government process?

Attendance aside, reporters should write far fewer stories about meetings they attend. It's often a highly orchestrated government process that bores readers.

Question: What kinds of information can you get at a meeting that you can't get from interviewing the council or board members?

You can learn more about citizen reaction to a particular issue and perhaps get an interview with one of the people affected by a pending action. You can see how board members act on stage as well as in the presence of fellow government officials. Finally, you can get an appreciation for how much

the board is truly involved in governing an agency and how much they are just caretakers.

I would stress, however, that unless there is great tension between council members, there is very little a seasoned beat reporter can obtain in a public meeting that cannot easily be obtained elsewhere—and turned into a more interesting story. We should be informing our readers before the final vote is made.

Question: What types of follow-up stories can help personalize meeting stories or demonstrate the impact of an agency's decision on citizens?

Stories that demonstrate what a particular agency decision means to everyday people: how does it affect their ability to work, play, raise their children and pay their bills? How much will it cost each person in your town? Answer the question of "What does it mean?" For example: "Jill Smith now has no place to take her children because new city regulations led to the closure of the home day care center she relied upon. As a single mother, she now must choose between losing her job and having someone care for her children."

Even the most mundane story about, say, snowplow routes can have a human element. Check to see if the main routes to the hospital emergency room get plowed before or after the street that the mayor lives on.

(continued)

PROFESSIONAL TIPS   Continued

Question: In an era of sound bites, is there value in covering speeches, particularly by elected officials and candidates for public office?

Like all highly orchestrated events, there might be value in attending for background, but there often is no reason to write a story about the event. We are not tasked to be stenographers for the boasts and bloated promises of candidates. If a news story is a must, ask for a copy of the speech in advance, and verify the claims the person is making. Or take that same action afterward. Tell your readers what the speech means to them on a practical level. And if it's all rhetoric, don't waste your ink.

Question: Does any real news ever come out of a press conference? Or could you get the same information elsewhere?

Press conferences held by politicians and public officials frequently are artificial news events with little real story value. If a press conference represents the only time a reporter can corner a public official and ask an important question, use that opportunity. Ask yourself if you could better spend the time interviewing the politician's former neighbors or checking to see if the mayor has delivered on his promise to deal with traffic problems in front of the elementary school.

If you must attend, use your highest standards in deciding whether to write a story. The best reporters know their beats so well that they can write about the most important news elements before the press conference takes place.

Question: How can a radio or print reporter keep the TV cameras and reporters from dominating a press conference? And how do you keep politicians from showboating for the cameras?

Be bold, but polite. Don't immediately yield the floor after you have asked a question if a follow-up question is warranted. Arrive early and figure out how you could corner the people you need to talk to after the event and ask a few questions "offstage." Call the politician's press aide in advance and arrange for a few minutes of the public official's time after the press conference.

As for showboating politicians, either ignore them entirely or, if it's over the top, mention it in a story. If politicians or public officials are frequent offenders in this category, consider not attending their press events at all.

A press conference typically begins with an opening statement: a formal announcement of candidacy, plans for a business to relocate to a community or a federal grant to support research at a university.

The announcement is often accompanied by a prepared statement, a press release or a media packet distributed to reporters (an enterprising reporter can sometimes obtain this background material in advance of the press conference, which helps in preparing questions).

After the opening statement, the main speaker typically opens the floor to questions. In some settings, the reporter with the most seniority asks the first question; in others, a reporter representing the largest or most powerful news organization has the honor. Protocol at more formal press conferences calls for reporters to take turns asking questions, but local customs might allow more aggressive questioners to dominate.

Reporters typically have the right to ask one follow-up question before giving the floor to another reporter. If a politician or public official is being evasive, it's entirely appropriate for the next reporter to rephrase the question or observe that the previous question had not been adequately answered.

A reporter pursuing a different angle on the event might sometimes avoid asking a provocative question, in hope of being able to ask it privately. On the other hand, there are sometimes advantages to pinning down an official in front of other reporters (and especially TV cameras). It then becomes more difficult for the speaker to disavow an answer, back away from a position that he or she is uncomfortable with, or claim that a quote was taken out of context.

The presence of TV cameras is an unavoidable nuisance at most events. The cameras often get in the way of a lively exchange, in part because the speakers choose their words more carefully and assume a more dramatic persona. Because of time limitations, TV reporters are usually most interested in the opening statement than in the Q&A that follows, though they rarely miss an opportunity to insert themselves into the story by asking the speaker to restate the obvious in responses to their question.

If a press conference is held in an unusual location or includes a demonstration or display, consider including it in the story. When the University of Idaho announced a new center to combat invasive species, the press conference was held in a grove of white pine trees on the edge of campus. Associated Press reporter Rebecca Boone described it as follows: "The school announced the center in a press conference held in the shade of a stand of white pine trees. The northern Idaho tree, which once provided much of the wood for American homes, was nearly wiped out by white pine blister rust."

Other Events

The press conference has several close cousins: candidate forums, panel discussions and symposiums.

- **Candidate forums:** These are often sponsored by the League of Women Voters or other nonpartisan groups, and are staples in the weeks leading up to an election. They typically give candidates time for short opening and closing statements. Questions are sometimes asked directly by the audience but are often screened and sorted by a moderator. Answers are short—one to two minutes. Forums can provide insights into what's on the public's mind but rarely provide any answers of any substance because of the time limits on answers. For reporters, they may be more valuable as a source of questions for follow-up interviews with candidates.

- **Panel discussions and symposiums:** These are often organized as part of academic conferences and trade shows. They usually consist of short presentations by several speakers, discussion by the panelists and questions from the audience. Tips for covering a speech—finding a theme, using quotes sparingly and including audience reaction—apply to these events. At academic conferences, it's often possible to obtain a copy of the speaker's prepared remarks or a scholarly article on which the presentation is based. Don't feel obliged to devote equal time or space to all speakers; one might have more interesting or important comments than the others.

All of these events—meetings, speeches, press conferences, forums and panels—share a common problem. They often are more staged than spontaneous, and can consume reporting resources better spent digging through documents or conducting interviews that actually produce news.

If an issue is especially contentious, elected officials will usually talk one-on-one away from the eyes and ears of reporters. Spontaneous decision making in the public spotlight is rare.

Access to Meetings

One of the foundations of democracy is the belief that government should conduct its business openly. The responsibility for policing open meetings often falls, by default, on journalists. Every state has laws requiring governing bodies of public agencies to meet in the open except in certain specific circumstances. Although each law is different, they share the same general principles. Public affairs reporters need to not only know the law but also keep a copy handy.

- **Who's covered:** If the government sets up a group to make decisions, create policies, spend tax dollars or conduct other public business, then that group's meetings generally are open to the public. "Sunshine" laws typically cover most governmental entities in the state, including state boards, counties, cities, school districts, public universities, fire districts and even weed-control districts. In most states, a meeting should be public if a majority of members (a quorum) are together at any time or place.

- **Advance notice:** A city council, school board or other public group usually must let people know when it's going to meet. Often, notices for regular meetings are posted anywhere from a day in advance to a month in advance, sometimes in newspaper legal ads or on a schedule at the government agency's Web site or at their offices. Reporters should ask the agency for an agenda ahead of time.

- **Secret meetings:** Although the presumption is that every public meeting shall be open, sometimes it's in the citizens' best interest to let government officials discuss some business in secret for specific reasons allowed by law. Government officials usually must cite a law that allows them to meet in secret. Some of the most common legal reasons for meeting in "executive session" include potential litigation, property deal negotiations, qualifications of job applicants and complaints against public officials. Often, government officials will simply say they are meeting in secret to discuss "personnel" or "litigation" matters. Reporters should ask for the specific law the officials are relying upon to justify secrecy.

If you believe a proposed executive session violates the law, challenge it:

- **Step 1—ask for the legal reason:** Stand up and ask politely for the provision under the state law that allows them to close the meeting. They should cite the specific exemption in the law. You should be familiar with the law before the meeting. It's helpful to have a copy handy, perhaps taped inside a reporter's notebook. Public affairs reporters need to be authorities on access law.

- **Step 2—get advice quickly:** Consult an expert if you have time. Call your boss, a media law attorney or someone else who is an expert on access in your state.

- **Step 3—ask for a vote:** Ask for the group to take a vote on whether the meeting should be closed. This puts the pressure on public officials to state publicly their position on excluding the public. You can also ask them to delay the meeting to allow you (and them) to find out if it is legal.

- **Step 4—object for the record:** If you still object to the closure, say it. Many state press associations provide wallet-sized cards that provide the law and a statement to be read, such as "I object to the closure of this meeting, and I note for the record that any action taken in an illegally closed meeting is null and void. I also remind the board that even in a valid executive session, no final action or decision can be made. I ask that my objection be noted in the minutes."

- **Step 5—stay cool:** Don't be disruptive. One reason an agency can sometimes evict people (or arrest them) is for causing disruption. So be polite and calm, but get your point across. You can always follow up later.

- **Step 6—follow-up stories and litigation:** Consult access law experts to find out if the executive session was legal. Tell the public about the secret meeting. Write about it. They did not shut you out—they shut out the public. Discuss with your bosses about taking the agency to court. In many states, if you win in court, you can be reimbursed for attorney fees.

Checklists for Meetings and Speeches

Advances

- Date, time, place.
- Public hearings.
- Continuing controversies.
- Background on major issues.
- Quotes from board members.
- Logistics: parking, seating, TV.

Follow-Ups

- Use an action verb in the lead.
- Look for impact on people.
- Recap major actions.
- Put decisions in context.
- Tell what happens next.
- Summarize other decisions.
- Identify future story ideas.

Speeches

- Find a theme.
- Give speaker's background.
- Provide context for remarks.
- Describe surroundings and reaction.
- Ask speaker to clarify.
- Use quotes sparingly.
- Identify the sponsor.

Quotations

- Complete sentences make the best quotes.
- Limit use of partial quotes.
- Don't diminish a quote's impact by using paraphrased words.
- If quote is ambiguous or the grammar is imprecise, paraphrase.
- The best attribution verb is *said.*
- Avoid verbs that characterize a quote (*admitted, emphasized,* etc.).

CHAPTER EXERCISES

1. Obtain a meeting agenda from the city council. Prioritize the items, according to your instincts, in the order of citizen importance and interest.

2. Write an advance story for the meeting.

3. Attend the city council meeting and see how close you were to prioritizing the order of importance/interest.

4. Write a two-page story about the meeting.

5. Find an audio and video speech online made by one of your university administrators or faculty members. Write a two-page story.

6. Research your state's open meeting laws, and write a one-page paper summarizing them.

7. Attend and cover a press conference.

8. Attend a speech and cover it. Service clubs such as Rotary and Kiwanis have guest speakers nearly every meeting.

Ethical and Legal Issues

BY JOHN IRBY AND SUSAN ENGLISH

Jonathan Livingstone Seagull is a novel in part about people who make their own rules when they know they're right. But how do they know they are right? Ethics is similar: how do you know if you are ethical as a journalist?

The journalism professor asked the room of about fifty potential college students and their parents how many considered themselves ethical. Almost every hand was raised.

He then asked the same audience how many believed newspaper reporters are ethical. Less than half the hands went up.

It was clear to those attending the university recruitment day that many in the United States question the ethics of newspapers and reporters. A credibility gap—or disconnect—has developed over the years between the public and mainstream print media.

There are several reasons why more and more readers don't seem to trust what they read in newspapers. Inaccuracies come to mind as a reason. But then uninteresting content, and competition from traditional media such as television, magazines and radio, have also had an impact. And there is the added competition from the 900-pound gorilla, the Internet.

The actions of some newspaper reporters and editors—seemingly void of ethical context—are another reason, and many have become angered to the extreme of no longer reading newspapers.

The list of ethical breaches, or at least controversies, sometimes seems endless, with names such as Jayson Blair, Jack Kelley, Armstrong Williams and Maggie Gallagher becoming commonplace.

But when newspaper editors and reporters are asked if they are ethical, almost 100 percent raise their hands.

Why is there such a divide in ethical perceptions?

Any discussion about ethical issues needs to be framed in terms of considering the importance of basic moral principles and values, standards, character and conduct.

Determining what is ethical can sometimes be boiled down to determining what is right or wrong, or fair or unfair, or caring or uncaring, or good or bad, or responsible or irresponsible.

But it isn't always that simple. This chapter will not provide crystal-clear answers to all journalistic questions. It will, however, show the importance of understanding how to think and act ethically in making journalistic decisions. And it will pose a number of questions for discussion and ethical conversation.

Ethical Perspectives

Many might not realize it, but they subscribe to one of three basic ethical philosophies, depending in part upon how they might answer the following question: "Does the end justify the means?" In other words, would they ever do something that is not good to achieve a goal that is good? As an example, would it be OK to steal a loaf of bread to feed a hungry child?

Those who agree probably believe that what makes an act ethical are the results, not the act. They might reason that the end can, and many times does, justify the means, depending upon the circumstances. They would probably be termed a *relativist.*

Another example: would it be OK to lie to save someone's life? Would it be OK to kill a bad person to protect a good or innocent person? A major consideration in this belief, however, should be who determines good and bad people, and what is sufficient cause to lie, steal or kill.

Those who believe that some things are always right and some things are always wrong would be termed *absolutists* or *legalists.* That ethical perspective usually comes from a sense of duty or religious background, and believers will not deviate from a fixed set of principles or laws. The reasoning is that the end never justifies the means; if it is wrong to lie, it is always wrong to lie.

Those who answered the initial question with "maybe, sometimes, don't know" are likely *situational ethicists,* who hold the belief that everyone and every situation is unique, and that all decisions should be made on individual merit. The overwhelming majority of journalists seem to fall into this classification.

Ethics and Diversity

Although journalists should be vigilant about cultivating a diverse array of sources and, indeed, generating story ideas that represent the many voices of the community, public affairs reporters need to work even harder. Because public affairs reporting focuses on watching government and civic affairs, reporters should also watch that the interests of all segments of a community are represented in civic proceedings and discussions.

This, however, poses a challenge for public affairs reporters. Seldom are the diverse voices in the community represented among the journalist's sources at city hall. Outside the metro and regional government offices in large urban areas, white middle-class males still dominate local power structures. It is most often their voice we hear in policy-setting discussions and in news reports.

The sources that journalists often use are also often those who are readily accessible by phone or e-mail. This means they are white-collar workers who have an office, or at least their own phone and computer at work. They are articulate. They often hold college degrees.

The greeters at Wal-Mart are not picking up a phone and doing interviews with reporters or answering their e-mail while at work, nor are the workers sorting chicken parts at the meat-packing plant, or the migrant farm workers picking strawberries from dawn to dark in the fields. Migrant workers might not have a home phone, and if they are using a cell phone it is unlisted. They might speak limited English.

Journalists who don't leave their offices to do their reporting end up with stories biased toward those in the economic middle class and often toward one gender because their stories are sourced only with people in those groups.

This is an ethical problem because diversity is an ethical issue.

Journalists have a responsibility to cover the many perspectives and voices in the communities they serve. Too often, this is interpreted as simply seeking out perspectives and stories about ethnic groups. Diversity, however, extends far beyond multiculturalism interpreted as people of color.

A diverse news report represents the perspectives of those of varying religious faiths in the community as well as gays and lesbians, the elderly and teens, the working poor and the homeless. Diversity, though, goes even beyond race, religion, sexual orientation, age and income levels. Those in the rural United States have different views from urban dwellers, as do those in suburbia and exurbia.

Journalists have an ethical responsibility to look below the radar of official sources and seek the perspectives of the less educated and, yes, even less knowledgeable citizens. They, too, have a stake in the community. When journalists use only economics to determine who has the largest stake in issues, they will naturally return repeatedly to the same voices and perspectives.

Reporters and editors do need the perspective of official sources to give credibility and accuracy to their stories. It is not suggested that these voices be excluded in attempts to secure a broader perspective. But too often the effort to gather information stops when what appears to be enough information to write the story is garnered from a variety of official sources. The resulting story might be factually accurate, but it is probably not balanced and fair ethically, or complete.

So what can journalists do to represent diverse voices in their stories? First, it is critical to start thinking of diversity at the idea stage of the story process. All stories should not come from the courthouse, city hall or state legislators. Before the story idea begins to gel, ask: "Who is affected by this?" Begin to seek out their perspectives, and consider telling the story from their viewpoint.

Diversity needs to be built into the journalistic process at the beginning. But interviewing a person of color, a single mom on welfare, a migrant farm worker or an elderly person as the story is coming together, just to add a different perspective, will not result in a story with diverse viewpoints. That's like putting steak sauce on meatloaf. The true content hasn't changed; the quotes dropped into the story in the final stage are just attempts to disguise the lack of diverse voices—or bad-tasting meatloaf.

Awareness of the diversity of the community should begin when the reporter is building his or her beat. Look in the Yellow Pages under *churches* to get a feel for the diverse religious faiths in the community. Examine U.S. Census reports and other demographic devices to determine the range of income and education levels. Is there a gathering place for people who are not heterosexual? Cultivate sources through the local grange. If there is a retirement community, ask to sit in on the coffee klatch to peer through the window onto their perspective. Visit teen hangouts and ask what's on their minds. And during all of these efforts, be aware that men and women have different perspectives, even if they live in the same situation.

Farmers, for example, have a big stake in agricultural issues. And they clearly represent a rural perspective. But most farmers are men, and reporters miss an important perspective if they don't talk to the women who live on farms. They might be more reticent, but their perspective is also important and will add richness and depth to the story.

Self-Reflections

Your editor asks you to actively deceive the public to gain information for a story. She wants you to pose as someone other than a journalist. Would you go undercover (under any circumstances)? Is it ethical for a journalist to lie about his or her identity if it is the only (or best) way to get information for a story that needs to be told? How would you handle these situations?

- **Let's say you** need to interview a man in a hospital. The medical staff, however, has blocked your attempts to arrange for the interview. They have, in fact, asked you to leave the hospital. You leave and drive downtown to a costume store. You rent the type of shirt, collar and pants a priest might typically wear. You put the clothing on, drive back to the hospital and walk through the halls and into the man's room—unimpeded. The patient grants the interview and even commends you for your creativity. Did you act ethically?

- **If one night** you are sharing pillow talk with your husband, a social services health employee, and he tells you his agency received its first child AIDS case that day, would it be ethical to consider the information "on the record"? Would it be ethical to ask follow-up questions, then get out of bed, write a story and electronically mail it to your newspaper for publication the next day? Would you stay married?

- **ABC Apartments are** rumored to be turning down applications from Native Americans. You are assigned to check out the story tip. Although you don't need an apartment, you drive to ABC to question people. On the way, you decide the best place to start would be to fill out an application. When you turn in the application, you strike up a conversation with a clerk, and at an appropriate time you casually mention you're an enrolled member of the Choctaw Nation of Oklahoma, even though you really aren't. Did you act ethically?

- **You are writing** a story about the homeless in your city. Although you drive a sports car, live in a nice condo and wear trendy clothes, you change into dirty jeans with rips and tears and an old sweatshirt and knit cap with a fish smell. You have someone drop you off near the Main Street overpass so you can spend a day under it with homeless men and women in disguise, trying to pass yourself off as a homeless person. Did you act ethically?

- **Twenty new grand** jury members have been selected, but the court public relations person will not release their names even though, by law, they became public once they were approved by the presiding judge. There is a promise to release the names the next day at a news conference, which will be staged for television's purposes. A source tells you there will be an organizational meeting for new members early tonight in Room 201 at the courthouse. You go over early and set up a table with a sign on the wall: "Grand Jury Members Sign in Here." As the new members arrive, one-by-one they sign the paper you have supplied, providing their name, phone number and occupation. Did you act ethically?

- **You receive a** phone call from an arsonist, and then meet with and interview him. The arsonist tells you how he and others have set more than ten fires at homes being built in recreational areas, and suggests there will be more. You write a story but do not reveal the name of your "confidential source" (the arsonist), and police request the information. Is protecting the source/arsonist ethical?

- **You open a** parked car's door and take a videotape. Thirteen pit bull dogs had been seized earlier at the site, and the homeowner had been charged with staging dogfights. You make a copy of the video, review it, write a story and then turn over the original copy to authorities. The videotape was in plain view in the back seat of the car, and you simply reached through an open window and took it, but only after authorities had searched the property and missed the tape. Is this "aggressive reporting" or a criminal offense? Were your actions ethical?

Accuracy and Fairness

Although we earlier discussed how diversity is an ethical concern, it is also an issue of accuracy. Without the perspective of all of the important stakeholders in an issue, the news report is neither accurate nor fair.

Accuracy and fairness mean going beyond the extreme points of view in reporting and writing a story. The extreme viewpoints represent only a small percentage of the community, whereas the middle is usually a much larger segment. Although many people lean one way or another on an issue, they might still be in the middle if they aren't completely sure how they feel about an issue. If perspectives were measured on a scale of 1 to 10, most people fall at 3 or 7. Those more moderate perspectives need to be represented in stories as well.

Ethics isn't black and white; there are many shades of gray. Some situations, however, have a much clearer focus than others. But ethical lapses contribute daily to the problems that newspapers face with the public over issues of credibility.

For instance, two reporters for the *Salt Lake Tribune* were disciplined—and later fired—after it was learned they were each paid $10,000 for providing information to the *National Enquirer* about the Elizabeth Smart kidnapping case. The reporters met with and had dinner with a reporter from the tabloid, and shared information without their employer's permission.

"I verbally wrung their necks and formally disciplined them for ignoring stated policy, but the act did not quite constitute a firing offense," *Tribune* editor James E. Shelledy said before all the details were learned. Shelledy also later resigned.

Forget considering—for a moment—the ethics involved with the *National Enquirer* headlines that week, which included:

- Rodney Dangerfield Laughs His Way through Brain Bypass
- Letterman Explodes
- O.J.'s Sick Plot to Get Rid of Daughter
- Lisa Marie Torments Nick Cage
- Monica Lewinsky Out of Control on New TV Show
- Laci Peterson's Final Moments: How Husband Murdered Her

But consider the following: would it be ethical for a reporter to share information with a competing publication? Would it be ethical to take money from another publication when your publication has already paid you for your work? Wouldn't it have been smart for the reporters to check with their employer, or go to the company policies and procedures manual, before making such a career-ending mistake?

Before being fired, the reporters admitted: "In hindsight, we made a bad decision by associating with the *National Enquirer*. We regret any embarrassment this brings to our colleagues or the *Salt Lake Tribune*."

But what happened in Salt Lake City was just one of many ethical concerns—or lapses in judgment—in newsrooms across the country, some of which were not even close to a shade of gray. For example:

A *Boston Herald* reporter, who had been embedded with the military in Iraq, was stopped by U.S. Customs agents who seized a large painting along with various Iraqi war souvenirs. The reporter defended his actions by saying, "These items were being routinely discarded and destroyed and clearly were of no value to the Iraqi people."

A satellite truck engineer for Fox News Channel, also returning from Iraq, was accused of trying to smuggle a dozen Iraqi paintings into the country, apparently looted from an Iraqi palace.

An editor in Washington agreed with law enforcement requests to run a fake story about a staged arson in an effort to help prove a convicted murderer was trying to hire someone to set fire to his mother-in-law's home. The editor stood by his decision and said: "We have a responsibility to the community."

A New York editor admitted making up eleven letters to the editor, positively referencing a column he wrote on the Vietnam War. He also admitted to authoring several other letters over a three-month period. "I wanted to make it seem that my columns provoked reader interest," he told the newspaper. His boss, the publisher, fired him and said: "He tampered with our single most important commodity: our credibility."

Jayson Blair of the *New York Times* was fired for gross plagiarism and faked reports.

Jack Kelley of *USA Today* was fired after, according to the newspaper, he "fabricated substantial portions of at least eight major stories, lifted nearly two dozen quotes or other material from competing publications, lied in speeches he gave for the newspaper and conspired to mislead those investigating his work."

Conflicts of Interest

A *San Francisco Chronicle* reporter was first suspended and later fired after he was arrested at a rally that opposed the U.S. invasion of Iraq. He later sued and reached a settlement with the newspaper over the firing.

Although the reporter was among more than 1,300 people arrested for blocking public streets the morning after the Iraq war started, his newspaper, unlike many in the United States, did not at the time bar reporters from participating in political events. It had, however, circulated an internal memorandum advising staff members to be cautious and gain supervisor approval in advance of participation in such events.

In a similar situation, a college newspaper columnist organized and led a walkout/rally protesting the war in Iraq. More than 1,000 students participated.

Ethical principles to consider in such cases involve conflicts of interest. Can a reporter participate in a political event and remain objective? Is there more ethical "wiggle room" with columnists because they write opinion and don't try to hide biases?

Codes of ethics nearly always include guidelines for dealing with inevitable conflicts of interest on the part of newsroom employees. In general, they advise journalists to avoid associations, relationships or activities that could taint their stories or their reporting abilities.

There are the obvious conflicts, such as membership or participation in organizations or groups associated with a reporter's beat. Identifying those conflicts is easy. The more difficult situations require the individual journalist to continually make judgments about his or her relationship to sources or organizations. When, for example, has the line been crossed between source and friend? Is it ever acceptable for a city hall reporter to date a person who works at city hall? Should sportswriters accept invitations to play golf with the coaches of teams they cover, or does this put their relationships on a less professional footing?

Reporters often must divine for themselves where the line between professional relationship and friendship has been drawn, and work continually to not cross the line. If they do, they must discuss the situation with their editors. This does not always mean they will be pulled from the story or the beat, but disclosure is always in order.

Many editors insist on a "no surprises" rule in their newsrooms, meaning they want to know of any potential problems before publication so they can avoid having to do damage control afterward. Disclosure fosters credibility when it comes to potential or real conflicts of interest.

That advice was apparently ignored by Armstrong Williams and Maggie Gallagher.

Conservative syndicated columnist Williams came under fire after revelations that he was paid $240,000 to promote the Bush administration's No Child Left Behind law. And syndicated columnist Gallagher, who often writes about issues on marriage, was paid $21,500 to consult with the Department of Health and Human Services on marriage issues.

Neither Williams nor Gallagher publicly disclosed the arrangements, perceived by many as conflicts of interest.

Attribution and Identification

Identifying the source of facts and viewpoints is critical to an accurate and ethical story. Most facts in the story should be attributed to someone by name and, if need be, the person's role in the issue. Take care to avoid mislabeling a source and in doing so marginalizing his or her perspective. To say that a source speaks for those on the right or left, or is a conservative or liberal, is seldom accurate, even if he or she claims this. What the reader needs to know is why the reporter chose to include the perspective of each source.

If the information came from official documents, say so. Public affairs reporters should go one step further. They should identify not only the source of the information, such as "court records," but also the method they used to obtain the information. If a freedom of information request was filed to obtain a document, tell the reader that in the story. First, this does not leave the reader wondering just how the reporter managed to get the information and whether it was done through legitimate means, and it also reinforces the need for the open records laws and the importance of the First Amendment.

In this era of public suspicion of the press and heightened attempts at domestic security, the press should use every opportunity to remind the public that freedom must include a free press, and that the highest calling of the press is ensuring that public institutions are acting in the best interests of the people.

Most news organizations have policies on the use of anonymous sources. But even if the policy allows liberal use of anonymous sources, reporters should strive to minimize their use. The public distrusts news reports that rely on unnamed sources. Studies repeatedly show that the use of anonymous sources hurts the credibility of the news story and of the reporter. Readers want to know from whom the facts came and how the reporter obtained them. For this reason, also, few newsrooms tolerate their journalists paying for information. The practice taints the information. Readers rightly suspect that the source invented a more fantastic story to warrant higher payment.

Public skepticism of press and news reports stems in part from beliefs that journalists skulk around digging up juicy tidbits on public officials, eager to ambush some public figure in print with minor missteps involving public money or time. Some readers assume that journalists go undercover like law enforcement officers or private investigators to catch public officials doing things they should not be doing.

PROFESSIONAL TIPS

Steve McClure

Steve McClure is managing editor of the *Moscow-Pullman Daily News* (Moscow, Idaho, and Pullman, Washington), circulation 8,000. The *Daily News* is a Monday–Friday afternoon newspaper with a Saturday-morning weekend edition. He was a reporter at the newspaper before moving into the top hands-on editing position at the newspaper, where he is responsible for day-to-day editorial department management and content supervision.

Question: Do journalists have the same understanding and concept of ethics as readers and the general public? Why or why not?

I think journalists and the general public may agree in principle on some areas of ethics. For instance, most would agree making up quotes and sources is unethical. Where we differ is our understanding of the ethics of journalists. In that regard, we're often on different ends of the spectrum. Journalists see themselves as upholding a strict ethical code while pretending our own biases don't exist. Most readers don't believe we're without bias, and it wouldn't surprise me if most believe our individual bias makes its way into how we cover people and events.

Question: Is it OK for a journalist to use deception to get a story?

That's a slippery slope. In general practice, I would say no. It's not OK to pretend you're something other than a reporter when you are, say, interviewing people for day-to-day stories. But is it deceptive to send a reporter into a nightclub to get a perspective on illicit drug use? Is it OK to send a reporter with no ailments to a clinic to see if the doctors push you toward a specific treatment or drug? I would say there's a certain amount of deception in that, but there's a public good involved in exposing that. I think editors and reporters need to be fairly specific on the goal

behind the reporting before sending someone off under an alias.

Question: In reporting, can the end justify the means?

When reporters go out on assignment, all they have is a notebook and their credibility. Lose either one, and you're not going to be very effective. A reporter who decides to lie to get a story may reap some short-term reward for his or her effort. Long term, however, selling your soul to get a good story undercuts your ability to get information and your ability to maintain trust with readers. If readers don't believe the information presented by a reporter, that reporter isn't of much use to a newsgathering organization.

Question: Is there an issue of credibility today with the media (and specifically newspapers), and if so, what can be done to restore credibility?

The media have a credibility problem, and it extends to newspapers. The problem has several fronts. We make too many mistakes and tend to dismiss the fact that spelling someone's name wrong is a big deal to readers. There is an adage that if we can't spell the name right, then what else in the story is wrong? There's a lot of truth to that. The way to address that is to be willing to promptly make corrections. Reporters and editors need to be less

(continued)

PROFESSIONAL TIPS   Continued

defensive when someone calls in asking for a correction, and reporters need to understand there are consequences for journalists who consistently make errors.

I also think most people are quick to lump all media together. The ethical lapses of Jayson Blair, for instance, were talked about at the local level with raised eyebrows toward reporters at small papers. And the biases of East Coast editorial pages are ascribed to all newspapers, despite stances that don't match.

One of the major sources of our credibility problem, in my mind, rests with the continued overuse of unnamed sources by the national media. What started as a reporting tool used in only the most exceptional of circumstances now dominates national reporting. Too many people have bought into the theory that granting anonymity is the only way to get the story out. That's a lot of hooey. Good reporting is being done by solid journalists who track stories without the benefit of handing out anonymity to people.

The use of unnamed sources is only effective if readers trust us to use that tool sparingly, critically analyzing the person and situation when we give anonymity, and the agenda they may be pushing. Well, readers don't trust us that much, nor should they. We haven't held up our end of the bargain.

We could take a major step forward if the big newsgathering organizations, which feed copy through the syndicates and wire services to newspapers across the country, dramatically curtailed this practice.

Question: What do you believe are the one or two most significant ethical lapses in recent newspaper history (and provide your comments on the reasons why)?

I think the Jayson Blair fiasco was significant because it happened at the *New York Times*. It's a newspaper many held up as the pinnacle of newspapers, immune to all the ethical flaps that had taken place to that point. That fabricated stories could make it through a newsroom filled with some of the best and brightest in the profession illustrated how widespread the problem is, and how long it could go unchecked. The recent shake-up at *USA Today* reinforces this position.

Question: Do you have any other comments on ethics in journalism?

I would really like to see more members of the media acknowledge that the problem of credibility and ethics is ours to address. It's not up to readers to figure us out and give us the respect we deserve. The burden is ours.

I'm not sure we've seen the bottom of this valley. As more newspapers are gobbled up by media corporations and with it an increased emphasis on profit over product, the push for the next sensational story will increase. Editors and reporters looking to make headlines will be tempted to take shortcuts, and that's when disaster happens. At some point, we risk losing our credibility with readers. When that happens, the profits and the product will quickly vanish.

Occasionally, journalists do go undercover. But they need to be aware that this newsgathering technique compromises the integrity of the news report. It requires deception on the part of the journalists. Some media ethicists say that because journalism is all about truth telling, any amount or form of deception is not acceptable behavior for journalists and they should never go undercover to get a story.

Most newsrooms have policies regarding journalists going undercover or at least not revealing their identity when gathering certain information. As a rule, journalists should always identify themselves prior to asking for any information from sources. Reporters should state their names and the organization they are working for, and, in most cases, identify the story for which they are gathering the information. It is unethical and dishonest to gather quotes for a story and then use it in a different story without checking back with the source to inform him or her or to get new information for the new context.

Identification becomes a legal requirement when the reporter uses recording devices. In many states, tape recording is illegal without the permission of the person being recorded. The best practice, whether it is a phone interview or one done in person, is to turn on the recorder before identifying yourself and your organization, then with the recorder running, ask the interviewee for permission to tape the interview. That way, you have his or her approval on tape should questions be raised later.

The same guideline applies to e-mail interviews. Try to send the e-mail from your news organization's file server so the return e-mail is clearly to your newsroom e-mail address. This will raise the trust your sources have in your legitimacy as a journalist.

Some newsrooms have e-mail templates with the publication's logo or newspaper masthead. Always identify yourself in the e-mail, the name of your publication and the story for which you want this information.

Some ethicists have raised questions about the credibility of e-mail interviews because it is more difficult to verify that the person answering the questions is the actual source. To raise the integrity of such interviews, ask in the e-mail for a phone number at which you can contact the source if you have last-minute questions or need clarification. Call the number to verify that the source received your e-mail and was indeed the person who replied.

Plagiarism

Recent cases of plagiarism such as the missteps of Jayson Blair, while he worked for the *New York Times,* and Stephen Glass, formerly of the *New Republic* magazine, have raised the profile of plagiarism and prompted new conversations about the ethical issue.

Plagiarism means using the work of someone else and claiming it is the result of your efforts. Plagiarism is always wrong. And in so many cases it could easily be avoided by attributing the phrase, sentence, paragraph or story to the person who wrote or spoke it. It's simple, really: give credit where credit is due.

Some of the recent situations have involved not only plagiarism but also outright fabrication of quotes and, in some cases, sources. That this is highly unethical should not need to be said. But the instances in which veteran reporters from major newspapers such as the *New York Times* and *USA Today* fabricated material and sources prompt the need to reiterate the need for truth telling and accuracy. Credibility in the news reports is the cornerstone of journalism.

Privacy

There will be times when the efforts to gather information intersect with a source's desire for privacy. One of the skills that journalists learn is how to respect the privacy of people involved in newsworthy situations as much as possible while still providing a fair, accurate and complete account for readers. Sometimes the intrusion into what might otherwise be considered private is necessary, but it should always be weighed against the legitimacy of the public interest. Pandering should be avoided.

Reporters should ask themselves why they need to overstep the generally accepted boundary of privacy and whether there is another way of gathering this information that would be less intrusive.

Reporting should be done with vigor and sensitivity. Journalists should also be aware that there are cultural differences regarding the types of information that are considered private or embarrassing. Information freely offered by one group might be considered to be highly private by those in another culture or ethnic group.

Journalists need to listen to the requests of those who ask that certain information be kept private. But they need to go beyond respecting verbal requests and simply be aware of the values and traditions of the diverse groups they are covering.

If a question arises about the imperative of using a fact that might embarrass someone, discuss it with your editor and colleagues. And it is not unreasonable to call the source, talk with him or her about the use of the material and explain why it is necessary for the credibility of the story. Remember that journalists are in the communication business and that extends beyond published stories.

Unlike some other ethical issues, privacy is a legal issue as well. The courts have carved out some practices that violate the laws of privacy. These generally fall into four categories:

- **Appropriation of another's** name or likeness
- **Publicity that unreasonably** places another in a false light
- **Unreasonable intrusion upon** the solitude or seclusion of another
- **Public disclosure of** private facts

Public affairs reporters need to pay particular attention to the last two. With the expansion of electronic record keeping and the access to electronic databases, the precedents involving privacy violations continue to evolve. Generally, the standard applied in the courts as to whether privacy was violated was whether the publication of material or the information-gathering process would be "highly offensive to a reasonable person." But in his book *The Unwanted Gaze: The Destruction of Privacy in America,* Jeffrey Rosen writes: "In an age that is beyond embarrassment, it's rarely clear what a 'reasonable person' would find highly offensive."

In some cases, though, the invasion of privacy charges bump against the freedom of the press guarantees. In other words, "reasonable people" would find it highly offensive if the same information about them was published, but the public's right and need to know such information outweighed the privacy concerns.

In general, reporters should ask themselves the following questions:

- **Is the information** vital to the credibility of my story?
- **In what ways** might it violate someone's privacy?
- **How did I** obtain the information?
- **Is there another** way of telling the story or of obtaining information that would still be credible but might avoid violating someone's privacy?

The extent of our lack of privacy in this country was revealed during the investigation of President Bill Clinton's affair with White House intern Monica Lewinsky.

During the investigation, the chief investigator, Kenneth Starr, subpoenaed the receipts of all the books purchased by Lewinsky from a Washington, D.C., bookstore since 1995. Prosecutors also retrieved unsent e-mails from Lewinsky's home computer, which included drafts of love letters to Clinton. Lewinsky said she was promised by prosecutors that the letters would be kept private. But they appeared in Starr's report to Congress, and Congress allowed the Starr Report to be posted on the Internet, then be published in book form.

Much information previously considered to be private is now included in records and documents open to the public and often broadly available on Web sites. In a move that outraged rape victim advocates, the judge in the Kobe Bryant sexual assault case in Colorado allowed the sexual history of the alleged victim to be examined during court proceedings, which makes it available to the press under open records laws.

Previously, defense attorneys were not allowed to explore the sexual history of the alleged victim in court, which kept it out of the public records (the sexual history of the alleged perpetrator, however, was often discussed in court proceedings, which does raise ethical questions).

Eager journalists need to remember the ethical caution: the right to publish is not the imperative to publish. It behooves journalists to help educate the public about the public nature of our lives in a democracy. Journalists should continually explain in their stories how they obtained the information they included and explain why they may have chosen to exclude some information.

Reporters should be able to explain why they are pursuing a story and how they are going about reporting and writing it. They need to be able to document the process of information gathering and the safeguards they took to avoid legal missteps.

Libel

The bedrock of libel law in the United States is the concept that truth is always a defense. Almost from the beginning of libel law in the United States, however, Congress defined circumstances under which published and later broadcast reports could be both true and not allowed. These generally are deemed to be reports that could compromise national security or endanger the democratic government.

Public affairs reporters should be aware of current legal precedents concerning libel and national security issues, especially as the homeland security rulings evolve. But more often, reporters deal with the basics of libel law—the legal benchmarks of whether the person claiming he or she was libeled is a public figure and whether actual malice on the part of the journalist or publication can be proved.

The libel precedents vary from state to state. Journalists should be up-to-date on the status of libel law in the jurisdiction in which they work. In general, there are four broad issues when it comes to a libel suit:

- **Is the fact** or story in question substantially false?
- **Did the false** information result in tangible damages to the plaintiff?
- **Within the context** of the story, was the plaintiff a public figure?

■ **If so, can** the plaintiff prove that the journalist or publication published with knowledge that the information was false and with reckless disregard of its falsity? This is often called *actual malice,* the intent of the journalist to damage the plaintiff.

If the plaintiff were deemed by the court to be a private individual within the context of the story, he or she would need to still prove that the information was false and caused tangible damages. But the benchmark would drop to negligence rather than actual malice. The plaintiff would need only to prove that the journalist or publication did not engage in the usual process of ensuring accuracy when publishing the false information.

The statute of limitations for libel also varies from state to state. Journalists should keep their notes and even early drafts of their stories as well as any tape recordings that verify the accuracy of the information in question until the statute expires. An easy way to do this is to identify the source and date of the interview on the cover of the notebook, and tape and label the boxes in which they are stored.

The courts have set high benchmarks for successful libel suits to allow a vigorous and free press. The courts repeatedly have acknowledged that with the press of deadlines and the volume of information offered in news reports, some errors will inevitably creep into stories. If we are to have a free press, which is necessary for an informed populace, we must have some tolerance for minor missteps.

Indeed, a study in the 1990s showed that many libel lawsuits can be avoided simply by offering an apology to the person about whom false information was published, and publishing a correction. Many potential plaintiffs simply want their information corrected in a public way and become punitive only when journalists become pompous and arrogant and claim their right to publish as a defense.

Most newspapers have procedures for the timely correction of any inaccuracies they have published or for clarification when needed. Most of these policies depend on reporters and editors to be forthcoming about mistakes they have made, even when no one has called to point out the errors.

To maintain high integrity, reporters should self-report errors as soon as possible and editors should realize that this would only happen outside a punitive environment. Everyone wants to get the news right, and the best newsrooms work to foster a team effort to make this happen, to quickly correct mistakes and learn from them and to make changes to minimize errors.

Journalists have access to legal help concerning questions of privacy, libel and other media law issues at a number of journalism organizations as well as from their editors and news organization attorneys. One of the primary legal sources journalists use is the Reporters' Committee for Freedom of the Press. They can also turn with some issues to the Society of Professional Journalists (SPJ). Students can contact the Student Press Law Center.

Codes of Ethics

The Society of Professional Journalists has a code of ethics that is followed, or at least referenced, by many newspapers across the United States. It has four detailed prongs for journalists to consider:

- **Seek truth and report it.**
- **Minimize harm.**
- **Act independently.**
- **Be accountable.**

The code can be found at www.spj.org/ethics_code.asp.

Each prong of the code includes a mini-statement to aid in understanding, along with bulleted detailed suggestions:

- **Seek truth and report it:** Journalists should be honest, fair and courageous in gathering, reporting and interpreting information.
- **Minimize harm:** Ethical journalists treat sources, subjects and colleagues as human beings deserving of respect.
- **Act independently:** Journalists should be free of obligation to any interest other than the public's right to know.
- **Be accountable:** Journalists are accountable to their readers, listeners and viewers and to each other.

The American Society of Newspaper Editors (ASNE) also has a widely reviewed and used code of ethics (statement of principles) that includes six articles:

- **Responsibility**
- **Freedom of the press**
- **Independence**
- **Truth and accuracy**
- **Impartiality**
- **Fair play**

Originally written in 1922 as "the Canons of Journalism," the statement of principles was updated in 1975. The preamble reads:

> The First Amendment, protecting freedom of expression from abridgment by any law, guarantees to the people through their press a constitutional right, and thereby places on newspaper people a particular responsibility. Thus journalism demands of its practitioners not only industry and knowledge but also the pursuit of a standard of integrity proportionate to the journalist's singular obligation. To this end the American Society of Newspaper Editors sets forth this Statement of Principles as a standard encouraging the highest ethical and professional performance.

The Associated Press adopted a statement of ethical principles when the Associated Press Managing Editors (APME) made revisions to the APME Code of Ethics in 1994. The main points of discussion include responsibility, accuracy, integrity and independence. It begins: "These principles are a model against which news and editorial staff members can measure their performance. They have been formulated in the belief that newspapers and the people who produce them should adhere to the highest standards of ethical and professional conduct. The public's right to know about matters of importance is paramount. The newspaper has a special responsibility as surrogate of its readers to be a vigilant watchdog of their legitimate public interests. No statement of principles can prescribe decisions governing every situation. Common sense and good judgment are required in applying ethical principles to newspaper realities. As new technologies evolve, these principles can help guide editors to insure the credibility of the news and information they provide. Individual newspapers are encouraged to augment these APME guidelines more specifically to their own situations."

There are many other ethics codes that have been in place for years, or updated recently in response to ethical concerns. Many major newspaper groups and media have a code or statement of principles, including Dow Jones, Gannett, Hearst Newspapers, E.W. Scripps Co., Knight Ridder, the National Press Photographers Association, the Radio-Television News Directors Association and the Society of American Business Editors and Writers.

CHAPTER EXERCISES

A Case Study: 1,000 Questions

Photographer John Harte was just about to go on his lunch break when the police scanner crackled something about a young boy who had drowned at a body of water just outside of the Bakersfield, California, city limits. He was dispatched and arrived just in time to take the controversial photo shown.

John Harte, photographer, Bakersfield *Californian*

Answer the following questions:

- **Did the photo** present news or invade privacy? Was it ethical to take the photo? Was it ethical to publish the photo?
- **If you were** the photographer, would you have taken the picture? How would ethics enter into such a decision?
- **Would the high** quality of the photo—the story it tells, the composition, aesthetics— have a bearing on your decision to publish?
- **If you would** run this photo, where would you run it? How big? Why?
- **Was this a** private time for the family, a time when they should have been allowed to grieve? Was this visual intrusion? Why was it private if it occurred in a public area?
- **Some claim this** was callous disregard of the victim. Was it?
- **Does this case**—and others—show that journalists are seriously out of touch with readers' sensibilities?

Bob Bentley, the Bakersfield *Californian* editor when the photo was published, justified running the image because it might serve as a water safety warning to parents and swimmers. The ethical discussion surrounded the hope that publishing the photo could prevent drowning in the county. Answer the following questions:

- **What do you** think of Bentley's ethical rationale? Are the potential benefits enough to justify the harm? Are there any other justifications—and, if so, what are they—for publishing the photo?
- **Did this photo** inflict additional harm on the victims? How?
- **How do you** define taste and canons of ethics or standards of publication for newspapers?
- **Was this an** accurate image of the world? Wouldn't it be dishonest and deceptive to hide these events from readers? Doesn't "ugly reality" often lead to action?
- **Do photos like** this have the potential to plant haunting images in our mind? Is that bad?
- **Could the photo** have been cropped to make it less offensive?
- **Is there an** ethical difference between the impact of a newspaper photo and fifteen seconds of television video?
- **Do journalists have** a moral obligation not to publish offensive photos? Is it OK if it advances the greater public good?

Naming Juvenile Victims

An 11-year-old sixth grader was infatuated with her 28-year-old principal at a private Christian school. The two fled after the young girl told her parents and police she had sexual contact with the man during a school camping trip. The man, according to his family, said he was depressed about not having a wife.

A nationwide manhunt followed. After eluding police in several states for a week, the two were found in Las Vegas as a patrolling officer recognized their vehicle driving down a street. The man quietly surrendered to police, who spotted the sport-utility vehicle as it was approaching the hotel where they were staying. The man faced federal charges of coercing and enticing a minor into sexual acts and transporting a minor across state lines for sexual purposes.

During the search, most of the media across the nation printed the young girl's name and photo. Upon the arrest, some stopped using the name and others continued. What would you do? Write a two-page essay addressing the following questions:

- **Should the names** of juveniles be broadcast or printed in newspapers? Should there be restrictions or limitations?
- **Should the media** identify crime victims by name (any exceptions)? Should the media identify sex crime victims by name (any exceptions)?
- **Were newspapers right** or wrong in initially publishing the name of the 11-year-old victim? Do situations sometimes dictate ethical decisions that can deviate from a policy that would include not publishing juvenile names? Is it ethical to violate policy?
- **Would you have** published the name of the victim after the child was found?

7

Access to Public Records

BY DAVID CUILLIER

A growing trend to try to keep information secret has made it even more important for reporters to understand the laws that aid access.

Part of being a good reporter is knowing not only what information to get but also how to get it. As government watchdogs, many journalists know more about freedom of information laws than public officials, even the agencies' attorneys. Their desk copies of their state open records laws are worn, and they develop a herd of access experts to help them navigate the law and overcome roadblocks. As explained earlier, government records are crucial to public affairs reporting, and journalists simply need to know how to get at the information that keeps democracy strong.

If reporters won't do it, who will?

In this chapter, you will learn how access to public records helps journalists and citizens—it can even help you at home. You will learn the overall principles of access laws; how to request government records at the federal, state and local levels; and what to do when you are denied—which, frankly, will happen a lot.

The Right to Know

Nowhere in the U.S. Constitution will you find a public "right to know." There is no guaranteed right to access government information, no matter how hard you look. In fact, the Founding Fathers came up with the Constitution in secret session.

Yet, a right to access government information has evolved over the centuries in the United States and is now codified in statutory law. After all, one of the Founding Fathers, James Madison, once said: "Knowledge will forever govern ignorance. And a people who mean to be their own governors must arm themselves with the power knowledge gives."

Americans want transparent government. A foundation of democracy is that citizens know what their government is up to. Thanks in part to freedom of information laws, journalists are able to shed light into darkness by tapping into public records.

Through the use of records requests, the *Dayton (Ohio) Daily News* found out that women Peace Corps volunteers were often at risk of violence, accidents, disease and suicide.

The *Albuquerque (New Mexico) Tribune* exposed problems for victims of governmental radiation experiments.

And the *Idaho Statesman* in Boise used public records requests to identify police officers who were prone to beating criminal suspects. The newspaper also exposed the diversion of millions of dollars intended to help the poor to instead subsidize big business.

Requests for records are often met with hostility by officials, particularly in an age of fear. Because of identity theft, the increased availability of information on the Internet and terrorism, people are more wary of information being broadly disseminated. In many cases, it is getting harder to get public information.

Following the terrorist attacks of September 11, 2001, government agencies began closing records. "In the three years since September 11, an astonishing amount of information has been taken away from the American people," said Lucy Dalglish, executive director of the Reporters Committee for Freedom of the Press, in the group's *Homefront Confidential* report that documents increasing government secrecy.

In nearly every state since 1995, media groups have organized "access audits" to find out how well government officials are complying with freedom of information laws. The findings have been disappointing. For example, on average officials deny access to police records half the time, even when the records should be public by law.

Sometimes public officials aren't too pleasant about it. During an access audit in Indiana, a clerk laughed at a requestor, another official pretended a requestor didn't exist, a jailer ran a criminal background check on a requestor, and a sheriff wadded up a copy of the state law, tossed it in the garbage and said, "I don't have to tell you nothing."

Getting access to public records is more than just knowing the law. It's about knowing people, and knowing that access can benefit not only the public, but also you.

Access for Real Life

Without access, I would be a mess. Access to public records has saved me the headache of living next to a highway. Getting access has allowed me to sleep soundly and have backyard barbecues with friends. It has helped me on the job and at home.

Every time my family and I move to a new community, which can be often for journalists, I access public records to check out neighborhoods and potential homes before ponying up thousands of dollars for a down payment.

One house we considered was a great deal, and was nestled next to an open field, where quail and rabbits played. When I checked the six-year road plan at City Hall I found officials were planning to build a five-lane major arterial through the field, about six feet from what would have been the vegetable garden. We didn't buy the house.

Several years and another journalism job later, we moved to another city. I asked the local public airport for a map of the flight patterns and found out that jets flew directly over a home we were considering buying. The map even showed the sound levels. That helped us understand why people didn't spend much time outside in that neighborhood and seemed a little sleep-deprived. We looked elsewhere.

Like many skills you will learn in public affairs reporting, knowing how to access public records will help you in your personal life and on the job. Information is power, and it sometimes has practical benefits to find out the following:

- **Home values:** Property tax records are public at county courthouses. You can find out how much homes in your neighborhood are worth and what they sold for, along with details such as the homes' square footage and the number of bedrooms. This helps you in buying or selling a home to compare homes and values.

- **Criminal records:** A person's criminal record is public information. If you want to find out if a babysitter has a clean record, you can check for free at your county courthouse. Lists of registered sex offenders' home addresses are often posted online. Many police departments track criminal activity, such as burglaries, car break-ins and violent crimes, by neighborhood.

- **School performance:** Overall standardized school test scores are public. Check with your school district to get a summary of the results for the past several years.

- **Development plans:** Cities and counties are always planning new development and infrastructure. Some useful records include:
  - **Six-year road plans:** Find out if new highways or main roads are planned for your neighborhood.
  - **Parks plans:** Find out if new parks are planned in your area (or if current parks will be phased out).
  - **New construction:** Stop by the planning department at City Hall to find out what new housing developments or businesses are planned. Even finding the zoning in your area is important before buying a house because that nice open field in back might be zoned for industrial use and could end up being the site of a gravel pit.
  - **Comprehensive plans for** cities and counties also provide a good indicator for what public officials have in mind for the future.

As you learn in your career about what public records are available to citizens and how to access them, remember that the information can help you, your family and your friends. Share that knowledge in your reporting and writing, and it will not only help your readers but also reinforce the need for open government so you can keep doing your job well.

The Freedom of Information Act

As mentioned earlier in this chapter, the Founding Fathers generally didn't talk much about access to public records. A specific protected right to access really didn't develop nationally until 1966 with the passage of the Freedom of Information Act (FOIA).

The FOIA (often pronounced *FOY-uh*) is the granddaddy of access laws and is something reporters need to know. The purpose of the act was to guarantee the right for citizens to access government documents from the federal agencies, unless there were specific reasons for keeping the records secret. The presumption was that all government records are open to citizens unless there's a specific reason they should not be.

FOIA applies only to the executive branch of the federal government, such as the FBI, Department of Education and Department of Energy. It does not apply to the courts or Congress. Yet, its influence is broad as many states adopted their own public records laws to cover state and local government agencies.

FOIA requires agencies to respond to records requests within twenty days, allowing them to take more time in fulfilling the request if necessary. A reporter can ask for "expedited review" to hurry things up, and can also ask for photocopying fees to be waived.

In some cases, records or parts of records can be kept secret if the information would be covered under nine exemptions:

- **National security**
- **Internal agency rules**
- **Statutory exemption** (some other exemptions put into law)
- **Trade secrets**
- **Internal agency memoranda**
- **Personal privacy**
- **Law enforcement records**
- **Bank reports**
- **Oil and gas well data**

Although FOIA is helpful for getting access to government records, delays can cause a request to drag on for years, hurting its usefulness for reporters. Also, for many reporters, the information they need for their hometown stories is often held by local or state agencies, so FOIA is not used that often. Most reporters rely on their state public records laws, which have a lot in common with FOIA.

For more information about FOIA, see the Reporters Committee for Freedom of the Press's "How to Use the Federal FOIA" publication at www.rcfp.org/foiact/index.html.

State Public Records Laws

Many public affairs journalists won't deal much with FOIA, but most will need to use their state public records laws. Every state has a law that guarantees citizen access to public records. The laws vary on some specifics, particularly on what records are allowed to

PROFESSIONAL TIPS

Christopher Smith

Christopher Smith is the Boise correspondent for the Associated Press. Previously, he was a Washington, D.C., staff reporter for the *Salt Lake Tribune.* He has worked as a print or broadcast journalist the past twenty years for small newspapers and radio stations in Idaho, Nevada and Utah, and he has written for *Outside* magazine, *High Country News* and the *New York Times.* His first book, *That's Amore: A Son Remembers Dean Martin,* was published in 2002 and was released in paperback in 2004.

Question: What strategies do you employ for accessing government records?

I generally try to have a targeted request for access to specific records when I make an application, since that usually allows faster responses. But if it's a fishing expedition you want, a good search target to request is any correspondence to the agency from members of Congress or your local elected officials. This is a good way of finding out what's on their radar, plus many times constituents will bring a particular problem with a federal agency to their member of Congress and, sometimes, members of Congress will try to exert a little political muscle to get an agency to do their bidding. And one of the sneakiest things to do is to FOIA the FOIA requests received by the agency— a practice that journalists sometimes call FOIA poaching. All FOIA requests are public records, and getting copies of other requests (and filing your own duplicate request) is a good way of finding out what tips or projects other reporters are working on, what lawsuits are being contemplated against the agency and what records are being sought by the public.

Question: What are the main differences between state open records laws and the federal Freedom of Information Act?

My experience has been that state sunshine laws are very hit and miss in how promptly a response is generated, how thorough the records search is and how exemptions for disclosure are understood and applied. The FOIA is usually administered by trained federal employees whose primary job is understanding the law, keeping track of requests and applying exemptions properly. That's not to say I've never had to appeal a federal FOIA, but many times the newspapers I've worked for have had to bring lawsuits to get state open records laws to be administered the way they were enacted. It seems like state agencies don't follow their own sunshine laws unless they get sued.

Question: How specific should a records request be?

I always try to identify a specific time window for the search period, such as all records related to Project X that were generated from last January until the receipt of this request. As far as the specificity of the actual records you are seeking access to, that cuts both ways. If you know precisely the

(continued)

PROFESSIONAL TIPS   Continued

form number you want, ask for it; but it's sometimes wise (although it takes longer) to ask for "all related correspondence or records," or something to that effect. One of the big complaints that FOIA officers have is that so many requests don't define the "universe" of records being sought; people just write in and say, "Give me all the information you have on Project X." Putting some sort of manageable timeline and type of record in the search universe can speed up the fulfillment of the request and, if you discover that you need to dig farther back in time, you can file a separate request.

Question: What's the biggest mistake reporters make in submitting public records requests?

Some of the obvious are not requesting expedited review (which most daily media can usually get by noting that the material being sought is of a timely nature) and not identifying a clear universe of records to draw from. Also, emphasize in the letter that you are happy to respond to questions about your request by phone. It doesn't always work, but if I'm stuck on how to properly word something to pinpoint what it is I want access to, I'll call the FOIA officer and ask them for suggestions on how to word my request to avoid any misunderstanding or confusion, avoid having something withheld due to an exemption and to speed up fulfillment. It's also a good way to build a source relationship with the person who will be herding your requests up the chain of command, and who sees a lot of the agency's dirty laundry.

Question: How has the availability of records on CD-ROM and other electronic forms affected public access to information?

It's certainly made everyday things, like court records and incorporation papers, much more accessible for tracking down during reporting on

breaking stories. But most of the time, the really interesting stories still come from the pile of paper that you get back from a FOIA request. It never ceases to amaze me how federal employees forget that their agency e-mail correspondence is a public record that is regularly released under FOIA. Even the heads of federal agencies seem oblivious that notations made in their official calendar in the ubiquitous Microsoft Outlook software can be released under FOIA.

Question: What general advice do you have for dealing with records custodians and archivists at government agencies?

Know thy enemy and understand thy enemy can be your best friend. One of the best investments of my time was attending a training session put on for federal FOIA officers by the American Society of Access Professionals [ASAP, www.accesspro.org]. This group holds two training sessions annually (one in the East, one out West) outlining how FOI laws and Privacy Act laws work, how to respond to requests, what sort of exemptions apply, etc. Instead of going to yet another war-story laden IRE [Investigative Reporters and Editors] or SPJ [Society of Professional Journalists] session on how to use the FOIA, I found that learning how the other side operates was the best way to get what I wanted faster. The first ASAP training I went to several years ago in New Mexico, I was the only journalist attending among about 300 FOIA officers. While I endured some barbs, I ended up getting business cards passed to me with story tips on the back, or people button-holing me in the hallway, their conversation starting with "What you ought to send me a request for is . . . " With few exceptions, I've found FOIA officers in the federal ranks to be very helpful and friendly, contrary to the image you may get at some journo [journalism] confabs.

remain secret and how you can get them. Most states have a guide to the public records law provided by a press organization or government agency, such as an attorney general's office. You'll want to get a copy and keep it handy.

In general, state public records laws throughout the nation share similar concepts:

- **Public record defined:** Typically, any "recording" kept by a public agency is considered a public record. That can include written documents, such as a memo or council meeting minutes. It can include electronic records, such as the mayor's work e-mails or an Excel file containing a university budget. It can include audio records, such as a tape of the school board meeting. It can even include something scribbled on a Post-It Note and stuck to a computer monitor.

- **Presumed open:** The presumption is that a record held by a government agency is public unless there is a specific law that says otherwise. This is important to remember: it's not *your* responsibility to prove why you have a right to the record. It's *their* responsibility to prove why you can't have it. If you remember that, then asking for public records becomes a lot easier. It shifts the pressure off you and onto the government.

- **Public agency defined:** Open record laws primarily apply to state and local governments, such as state departments, county commissions, city councils, school boards and mosquito control districts. In some states the courts and legislative bodies are covered under common law rather than the state public records law. The laws usually don't apply to nonprofit agencies or businesses, except for some information that might be required to be made public.

- **Anyone can ask for information:** Most laws allow anyone to request public records without having to identify themselves or explain why they want the record. Sometimes you might be asked to fill out a form asking for basic contact information to reach you. In some states you might be asked whether you intend to use a list, such as a database of registered voters, for commercial use because using public information for marketing or advertising can be against the law in some places.

- **Free to look:** You should be able to look at a public document for free. If you want to get a copy of it, you will likely have to pay for the photocopies. Sometimes a search fee is assessed if the request would require a lot of staff time to fulfill.

- **Ball is in their court:** Once you submit a public records request, the responsibility is on the shoulders of the agency to give you a response, usually within a week's time, depending on the state. If the agency wishes to deny your request, then it must tell you in writing and cite the specific law that allows it to do so. Again, everything is open unless there is a law (exemption) that says otherwise.

- **Exemptions:** Not every public record is public. There are times when it makes sense to keep government records secret to protect taxpayers, troops or individual citizens. In most states there are hundreds of exemptions to the public records law, often to protect the commercial interests of businesses or citizen privacy. For example, medical records at a public hospital are typically closed. Memos between city council members and the city attorney discussing legal strategy in a lawsuit might be closed. Other typical exemptions include library check-out records, the location of sensitive archaeological sites and trade secrets.

- **Penalties:** Most states provide some penalties that can be levied against officials for violating the public records law. If you sue the agency to get the records and win, the court might make the agency pay your attorney fees and perhaps a penalty. In most cases, however, it can be difficult to enforce the public records laws.

How to Request Records

Knowing the law is just the first step in accessing public records. Knowing people is even more important.

Government officials generally don't think much about access. For the most part, they are more concerned about how to make sure records aren't released that might hurt their agency or citizens. The general presumption among many officials is to keep records secret unless someone can prove they should be released. Officials are wary of people who request information. In some cases, officials have been known to interrogate requestors, delay providing records and check requestor's criminal records.

That makes your job more challenging, but there are a variety of techniques that can improve your chance of success:

- **Be prepared:** Bring along a copy of the law in case you run into a question. It doesn't hurt to have a copy produced by a government agency, such as the state attorney general's office, because that can hold more sway with government officials who question your right to obtain information. Read through the law with a reluctant clerk, if necessary.

- **Know what you want:** Be specific in your request. It speeds the process, and in some states officials can deny requests that are too broad. Understand that some records, such as budgets or meeting minutes, are relatively simple to get (about 90 percent of the time you shouldn't have any problems). However, law enforcement records can be more difficult (you are likely to be denied about half the time). Also, understand that in general, larger agencies are more likely to comply than smaller jurisdictions. In an Illinois access audit, a thwarted requestor was pulled over by a sheriff's deputy in a small town and told, "You can't come to a small community like this and act like that."

- **Ask in person:** You'll have more success if you first ask for a record in person rather than by mail or e-mail. When access audits around the country have asked for meeting minutes by mail, the compliance rate is about 50 percent. When asked in person, it jumps to about 90 percent. E-mail requests don't work well unless you already have an established relationship with the agency.

- **Be polite:** Although nicety is not a requirement in the law to have access to public records, the reality is that officials are people and they respond better through courtesy, particularly in smaller communities. In Florida, a public official refused to give out a record because of the requestor's long hair, sloppy jeans and "look in his eyes." Although shiftiness is not a legally defensible reason for denial, the reality is that congeniality can go a long way toward getting information. In other audits, requestors who were deemed as unfriendly were threatened with arrest and kicked out of the office. One school superintendent in New Mexico complied with the law, but waited the allowed seven days to supply the information because he thought the requestor was "not courteous." Again, the agencies aren't supposed to respond that way, but courtesy might have prevented animosity and delay.

■ **Be up front:** It's not required that you provide your name, but often it smoothes the way and provides a way for the agency to reach you. Public officials ask about half the time anyway, and one of the most common reason for record denials is that the officials didn't trust the requestor or know how the information would be used (even though requests cannot be denied on that basis). In some cases, as mentioned ealier, officials have been known to interrogate requestors, delay providing records and check requestors' criminal records via their license plates. If you do not want to explain who you are or why you want the information in order to avoid tipping off sources to a story, simply politely decline.

■ **Put it in writing:** If the officials deny your in-person request or don't respond, then submit a request in writing. Sometimes officials will ask you to submit a request in writing anyway. Submitting a written records request starts the clock ticking, as most states require that officials respond in a certain amount of time. Also, it prevents confusion later. Try out the online records request letter generator discussed in the Exercises section at the end of this chapter. A sample letter is provided later in this chapter.

■ **Look for free:** You can look at records for free, but if you want copies you are more than likely going to have to pay. Make sure you know how many pages you have to photocopy before agreeing to pay for copies. In many states, you can request that no fee be charged because you are gathering the information for the public good. Most state laws do not allow government agencies to charge you more than the actual cost of photocopies.

■ **Follow-up letters and calls:** Access audits have found that if a follow-up letter is mailed or e-mailed after a records request, then you will increase your chance of success by about 50 percent. Let them know that you are serious and really want the information.

■ **Keep at it:** If you have a right to the information, do not give up. It takes time and tenacity. Officials will tell you something is closed (either through ignorance or arrogance) when it should be open. A reporter at the *Tri-City Herald* in Kennewick, Washington, once hounded the state Parks and Recreation Commission for two years to get a database of boating accident records. Be polite but firm. Don't give up. Get help if you need it.

SAMPLE REQUEST LETTER

Joe Smith
111 Main St.
Everytown, State, 55555
555-234-5432

January 1, 2006
Department of Energy
Director, FOIA/PA Division, ME-73
1000 Independence Avenue, SW
Washington, DC 20585

FOIA Request

Fee waiver requested

Dear FOI Officer:

Pursuant to the federal Freedom of Information Act, 5 U.S.C. § 552, I request access to and copies of all records regarding the transportation of nuclear waste through my city for the past five years.

I would like to receive the information in electronic format.

As a representative of the news media I would request a fee waiver for photocopies. Through this request, I am gathering information on nuclear waste issues that is of current interest to the public because of safety concerns on the roadways. This information is being sought on behalf of the *Daily News* for dissemination to the general public. Please waive any applicable fees. Release of the information is in the public interest because it will contribute significantly to public understanding of government operations and activities.

If my request is denied in whole or part, I ask that you justify all deletions by reference to specific exemptions of the act. I will also expect you to release all portions of otherwise exempt material.

As I am making this request as a journalist and this information is of timely value, I would appreciate your communicating with me by telephone, rather than by mail, if you have questions regarding this request.

Thank you for your assistance.

Sincerely,

Joe Smith

What to Do When Denied

No. Sorry. Not this time. Buzz off!

Occasionally you will be rejected in this business, and even more if you ask for public records. Don't take "no" for an answer. And certainly don't buzz off. Here are some tips for dealing with rejection.

- **Know how to respond to bluffs:** Over time, you'll start to figure out when you are being denied a record for a legitimate reason and when it's simply to get rid of you. Here are some responses that might come in handy:

  - **Denial reason:** We don't give that out. **Response:** Can you please cite in writing the exact law that allows it to be secret and explain why the law pertains to the information, as required by law?

  - **Denial reason:** The record includes some private information exempt by law, including bank account information of those involved, so you can't have it. **Response:** How about if you blot out the exempt material and give me the rest, as required by law? I don't need to know someone's bank account number anyway, just the rest.

  - **Denial reason:** We don't have time to dig that up. **Response:** Sorry, because I know you are busy, but I don't know of any part of the law that allows records to be kept secret because you don't have time. Maybe I can help you out.

  - **Denial reason:** Who are you, and why do you want the information? **Response:** Is that a requirement for me to get the information? If I'm not mistaken, the law states that anyone can look at information without explaining themselves. Why is that different here? (It is up to you, depending on your reporting needs, whether you want to push the issue.)

  - **Denial reason:** Your request was too vague. I don't know what you want. **Response:** I'll be a little more specific. Let's narrow the request.

  - **Denial reason:** No document exists that you are asking for. **Response:** What document does exist that would include the information? Better yet, what documents do you keep at your agency? I could pick what I want from your document index.

  - **Denial reason:** That will cost $1.3 million for a copy of the files you requested. Will that be cash, check or credit card? **Response:** I will need an itemized explanation of why it costs that much money to make copies. If it truly costs you that much money to make that copy, then I would be happy to just look at it for free in your office. Maybe by looking through the records, I can whittle down the number of pages that need to be copied.

- **Make them prove it:** If the agency balks or denies your request, put the burden on them to prove why it isn't public. Remember, the presumption is that everything is open unless there is a specific law that states otherwise. Many state laws require agencies to put denials in writing, citing the specific law that allows them to keep the records secret. A denial might sound legitimate, but check with access experts to make sure they aren't playing you for a chump.

- **Go up the chain:** Often clerks or assistants who handle requests might be unfamiliar with the law. If they turn you down, talk to the people in charge, including their attorneys or the governing body, such as city council members. Some states provide an administrative appeal process.

- **Get help:** Contact your state's press association to find out who can help provide tips or guidance for getting access.

- **Tell readers:** If an agency keeps information secret that should be open, write about it. They aren't only denying *you* the information, but they are also denying *citizens.* Sometimes journalists are reluctant to write about issues they are involved in, such as asking for public records, but they forget that officials are saying no to the public, not just to the media.

- **Sue:** Sometimes the only recourse is a lawsuit. This should be the last resort, but sometimes it is necessary. Unfortunately, some news organizations don't vigorously pursue these issues in court because of the cost or lack of interest. Let's hope you don't end up working for one of those companies.

- **Don't get mad, get busy:** Try to get the information through other (legal and ethical) channels. Sometimes, other agencies will have the same information and are more than happy to hand it over.

CHAPTER EXERCISES

1. Go to: www.splc.org and find the online records request letter generator toward the bottom right of the Web page. The Student Press Law Center provides this easy form that automatically provides legal citations for your state. Fill out the online form and click on the "Create letter" button. A complete letter is now ready for you to copy and paste into a Word document for presenting to a public agency. A similar letter tailored for requests of federal agencies through the Freedom of Information Act is available at www.rcfp.org. A word of warning: these letters are strongly worded and threaten legal action for noncompliance. You should probably request the records in person first and then use the letter if the agency is reluctant, denies your in-person request or wishes a request in writing.

2. Request the list of registered sex offenders in your area from the local police, or go online to see if your state provides the registry online (many states do). Go to a centralized Web site for links to state criminal data at www.publicrecordfinder.com/criminal.html

3. Go to www.securityoncampus.org to find out how much crime is reported on your campus by your university. Click on the "Crime Stats" button, and enter the name of your university. You can also look up the same information at the Chronicle for Higher Education Web site (http://chronicle.com/stats/crime/) and find stories about the reporting of crime on campuses, as required by the federal Clery Act. Once you find out what crime numbers your university reports, find out through public records requests of campus police or city police their crime statistics to see if they match. With some good reporting you might find, as many newspapers and journalism students have found, that the university underreports its crime.

4. Ask your university for an electronic database (such as an Excel file) of every employee and their start date, department, title, salary and position type (9- or 12-month). Find out

who is paid well on your campus and who is not. Take it further by requesting your university's line-item budget, also in an Excel file, as well as the expense report items of your university president to find out how he or she spends your tuition dollars. Keep a copy of your state public records law on hand, and consult it and experts in case the university denies your requests. Make sure the denial, if any, is legitimate. If not, challenge it and write about it.

5. Go to www.spj.org/foia.asp, at the national Society of Professional Journalists Web site, to find the "FOI Audit Toolkit." It's a PDF file you can download to find out how to conduct an access audit on your campus. Get a couple of classmates together to ask for a variety of public records from your university, and see how your university compares to others nationwide. For more information about university access audits, check out an audit conducted by students at Washington State University who asked for records from twenty different universities in five different states (www.wsu.edu/~accessnw/resources/cleryact/campuscrime.htm)

8 Documents, Databases and Computers

BY KENTON BIRD AND DAVID CUILLIER

There is an explosion of information that is available today, and the most successful reporters take advantage of and understand the necessity of computers, technology, documents, databases and computer-assisted reporting.

A scene in the movie *All the President's Men* gives a glimpse of investigative reporting techniques of the not-so-distant past. In it, *Washington Post* reporter Carl Bernstein (portrayed by Dustin Hoffman) pores over canceled checks that had been deposited in the bank account of one of the Watergate burglars. When he finds a $25,000 cashier's check payable to Kenneth H. Dahlberg—a name he doesn't recognize—he calls his colleague Bob Woodward in Washington.

"Bob, listen, I think I've got something, I don't know what it is," Bernstein says breathlessly. "But somewhere in this world there is a Kenneth H. Dahlberg, and we gotta get to him before the *New York Times* does, because I think they've got the same information."

Woodward (Robert Redford) goes to the newspaper's morgue seeking Dahlberg's identity. A librarian brings Woodward a clipping of a photograph of Dahlberg that lists his hometown as Wayzala, Minnesota. Woodward then rummages through a shelf full of telephone books and finds a directory for Minneapolis. There, to his surprise and delight, is Dahlberg's phone number.

Using a rotary dial telephone (this is 1972, after all), Woodward calls Dahlberg at home and discovers he is the Midwest finance chairman for the Committee to Re-Elect the President (CREEP). It is the strongest link so far between the break-in at Democratic national headquarters in the Watergate office complex and President Nixon's reelection campaign.

The sequence is a classic example of how the two *Post* reporters used documents to establish links among participants in what proved to be a tangled web of espionage, dirty tricks and deceit. It illustrates the combination of good luck, hard work and determination that enabled Bernstein and Woodward to establish a connection between the burglary and the White House, triggering a series of events that led to Nixon's resignation in 1974.

Today, the reporters would still need a tip to get them started, but their follow-up strategy would be much different. Woodward could use an Internet search engine to quickly locate Kenneth Dahlberg; he probably would find Dahlberg's phone number, employer and political affiliations in a matter of minutes. As a result of the campaign finance reforms passed in the wake of Watergate, the Federal Election Commission (FEC) tracks contributions to presidential campaigns and makes them available on its Web site. Using the FEC's data, Bernstein could sort contributors by name, date, occupation or zip code—and could easily match them with interest groups, causes or political connections.

Similar information on congressional and legislative contributions is available at the state level. Campaign finance watchdog groups provide far more information than a reporter would be able to use in a single story.

Paper documents, particularly at the local level, are still critical to a public affairs reporter's job, of course. Increasingly, though, many documents are available online or in digital form. The World Wide Web puts millions of documents at a reporter's fingertips—but carries no guarantee of legitimacy or timeliness. The reporter's challenge, then, becomes to determine which records are most useful, determine the best format in which to obtain them and verify their accuracy. There remains no substitute for the curiosity and skepticism that Woodward and Bernstein possessed—and their determination to pursue a hunch.

Getting Started on a Beat

Before setting foot in a courtroom, visiting city hall or covering a school board meeting, a reporter can identify key players and issues through a virtual tour of the beat. The most obvious place to start is the desk of the previous reporter on the beat. Even in an era of personal digital assistants (PDAs) and cellular phones with extensive contact lists, a Rolodex or similar device for holding and alphabetizing names, addresses and business cards is a valuable tool. A visit to the department's or agency's Web site will provide additional names, addresses and phone numbers—usually under a "Contact Us" link. Even small towns and rural counties provide this information on the Web.

Most newspapers' archives have been computerized since the mid-1990s; clippings of earlier stories might be saved in folders or on microfilm, useful only if the reporter knows the date a story was published; if not, an index is essential. Discover how the printed and electronic files are organized—by author, date, subject or keyword. And find out who assigns categories to each type of story: a librarian, news clerk or copy editor at the end of his or her shift.

Are crime stories filed by locale, by investigating agency or in a generic category such as *law enforcement*? Knowing the quirks of the classification system will help you locate stories later on. Some newspapers supply electronic copies of their stories to a database service such as LexisNexis. This provides reporters with an easy way to retrieve stories from their own paper, particularly if they're working at home or on an out-of-town assignment.

A visit to the agency is the next step. Bulletin boards in a hallway or waiting area at the courthouse or city hall might show calendars, minutes of previous meetings, notices of public hearings, departmental newsletters and even a flier for a going-away party for a longtime employee. A reporter can easily begin to piece together the social networks that overlay the bureaucratic structure. Knowing the existence of a publication enables a reporter to ask for it on a regular basis or request to be on the mailing list. Many of these documents are distributed by e-mail or posted regularly on an agency's Web site. A clerk or departmental administrator can often suggest the best way to receive press releases, meeting notices and personnel changes.

One key document to understanding an agency is an organizational chart. Some departments update these annually; others might list positions but not names. Knowing lines of authority and relationships among officials at different levels is useful, particularly when pursuing a story up the chain of command.

A map indicating locations of offices is useful, too. Proximity is power, and knowing who has direct access on a daily basis to a department head or elected official often gives an indication of influence over decisions. In the absence of a map, a directory showing office numbers will serve the same function. Finally, obtaining a directory or reference card showing names, e-mail addresses and phone numbers is essential to bypassing receptionists and secretaries and going directly to the people in charge. A publication that lists home telephone numbers is especially valuable to reporters seeking to reach sources on evenings, weekends or holidays.

Finding Helpful Records

"The first and great commandment of investigative reporting is this: get the record," the late Paul N. Williams, a professor at Ohio State University, wrote in his landmark 1978 book, *Investigative Reporting and Editing*. Williams suggested building a solid foundation of records before the first interview for a story, pointing out that documents provide a basis to verify the accuracy of what people say later. The need for records, he argued, "is based on the premise that every hypothesis, every biased allegation a tipster may have made must be checked but in the best possible way."

Records germane to particular beats are discussed in other chapters in this text. The following are categories of records applicable to almost all public affairs beats:

- **Agendas for meetings of a governing body, board or commission:** Agendas often become the cover page for packets that contain background and supporting documents for each agenda item.

- **Staff reports:** These might respond to inquiries from elected officials or make recommendations for policy decisions.

- **Minutes of regular, special and closed meetings:** These are great tools to verify the spelling of names and obtain addresses of citizens who speak at public hearings. Exhibits entered into the record of public hearings also provide additional background. Open-meeting laws usually require generic minutes of "executive" or closed sessions that sometimes give hints of the topics discussed.

- **Legislation:** Drafts of bills, ordinances and resolutions are essential to helping citizens understand the workings of government.

- **Budgets and financial reports:** Knowing an agency's spending plans and practices helps taxpayers know whether their dollars are being spent wisely. Monthly expenditure reports and accounts payable indicate whether the office or program is staying within its budget.

- **Expense accounts:** Which officials are traveling regularly? Why? Where do they stay, and how much do they spend? Scrutinizing travel and entertainment vouchers often provides insights into a department's frugality or extravagance.

- **Reports to state or federal agencies:** Almost every government grant carries with it a requirement to report regularly on how the money is spent and the effectiveness of the program. Similarly, state agencies often audit municipalities and school districts; copies of those audit reports might provide evidence of financial mismanagement.

- **Contracts:** Learning which companies and individuals provide goods and services to an agency can be the first step to learning of cronyism, cost overruns and mismanagement.

- **Correspondence:** Letters from citizens requesting services or complaining about policies provide an early warning of disputes and controversies before they surface publicly.

- **Court records and legal opinions:** Tort claims are a request for payment for damages from a government agency; they are often a first step before filing a lawsuit. Be aware that "pending litigation" is usually a justification for a closed meeting, but usually the financial implications of a possible legal justification must be discussed in open session.

- **Federal documents:** Even though most federal agencies provide considerable information on their Web sites, some reports are available only in printed form. Every state has at least one library designated a U.S. Government Document Repository. Check with your university or public library to discover the nearest one.